3.50

22nd Feb.
195 Upper Bridge Road,
Chelmsford, Essex.
CM2 0RU.

Office Administration

Office Administration

Edited for The Institute of Administrative Management

Geoffrey Mills
F.C.I.S., F.B.I.M., F.Inst.A.M.

and

Oliver Standingford
O.B.E., F.C.I.S., F.B.I.M., F.Inst.A.M.

Pitman

Third Edition 1977

Pitman Publishing Ltd
Pitman House, 39 Parker Street, London WC2B 5PB
PO Box 46038, Banda Street, Nairobi, Kenya

Pitman Publishing Pty Ltd
Pitman House, 158 Bouverie Street, Carlton, Victoria 3053, Australia

Sir Isaac Pitman (Canada) Ltd
495 Wellington Street West, Toronto, M5V 1G1, Canada

The Copp Clark Publishing Company
517 Wellington Street West, Toronto, M5V 1G1, Canada

© Office Management Association 1958
© The Institute of Office Management 1966
© The Institute of Administrative Management 1977

0 273 00793 9

(186:63)

Phototypeset by Galleon Photosetting, Ipswich; printed photolithography and
bound in Great Britain by Unwin Brothers Ltd.

Editor's Preface

Much of the material included in this volume was originally prepared by its authors to be delivered before an audience rather than read. The Editors have, therefore, had the task of making the amendments which this situation demanded. In so doing they have, however, endeavoured to retain the style of the author in the belief that the value of each contribution lies as much in its mode of expression as in its content.

They are grateful for the permission, so generously given by contributors, for their work to be adapted as necessary in order to avoid duplication and to enable the editors to prepare a book which they trust may be read as a connected whole rather than a series of monographs.

Preface to Third Edition

In this third edition the text and illustrations have been fully revised and such amendments made as are necessary because of recent developments. Computers are now more commonly used and a new Chapter on the designing of computer methods has been added to Part V.

The recent spate of legislation has made it impossible to deal with the law relating to employment in detail, as was done in the second edition. This branch of the law is now a subject in its own right. It is still, however, necessary for the administrative manager to be aware of the areas in which Acts and Regulations apply. A brief summary sufficient for this purpose is provided as an Appendix and the Editors are grateful for the authoritative assistance of Mr. M. Clipsham of the Midland Bank Limited in ensuring its accuracy.

The use of the masculine gender throughout this book is for convenience only. Office work is, of course, also done by women who occupy posts at every level of responsibility.

List of Contributors

Miss A. Atkinson
(Chapter 11)

P. N. Blackaby, M.A.
(Chapter 13)

H. L. Connor
(Chapter 12)

H. A. Cubbon, M.A.
(Chapter 8)

L. E. Leslie
(Chapter 7)

G. J. Mills, F.C.I.S., F.B.I.M., F.Inst.A.M.
(Chapters 3, 15, 16, 17)

O. G. Pickard, C.B.E., Ph.D., B.Sc.(Econ), M.Com., F.Inst.A.M.
(Chapters 9, 10)

N. C. Pollock, M.B.E., F.Inst.A.M.
(Chapters 18, 19)

J. R. M. Simmons, M.A., F.Inst.A.M.
(Chapters 2, 6)

O. W. Standingford, O.B.E., F.C.I.S., F.B.I.M., F.Inst.A.M.
(Chapters 1, 5, 6, 12, 14, 20)

V. J. S. Warrell, B.A.(Lond.), F.Inst.A.M.
(Chapter 4)

Contents

PART I
Office Organization

1 The Office Service

Since the beginning of the century the office has undergone probably a greater revolution than any other activity in the economic and governmental life of the civilized world. The proportion of the total workers employed in clerical work has increased, and this in spite of mechanization and other improvements in method. The conception of the clerical service has changed completely.

At the end of the nineteenth century the office and the clerk who worked in it were regarded as necessary evils and little more than incidental to the running of industrial, commercial and national affairs. Today the office is a vital department of every organization and the clerk an important member of the team.

The reason for this change lies in the complexity of affairs, be they industrial, commercial or governmental. In days gone by, manufacture was generally from a limited number of materials, often all obtained locally, and marketing was in a limited field. Now, for example, the making of a motor-car demands the drawing of material from the four corners of the earth. Many businesses are involved in the making of components. And the finished product may be sold, and serviced, all over the world. This is, perhaps, an extreme example, but it is nevertheless illustrative of the trend of events.

In the sphere of government there has been an increase in the control and co-ordination of affairs.

The greater the complexity and the greater the degree of specialization, the greater the need for co-ordination.

The street trader has no need of a clerk. He can know at first hand the cost of his merchandise and the state of the market. His overheads are few and he can calculate his profit in his head. He rarely corresponds and his business decisions are made without recourse to minutes or reports. He is a "one-man team" and is both captain and player.

The managing director of a multiple store on the other hand has to control and co-ordinate the work of many people dealing with a range of merchandise in shops spread over a wide area. He cannot hope to conduct his business by word of mouth nor can he hope to remember every incident, however important. For this reason an office is established to

3

correspond with suppliers and shops, keep accounts and records and supply information generally from which the trend of affairs may be known and future policy determined. And the amount of paper work involved is not necessarily in direct proportion to the number of people employed in an undertaking. There are, unfortunately, no statistics available to show the relationship between the size and complexity of an undertaking, and the volume of office work. Observation and experience suggest that the amount of paper work increases disproportionately as the undertaking grows. Fortunately its cost can often be offset by savings resulting from mechanization and more efficient organization within the office.

The "clerical service" is often not provided by a central office alone. The Head Office, Accounts Department, Counting House— by whatever name it may be known—may be and probably is the chief centre of this service. But it is supplemented by the factory office, the sales office and other local or departmental offices giving service to departmental managers as well as passing information to the central office. Furthermore, it is important to bear in mind that clerical work is not confined to the offices as they are generally recognized.

Offices usually work from information received in the form of documents such as time cards, invoices, goods-in notes, dispatch notes, etc. These documents are prepared often by people who are not primarily clerks, but engaged as gatemen, porters, drivers, storemen and the like. These non-clerical workers are a vital link in the chain of information. It is they who witness at first hand the events which they record. If they fail, no amount of good work in the office will produce correct records or enable reliable information to be given. This is indeed a solemn thought for those engaged in office administration. It is not sufficient to organize an efficient clerical machine within the office. The links which bind the records of the office with the realities of the remainder of the organization must be well forged. Time is well spent in ensuring that those responsible for originating primary documents know what is wanted of them and have the facilities necessary to do their simple clerical tasks.

The function of the office has been described as the provision of a service of communication and record. Whilst this was perhaps sufficient definition in the past it is inadequate today. A more recent definition* suggests five major functions—

(1) Receiving information.
(2) Recording information.
(3) Arranging information.
(4) Giving information.
(5) Safeguarding assets.

*Mills and Standingford, *Office Organization and Method* (Pitman).

In the business office, these functions are all readily distinguishable.

Information is received in the form of letters, telephone calls, orders, invoices and various forms and memoranda reporting what has taken place. The receiving of information is not, however, entirely a passive function. There is a duty to see that the necessary information is complete and to take active steps to obtain it.

The information received is recorded with a view to its being readily available when required. In some cases records are required by law to be maintained, but the majority are for use in the conduct of the business.

A letter placed on record in the files is given out, when required, exactly as it was received. Such simple fulfilment of the functions of receiving, recording and giving information has, however, become a minor part of the work of the office as a whole. More often the information received has been rearranged in the course of recording. Invoices, whilst filed and available, have been posted to accounts and analysed for statistical purposes. Stores requisitions have been valued and incorporated in stock accounts, in production cost accounts and consumption statistics. This rearrangement of the information received has now become one of the most important jobs within the office and one on which the more experienced and highly trained clerks are employed. Whilst much of the rearrangement and presentation of information is routine, there is also the task of preparing special statistical and other reports to assist the management in the formulation of policy.

In addition to giving information on request or as a matter of routine, the office has the duty of drawing attention to anything which from the records appears to be abnormal. Those who undertake clerical work are not taking their full share of responsibility if they merely follow a procedure blindly without thought as to the practical implications of what the records show. Clerical records should be designed so as to present a reflection of reality; a picture in words and figures of what has occurred. This picture if observed intelligently will show when anything unusual occurs. And it can be assumed that such an occurrence will be of importance to management and that they will wish to be informed without delay.

Finally the office has the function of safeguarding the assets of the business; it must see that cash and stock are accounted for, debts collected and that the vital records in its custody are protected.

Each of these functions can in part be carried out as a matter of routine according to a set procedure. Documents can be received, identified, scrutinized, sorted, posted, filed and so on, much as material is processed along a factory production line. Indeed, it often happens that a large part of the administrative manager's day is spent in ensuring the smooth flow of these processes. At each stage, however, accuracy must be checked and abnormalities observed and reported. For this reason those who supervise the work must not only be knowledgeable clerks but have a fair knowledge of the affairs of the business which the various documents and other records purport to depict. To this extent there is a special aspect to every routine process.

Beyond the routine processes lies the preparation of financial, cost and management accounts and the various statistical reports produced by more senior staff. It is at this point that the office comes into close contact with management as a direct and personal servant rather than as merely doing a clerical job. The accounts and statistics which are produced are the tools of management. From the study of these, ideas will be stimulated, policies determined and action taken. There is then no doubt that in this field lies the most responsible function that the office has to perform.

It has been said that statistics can be made to prove anything—a somewhat bald statement but one having some measure of truth in it. If selected figures are presented whilst others having a bearing on the matter are left out, an inaccurate picture is presented and a wrong impression given. If all the facts are presented, but in a jumbled order, a distorted picture may be given. There is an art in presenting information in a complete and appropriate form, an art which demands an assessment not only of the purpose to which the information will be put, but of the personal peculiarities of those for whom it is intended. A statistical statement should be an aid to reasoning; it should present data in such a form that the mind of the receiver may work upon them to draw a proper conclusion from them. Whoever prepares and presents information to management is presuming in some degree to lead their thought-processes along certain lines, and this is no light responsibility.

The administrative manager, the accountant, the secretary and the senior clerks should be constantly aware of their responsibility in this direction. If the service which they give is to be good service they must understand the needs of management so as to be able to interpret their requirements. This demands service without servility. Whenever the situation demands, the management must be asked what is the purpose of the information which they require; how will it be used, and by whom. If the office is preparing a report on some special subject, attention must be drawn to assumptions and any deficiencies in information. And, whenever appropriate, the conclusions to be drawn from the information presented should be suggested.

The office service is not an end in itself. Its purposes are manifold but they have something in common. The results produced should present in terms of word and figures a picture of reality. A sales invoice should present in the simplest terms possible the facts about a sale. A customer's account should present clearly the facts about trading with that customer. These are simple examples and there are much more difficult problems in presenting the facts. Financial statements, statistics showing trends of trade, cost and profit, estimates of cost and of the probable effects of policy require more than the mere presentation of simple facts. To give a realistic impression they must contain all the relevant information, and be arranged so as to bring the facts into a proper relationship one with another.

Facts and figures are to many people "as dry as dust." The administrative manager must present his products so as to make them live. He must present to the practical man a picture which is recognizable and which stimulates thought and action. To be able to do this demands an appreciation of the work and problems of the other departments of the organization. This appreciation can come only from frequent contact with the managers of these departments. The office is not a department set apart to observe, record and inform; it is a member of a team and an active member. Its manager must therefore be fully aware of what is going on within the organization and must take active steps to keep himself informed. And the general management has a duty to give him every encouragement and facility to this end.

Of what, then, does the clerical service consist? An office receives information from all manner of sources, often recorded by those who are not primarily clerks. It stores this information so that it shall be readily available when required. It gives out information on request and, as perhaps a more important function, when in the judgement of its manager or even of a senior clerk it appears desirable. It gathers, arranges, relates and presents information so as to tell a story—a true story told in a manner both realistic and stimulating. It has a duty to protect, in the widest sense, the assets of the business.

These in the smaller businesses are in a large measure the personal functions of management. In the larger business they are, though delegated, still an extension of these same functions. The office can be likened to the eyes and ears of management in that it receives information on their behalf. It can be likened to the voice of management in that it communicates with other departments and with the outside world on their behalf. It is perhaps not carrying the likeness too far to say that the office is an extension of the mind of management in that, by arranging and presenting information in logical form, it aids reasoning and judgement.

The service which the office can provide to management is not only the routine processing of paper work. It is a service which can be almost part of management itself; it is in part a highly personal service, personal in the sense that it must be designed to satisfy the particular needs of specific people. The administrative manager must therefore be more than the person responsible for the work of the clerks, he must be a full member of the management team.

Whilst it is possible to discuss the office service in isolation, it is unrealistic to do so with regard to the person giving that service—the administrative manager. He is often not known by this title; he may be styled as Accountant, Secretary or Chief Clerk, or he may even be the general manager who has assumed direct responsibility for the office function without the aid of a departmental manager. In some organizations the clerical work is broken up so that each department has its own small office under the direct control of the departmental manager, with little more than the financial accounts kept by the main office. Policies in this respect vary considerably.

On the one hand it can with justification be argued that the clerical work should not be remote from the practical work to which it relates. One of the main purposes of clerical work is to mirror accurately what occurs in the business. The more remote the clerks are from reality the more is the clerical reflection likely to be distorted. Clerks who write and figure blindly about things which they do not understand and which they have never even seen, can scarcely bring to their work the imagination necessary to raise queries and prevent errors. The departmental local office can often, therefore, give a quicker and better service to the departmental management and at the same time render more accurate returns to head office.

On the other hand it is scarcely economical to have at each departmental office a manager capable of obtaining the best results from the clerks employed there. Often such an office is the responsibility of a senior clerk who cannot be expected to do more than maintain the routine. The functions of administrative management then rest with the departmental manager to whom they are only a secondary function. The sales manager who has to concern himself with a sales office has still the prime duty of selling, and his particular skills and most of his interest will be in this direction. The factory manager's skills will be in his ability as, for instance, an engineer and as a production executive. The management of an office calls for its own skills, skills which have increased in their complexity with the increasing use of office machinery, including computers, and with the development of accounting and statistical techniques.

There is then advantage to be gained from the decentralizing of the office service, with local offices giving service to the various departmental managers and rendering information to head office. And there is considerable advantage also to be obtained from the employment of an administrative manager skilled in those techniques peculiar to the office. Whilst these two situations may appear to be in conflict one with the other, there are organizations in which both advantages have been obtained. This has been done by physically decentralizing the clerical work, whilst leaving the responsibility for running the departmental offices in the hands of one specialist administrator. This manager is responsible for the staffing, systems, equipment and general conduct of the offices, each of which is under a supervisor or senior clerk appointed by him. He must ensure that the local departmental manager receives the clerical service which he may reasonably demand, and that the work of the departmental and head offices is co-ordinated so that the clerical service to the organization as a whole is economical and efficient.

What is there in administrative management which makes it a special skill, different from those of the accountant, cost accountant or company secretary? The distinction is perhaps no different fundamentally from the long-accepted distinction between the engineer and the engineering factory manager. The engineer may employ his professional skill as a consultant or designer; he may be responsible for plant maintenance or installation. When, however, he becomes a factory manager his responsi-bilities and interests widen and include entirely new fields. He must become expert in plant layout, production methods, progress and output control and, now that he is concerned with the direction of others, in personnel matters. The factory manager is primarily a leader of a team, charged with the duty of directing their efforts to a common end. Similarly, the accountant can employ his professional skill, as indeed many do, without being concerned in the management of more than a few assistants. The accountant who becomes an administrative manager also, is faced with problems and duties widely beyond the field of his accounting skill.

In 1963, The Institute of Administrative Management re-defined its objectives as follows—

The objectives of the Institute are to study and promote that branch of management which is concerned with the services of obtaining, recording, and analysing information, of planning, and of communi-cating, by means of which the management of a business safeguards its assets, promotes its affairs, and achieves its objectives.

In this definition it will be seen that, whilst the factors included in other definitions remain, there is emphasis on the ultimate aims of promoting the affairs of a business and achieving its objectives. Good administrative management must be broad in outlook, realizing that office work is not an end in itself; the services which are provided should be seen to contribute to the overall productivity of the organization.

In amplifying this definition of its objectives, the scope of the activities of The Institute and its members is stated in the following terms—

Members of The Institute are expected to study, and to contribute towards the body of knowledge of, that part of the following which is appropriate to their responsibility:

(1) *Top Management Plans*

(*a*) The nature of the plans, financial policies and budgets made by top management for achieving the objectives of the business.

(*b*) Obtaining reliable information, sifting that which is relevant from that which is not, in order to maintain the accounts, records and reports required to enable the plans to be prepared.

(*c*) Analysing alternative plans and evaluating them in a practical manner to enable the best alternative to be selected.

(*d*) Formulating practical plans for consideration along with other alternatives.

(2) *Subordinate Managers' Adaptations of the Plans*

(*a*) Interpreting and communicating the top management plans to subordinate managers in terms which are meaningful to each.

(*b*) Giving assistance to subordinate managers in formulating their own plans and in making proposals for changes to the top management plans in the form of amended budgets or otherwise.

(*c*) Analysing the proposed changes to enable top management to make decisions on them.

(3) *Subordinate Managers' Accounts and Records*

Planning, installing and controlling suitable systems of accounts and records on behalf of each subordinate manager, making use of central clerical services whenever it would be desirable to do so.

(4) *Accounting to Top Management*

(*a*) Summarizing the subordinate managers' accounts or records to enable top management to control the total operations of the business.

(*b*) Ensuring the security of cash and cheques, stamps, contracts, title deeds, share certificates and any other instruments and documents of value.

(*c*) Adequately controlling and accounting for—

Moneys received and paid out,

Goods and services supplied to customers, credit allowed to them and collection of amounts owing by them,

Goods and services received from suppliers and payment of amounts owing to them,

Payments of wages and salaries,

Amounts disbursed by employees in the course of their duties,

Capital expenditure and depreciation thereof,

Stock valuation,

and providing any required reconciliation between the subordinate managers' accounts and the financial accounts of the business without requiring the subordinate managers to maintain records which are not needed by them for achieving their objectives.

(5) *Efficiency*

(*a*) Providing the services for which he is responsible according to the required timetable.

(*b*) Providing his services according to any control, security or other policy laid down by top management.

(*c*) Providing his services with technical efficiency and due economy, enlisting effective help from subordinates and colleagues and making effective use of the means available to him.

Knowledge and understanding are in themselves not all; the true skill lies, of course, in the application of these in practice. Management is essentially leadership, the leading of people so that their efforts may achieve some common purpose. The purpose is the provision of a service to industry and commerce which facilitates the work of other departments and so contributes to efficiency generally. The means employed are good organization, sound methods, proper forms, equipment and machinery. But these means can only be as effective in use as the people employing them can make them. The key to efficient service lies, as in any human enterprise, in the people. And the effectiveness of the people depends on sound management.

2 The Organization of an Office

The manager of an office, by whatever title he may be known, gets things done by his subordinates. He has the task of allotting duties to clerks, stimulating them to action and checking to make sure that everything has been done properly. If his office consists of more than just a few clerks he will have executive assistants, each responsible for a section of the work. In a large office he may well make use of specialist assistants dealing with such matters as organization and methods, engagement, training and internal audit. Whatever the size of the office, the manager's task is the same—the co-ordination of the work of his principal assistants and through them the work of his clerks.

The pattern of organization adopted for an office will depend to some extent on its size. This does not, however, mean that there are no common principles of organization applicable generally. The differences will be more of emphasis than absolute. In examining this subject it is usual to choose examples from among the larger offices. This is quite natural; it is easier to identify characteristics in a large specimen than in a small. Often the manager of the smaller office can gain much by consideration of the magnified example given by the larger office. On the other hand some quite important points emerge from an examination of the evolution of the larger organization from the small.

For these reasons that which follows is a succession of studies of actual offices of varying sizes from which a number of conclusions will be drawn.

The office represented in Fig. 1 is a typical small office—in this instance the office of a small ice-cream company selling to agents in its locality through the medium of roundsmen's vans.

One can imagine how this office has grown up with the business, and how it is likely to continue to grow. Everyone knows his or her own job thoroughly so that, even if the secretary is away, the work will go on satisfactorily for quite a time, but no one is expected to take any formal responsibility beyond that of his own job. If the office continues to grow in this way there are, however, likely to be serious difficulties, which can be more clearly seen from a formal organization as in Fig. 2.

The chart suggests that ten people are directly responsible to the

A SMALL OFFICE

Company Secretary and Accountant—personally responsible for keeping Private Ledger, reconciling Bank Pass-Book and preparing statistics for the Managing Director.
Cashier—responsible also for balancing roundsmen's stock and takings.
Private Secretary to the Managing Director and the Factory Manager.
Private Secretary to the Sales Manager.
Wages, Stock Records and Bought Ledger Clerk.
Sales Invoicing Clerk.
Sales Ledger Machine and Calculator Operator.
Shorthand-typist.
Sales Records Clerk.
Telephone Operator/Receptionist.
Junior Clerk—Postal, Messenger and Filing.

Fig. 1

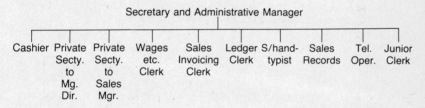

Fig. 2

secretary; not ten people doing similar jobs, but all performing very different work.

Such an organization could not work if it were exactly as the chart suggests; fortunately it is not. For example, the two private secretaries are not really subordinate to the office manager, but in practice report to their respective chiefs; the senior clerk responsible for wages, stock records and bought ledger regards the junior clerk as being at his particular disposal; the sales records clerk assists the sales invoicing clerk; the telephone operator reports to the managing director's secretary. A truer representation of the organization of this small office is therefore that set out in Fig. 3.

It can now be seen that the office manager has, in fact, only five immediate subordinates, which is much more likely to be an effective arrangement. Note, too, the notion of seniors and subordinates creeping in, even though the relationships in an office of this size are likely, and properly, to be of quite an informal character. If, however, for the purposes of illustration these levels of responsibility are formalized by

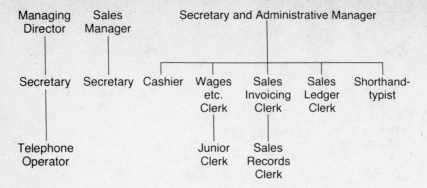

Fig. 3

making use of the I.A.M. Job Grading,* that part of the office which is the direct responsibility of the secretary and office manager could be represented as in Fig. 4.

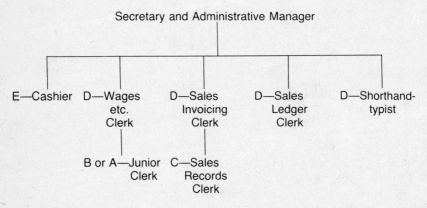

Fig. 4

A precise organization, such as that represented by this organization chart, is not really necessary at this stage in the development of the office. But if the company it serves is to prosper and if the administrative manager is not to find his job outgrowing him as time passes, he has got to be capable of devising a more formal organization when the time is ripe. In due course the question will be not whether he ought to have a formal organization, but what kind of formal organization ought he to have—one that has been thought out and planned on sound lines, or one that has "just growed" and developed from one expedient to the next.

* The Institute of Administrative Management Job Grading Scheme referred to here and subsequently in this chapter is described in Chapter 9.

In order to assess the lines on which such a small office ought to be developed as it grows in size, it will be useful to consider a larger office, one of about four times the size—this time the office of a large laundry.

Before discussing the organization of this office, however, there is another matter to be considered. In planning an office organization, at which end ought we to begin—with the manager and work downwards, or with the clerks and work upwards?

There is a great temptation for the manager to start with himself and with the senior members of his staff who are the key people. But the office exists not for the benefit of its manager but to do clerical work. The approach should therefore be to start with the clerks doing the work and consider how they can best be organized, grouped and supervised in order to do that work most effectively. The clerks must be able to work as a team, without duplication of effort or interference one with another, receiving guidance, information and help from the supervisors and manager when they need it. It would perhaps be more expressive of the truth if organization charts were drawn with the clerks spread out along the top and with the administrative manager at the bottom, like Atlas supporting the office on his shoulders.

In the laundry office there is work for some forty clerks, clearly too many to be each directly responsible to the manager. The work can, however, be grouped under convenient headings for examination as in Fig. 5.

LAUNDRY OFFICE

	Numbers and Grades	
Lists Group	1 E, 1 D, 8 C, 4 B .	= 14
Invoice Group	1 E, 4 D, 2 C .	= 7
Wages Group	1 E, 1 D, 3 C .	= 5
Premium Bonus Group . . .	2 E, 1 D, 3 C .	= 6
Company Accounts	1 F . .	= 1
Cashier	1 E . .	= 1
Services Group	2 D, 2 C . .	= 4
		—
		38
Secretary and Administrative Manager		1
		—
		39
		=

Fig. 5

The Lists Group is, in the main, responsible for the valuing of the laundry lists, their entry on the vanmen's journey sheets and the recording of the amount to be paid in by each vanman. The Invoice

Group is responsible not only for preparing invoices for the contract work undertaken by the laundry, but also for such other jobs as checking of bought invoices and the maintenance of stock records. The Wages Group speaks for itself, while the Premium Bonus Group calculates the laundry workers' bonus earnings based upon time study standards, and keeps various labour statistics. The company accounts clerk keeps the ledgers, including the private ledger, and is responsible to the secretary for the production of the Profit and Loss Account and Balance Sheet. The cashier controls all cash payments and receipts, including cash paid in by the vanmen, and also makes up and pays the wages. The Services Group provides a miscellaneous service to the company and to the rest of the office; for example, it deals with the incoming and outgoing mail and operates the telephone switchboard.

In this office the manager feels, quite rightly, that there are too many groups for him to supervise himself. Nor can he see his way to combining any of them together so as to reduce their total number; either the work is too diverse or, for reasons of security, they need to be kept separate. In any event, with his responsibilities, he needs a capable assistant. So, while himself looking after the work of the company accounts clerk and the cashier, together with the Wages and Premium Bonus Groups, he has appointed a senior supervisor, not only as his personal assistant, but also to take charge, under him, of a section of the office comprising the remaining groups. The resulting organization is given in Fig. 6.

The chart illustrates two other details of organization. Firstly, with thirty-eight clerks, the administrative manager obviously must have some spares to cover illness and holidays, although it is uneconomical to try to make each group entirely self-contained. He has therefore created a small relief squad of three clerks sufficiently versatile to step in and lend a hand wherever there is a shortage. When not so employed they are useful to help deal with the hundred-and-one special demands that are always being made on any office.

Secondly, he has decided that his senior supervisor ought to have a deputy, and accordingly the senior clerk of the Invoice Group combines this responsibility with that of group leader and this has justified his being promoted to the F grade.*

The chart in Fig. 6 is deliberately set on its side in order to illustrate the idea of first scheduling the work to be done and then organizing it into a complete office. From this chart, certain features are distinguishable.

The work is arranged in groups, each being what the term implies—a group of clerks working together on jobs which have at least something in common. Each group has a senior clerk or group leader in charge of the work done by the group, but he or she is a "working chargehand." This

---

* See Chapter 9 for a description of the Job Grading.

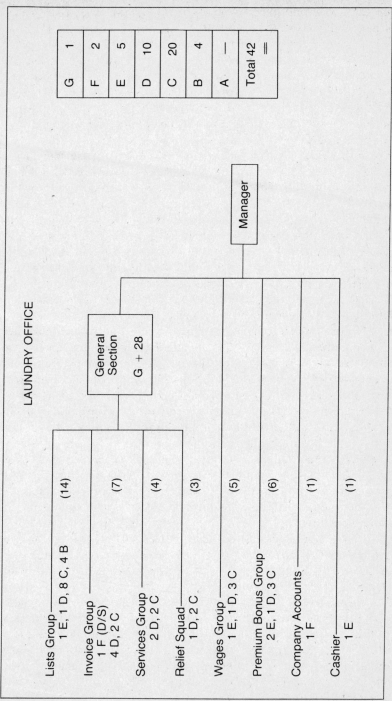

LAUNDRY OFFICE

Manager

General Section
G + 28

Lists Group
1 E, 1 D, 8 C, 4 B (14)

Invoice Group
1 F (D/S)
4 D, 2 C (7)

Services Group
2 D, 2 C (4)

Relief Squad
1 D, 2 C (3)

Wages Group
1 E, 1 D, 3 C (5)

Premium Bonus Group
2 E, 1 D, 3 C (6)

Company Accounts
1 F (1)

Cashier
1 E (1)

G	1
F	2
E	5
D	10
C	20
B	4
A	—
Total	42

Fig. 6

means that the group must be small enough for the supervision to be informal—that which the group leader can see going on under his own eyes. If, as in the case of the Lists Group, the work is so simple and straightforward that it would be uneconomical to have an experienced clerk doing it, the function of the group leader changes. He becomes instead the senior responsible for controlling and handing out the work, and the group itself can be made somewhat larger. It should still, however, be kept small enough for the supervision to remain simple, informal and personal.

Where the work is highly technical (as in the case of the company's accounts) or where it is desirable for security reasons (as with the cashier) groups may need to be kept quite small and may even consist of only a single clerk.

The typical group, therefore, consists of five to seven clerks including the group leader, but as we have seen, it may be larger if the work is simple and straightforward, or smaller if the work is complex or specialized.

There is, similarly, a limit to the number of groups, or rather group leaders, who can be responsible to one man. The actual number will, like the size of the group, depend upon the circumstances of the particular office but in general experience this "span of control" should not, ideally, exceed five or six. If there are more than this number of groups in an office it becomes necessary, therefore, to organize the groups into sections. An additional level of supervision, consisting of the section supervisors, has then to be introduced between the group leaders and the office manager. The section supervisor is responsible to his manager for all the work performed by his groups and, in order to provide for the eventuality of his own absence, it is desirable to appoint the senior group leader as his deputy to take over and act for him when necessary.

It has been seen that even in a relatively small office, one employing some forty clerks, it becomes necessary to introduce this conception of sections; even in this office we can see emerging a general pattern of clerks organized into groups, of groups into sections and of sections into the complete office.

Or to put it another and more practical way; even in an office of this size it is necessary to introduce at least two levels of supervisors between the manager and his individual clerks—the section supervisors and the group leaders.

The problem facing the administrative manager is how, with these intermediaries, he is to control the work of his individual clerks. Whilst in all but the smaller offices it would seem necessary to introduce these two levels of supervision between the manager and his clerks, the fewer intermediaries there are the better. Every additional one must weaken the manager's influence on the clerks who actually carry out the work for which he is responsible.

What then is the number of clerks that can be made subordinate to a manager without any more than two levels of supervision becoming necessary? In order to answer this question with any certainty it is necessary to examine a still larger office.

Fig. 7 gives the organization chart for an office some three or four times larger than that illustrated in Fig. 6. It is an office of 137 clerks serving the needs of a motor company. In this office the manager is the accountant, the secretary being fully occupied in attending to the board and to the legal side of the company's business. Apart from the secretary's office, the accountant is responsible for the whole of the clerical work of the company, except for one or two isolated clerks in the works and the branches.

The company's business is that of motor engineering and coach-building. Besides its head office and main works it possesses a number of branch garages of varying sizes in London and in the provinces. The main engineering workshop is engaged on general maintenance, running repairs and major overhauls of commercial vehicles and private cars. The greater volume of work is carried out under contract for commercial fleet owners. The coachbuilding workshop is concerned both with the building of specialized commercial bodies and also with the repairing and reconditioning of commercial vehicles and private cars. The men working on new bodies come within a production-bonus scheme. The branch garages provide the normal services of the motor trade but the clerical work is concentrated as far as possible at head office, leaving the branches to prepare the primary records and cash customers' bills only.

The accountant and administrative manager has an assistant who deals particularly with the cost accounting work of the office and is virtually the cost accountant of the company. There are six senior supervisors, namely the supervisors of the four sections, a female personnel officer, and an organization and methods specialist.

It will be observed that the Accounts Section consists of twenty-eight clerks with a G section supervisor and is divided into four groups. The Ledgers Group has an F group leader who is also deputy section supervisor, and the other clerks on this group consist of three E, two D and one C grade making, with the group leader, seven in all. Owing to the technical nature of some of the wages work, the Payroll Group also has an F group leader and he is supported by three E, four D and two C grade clerks. The other groups on the section have E grade group leaders.

The Stores Section consists of twenty-seven clerks with a G supervisor and is divided into six groups. The Costing Section has the senior section supervisor of the office, an H clerk, and is divided into five groups.

These three sections are relatively closely knit, but the fourth section, the Services Section, is much more loosely organized. The management secretaries spend most of their time with, or working for, their respective

Office	Motor Company
Date	

Accountant and Manager
Assistant Manager

H	G	F	E	D	C	B	A	Total
2	4	6	35	45	31	11	3	137

Organization and Methods
H

Personnel Officer
G + 10
3 E, 4 D, 3 C
- Relief
  3 E, 4 D, 3 C   (10)

Services
G + 33
2 F, 12 E, 9 D, 6 C, 2 B, 2 A
- Management Secretaries
  2 F, 6 E, 2 D   (10)
- Correspondence
  1 E, 3 D, 2 C, 1 B   (7)
- Postal
  1 E, 1 D, 1 C, 1 A   (4)
- Cashiers
  2 E   (2)
- Works Office
  1 E, 2 D, 3 C, 1 B, 1 A   (8)
- Telephones
  1 E, 1 D   (2)

Costing
H + 33
1 F, 5 E, 10 D, 11 C, 5 B, 1 A
- Repairs Costing
  1 F (D/S)
  1 E, 2 D, 2 C, 2 B   (8)
- Special Contract Costing
  1 E, 2 D, 3 C, 1 B   (7)
- New Bodies Costing
  1 E, 2 D, 2 C, 1 B   (6)
- Summarizing
  1 E, 2 D, 4 C   (7)
- Fleet Records Control
  1 E, 2 D, 1 B, 1 A   (5)

Stores
G + 27
1 F, 7 E, 9 D, 6 C, 4 B
- Works Bought Invoices
  1 F (D/S)
  1 E, 2 D, 1 C, 1 B   (6)
- Branch Bought Invoices
  1 E, 1 D, 1 C, 1 B   (4)
- Works Stores (Mechanical)
  1 E, 1 D, 2 C, 1 B   (5)
- Works Stores (Coach)
  1 E, 2 D, 2 C, 1 B   (6)
- Branch Stores
  1 E, 3 D   (4)
- Branch Audit
  2 E   (2)

Accounts
G + 28
2 F, 8 E, 13 D, 5 C
- Ledgers
  1 F (D/S)
  3 E, 2 D, 1 C   (7)
- Payroll
  1 F, 3 E, 4 D, 2 C   (10)
- Production Bonus
  1 E, 4 D   (5)
- Branch Control
  1 E, 3 D, 2 C   (6)

chiefs, and the section supervisor is responsible for little more than "rations and discipline." The Works Office Group is detached from the rest of the office, being situated in the main works. It is responsible for recording work to be done and issuing job numbers, maintaining works' personnel records and generally providing an office service to the works manager. Apart from holding these rather diverse groups together, the most important function of the section supervisor is to take responsibility for the company's cash and to supervise the work of the two cashiers.

The duties of the personnel officer are to assist her manager in a variety of ways concerned with the personnel of the office. She is responsible for interviewing all applicants for work and for virtually completing the engagement of junior applicants. She is responsible for keeping the personal records of the clerks, the attendance sheets, absentee records, and so on. She is also responsible for inspecting the working conditions in the office, particularly those affecting the female staff. Finally, as is shown by the chart, there is a relief squad consisting of ten clerks, and she is responsible each day for assigning them where their help is most needed.

Probably little needs to be said to justify the O & M specialist. In an office of this size and type there always seems to be ample work for him to do which, if he were not there, would fall upon the manager or his assistant and which would largely never get done because of their preoccupation with more urgent matters.

With no more than the same two levels of supervision, the section supervisors and group leaders, it is possible for the manager to be responsible for an office of at least this size. The manager has an assistant, but this is for no other reason than common prudence, so that if he is absent on holiday, through illness or for any other reason, there is somebody else free of sectional responsibilities able to carry on. Though his assistant specializes on the cost accounting side of the work, no particular part of the office is directly responsible to him as distinct from the manager.

In addition to the normal hierarchy of manager, section supervisor, group leader and clerk, it is found in an office of this size that specialist assistants can be employed to advantage. Examples in this instance are the personnel officer and the O & M officer.

This illustrates the fact that in a larger office it should be possible to get greater efficiency by specialization, in the sense that section supervisors do not need to be "jacks-of-all-trades," like the managers of the other offices illustrated who, with staffs no greater than that of one of the sections here, have to be responsible for doing everything themselves. Nevertheless the introduction of specialists means the necessity for co-ordinating the work of the executives (the section supervisors) and the specialists. The manager cannot have as many section supervisors directly responsible to him as he could otherwise have, because he also has two specialists to whom he must give an appropriate proportion of his total time and energy. There is no golden rule to enable a manager to decide whether he can get more assistance from having an executive or a specialist assistant. He must make his decision in the light of his own circumstances.

If it is assumed that the manager of an office should not have more than five or six section supervisors or specialists directly responsible to him, or with the help given to him by his assistant manager, say seven or eight as an absolute upper limit, this clearly sets an upper limit to the number of clerical staff which can be organized into an office of this pattern. The limit has not been reached in the office of the motor company—some of the sections could be allowed to grow larger and possibly another section, or even two, could be added. It would probably be true to say, however, that in a self-contained office of this kind once the number of clerks employed exceeds about two hundred an organization of another and more complex kind would need to be created.

In dealing next with a larger organization, it is not necessary to discuss the problems concerned with the whole of such an organization, but only with one office within the organization. The reason is that it is possible to organize up to about two hundred clerks into a single office organization, responsible to one administrative manager, an important characteristic of the office being that there are only two levels of supervision between the manager and the clerks.

This characteristic is fundamental to the theory of office organization. It is possible for a man in charge of an office of two hundred clerks to know each of his clerks, and to be known by them, in some degree. There is no need for him to be a remote authority, unknown to his subordinates. But as soon as the number of clerks makes it necessary to introduce a third level of authority between them and the man at the head, there is no reason why the total number should not be anything up to five or six times the number, say a thousand or more. With such a number it is just not possible for the man in charge to know every individual and to be known by them, and something very important in the practical and human needs of the organization is inevitably lost.

It therefore seems that any large office organization should be built up from units of individual offices, each office under the control of its own manager, and no office possessing more than that number of clerks which can be managed with the assistance of only two levels of supervision.

The manager of each office should in these circumstances have as much authority within his own office as is possible, so that the clerks in his office may feel that any rules and regulations spring from him, the man they know, and not from some remote authority almost unknown to them. This is not to say that there cannot be a higher authority; it merely means

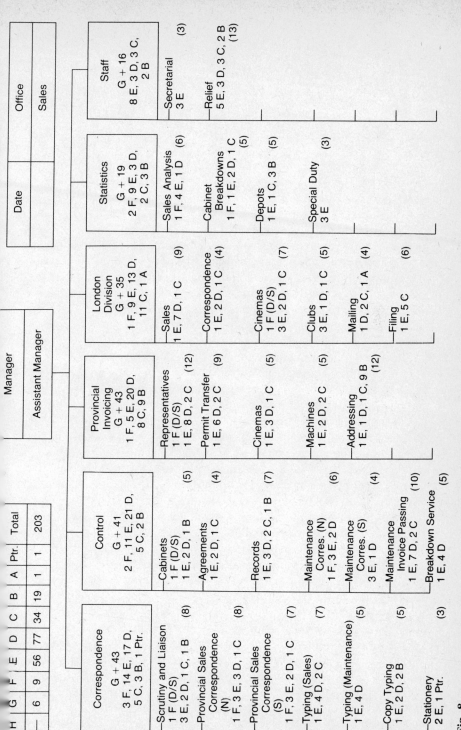

Fig. 8

that every care must be taken to see that the managers are parties to whatever authority is exercised over their clerks.

An office which is one of a group in a large office organization will possess certain characteristics different from those of a self-contained office.

Fig. 8 represents an office situated in London and giving a clerical service to a sales department, in this instance an ice-cream sales department.

The general pattern of the organization is very much the same as that shown in Fig. 7. There are, however, five sections instead of four and while there is a personnel officer in charge of the staff section, there is no O & M man attached to the office.

The Correspondence Section's main job is conducting the sales department's correspondence with its agents in the provinces, but all incoming correspondence for the whole office goes first to the Scrutiny and Liaison Group which is responsible for segregating urgent and special matters for immediate attention by the management, passing the remainder to the correspondence clerks both on this section and on the others. There are also three typing groups attached to this section which likewise serve the correspondence clerks on both this section and the others. The seventh group is a small one (including a porter) dealing with the stationery for the whole office. These are examples of the way in which groups may be linked together to form a section in a perfectly matter-of-fact, common-sense fashion so that, although the section is primarily concerned with the correspondence of the provincial agents, its total strength is built up by attaching to it other groups which are allied to its own work and which at least do not link more certainly to the work of any other section.

The Control Section is concerned with the refrigerator cabinets on agents' premises in which the ice-cream is stored for sale. It will be noted that there are two further correspondence groups dealing with maintenance matters and the typing for these groups is done by one of the typing groups on the Correspondence Section.

The third section is concerned with preparing invoices for sales to provincial customers, while the fourth is concerned with all the work connected with sales in London. To this fourth section there are also attached two more groups which serve the whole office in the tasks of mailing and filing.

The Statistics Section consists of four groups, two of which are concerned with keeping various statistical records. The third is responsible for stock control of the decentralized storage and distribution depots, and the fourth consists of three "special duty" clerks to whom reference will be made below.

The Staff Section consists of two groups, the first being a small group of shorthand-typists giving a secretarial service to the manager, his assistant and the section supervisors, the second being the relief squad for the office. At the head of this section there is the personnel officer, but her duties are somewhat different from those of the personnel officer in the motor company's office. The Sales office, being one of a large clerical organization, is served by a centralized staff-engaging office. The personnel officer is, therefore, not responsible herself for engaging staff, but under her manager is responsible for requisitioning on the central engaging office and screening the applicants submitted by the engaging office. Since vacancies at the higher levels are normally filled from inside the office, the personnel officer has the important responsibility of maintaining the standard strengths of all the sections and of ensuring that the most suitable clerks are recommended to fill vacancies. She is also responsible for making recommendations to the manager, after consultation with the section supervisors, on the progress and efficiency of the clerks. She maintains a personal history sheet for each member of the staff. Others of her duties are in connexion with training: for example, to assist the supervisors and group leaders in organizing training on the job, to make recommendations for training by the organization's central training school, to advise on classes to be attended by the younger clerks at day continuation school and to advise, in appropriate cases, on evening classes. She conducts an induction course for newcomers.

Finally, her most important duty, though difficult to define in precise terms, is to keep in touch with each member of the staff and to give any help or advice that may be required on personal problems. In short, she is there to see that the personal side of management is not neglected because of her manager's possible preoccupation with the technical side of getting the work of the office done.

Mention has already been made of the advantage of having a relief squad. This is an important item in the theory of office organization and it is based on the assumption that the bigger the unit of staff the easier it is to estimate the total number that are likely to be away at any given moment. If each group is to carry sufficient surplus staff to meet any reasonable eventuality, a much greater margin will need to be provided than if a surplus of staff is carried for the office as a whole.

It might be argued that on this theory it would be better in a large office organization to maintain a central relief squad to service the needs of all the offices. This, however, would strike across the principle of giving maximum authority to the manager of the office, and it is better, therefore, to organize each individual office on its own.

Nevertheless, there are certain other eventualities which need to be provided for—sudden awkward jobs which have to be undertaken. In this office organization, it has been found convenient to earmark a number of what are called "special-duty" clerks, who are capable senior clerks willing to undertake any job which may crop up. The allocation of these clerks to each job is done centrally, but they are attached to one or other of the sections. This is the explanation of the small group of three special-duty clerks included in the Statistics Section.

Attention has already been drawn to the lack of any O & M officer in this sales office and the reason is that there is a central O & M department serving the needs of all the offices in the organization.

There is one other central office which perhaps should be mentioned, although its primary task is not to provide a service to the various office managers. It is the Internal Audit Office and its task is to serve as the eyes of the higher management. Its members have the entrée to any of the offices, such as the Sales Office, to examine the way in which the records are being kept. However, if the manager of any office requires an audit or special check to be carried out the Internal Audit Office is there to assist him.

This completes the survey of this series of offices of differing sizes and types, from the small company office of ten clerks to the departmental office of some two hundred clerks working as part of a large commercial undertaking. As each office has been considered, various propositions have emerged which are worthy of consideration by those reponsible for the management of offices. These may be summarized briefly as follows—

(1) That the study of the organization of a large office can be helpful to the manager of a smaller office.

(2) That the manager of an office in an expanding business should have plans ready to deal with the fundamental changes needed when his office gets larger.

(3) That the organization of an office should be planned from the clerks upwards rather than from the manager downwards.

(4) That there is a place in the organization for group leaders who are "working chargehands" as well as for full-time supervisors.

(5) That the "span of control" at all levels should be about six people, this number being varied according to the simplicity or complexity of the work, or for reasons of security.

(6) That in a single office there should not be more than two intermediate levels of supervision between the manager and each of his clerks, these levels corresponding to the section supervisor and group leader in the examples given.

(7) That there should be deputies appointed to cover the absence of supervisors or managers.

(8) That in a large office there is a job for a specialist personnel officer subordinate to the manager of that office and not to some higher authority outside the office.

(9) That in the medium-sized or large office it is good practice to provide a relief squad in order to cover absence and emergencies whilst keeping the staffing of groups and sections to a minimum.

3 The Centralization of Office Services

On examination it will usually be found that the centralization of office services carries with it great potentialities for reducing the cost of these services. At the same time, however, there is a danger that the value of the service itself may be reduced. Therein lies the problem; centralized services cost less but they may be worth less, and it is necessary to weigh carefully the advantages and disadvantages in each case in order to resolve this problem.

In this chapter different types of office services are taken as examples of the problem, and in each case the probable advantages and disadvantages are discussed. There are some circumstances in which centralization may bring with it increased efficiency; there are other circumstances in which dispersal offers greater advantages.

In considering this subject it is essential that the meanings of "centralization" and of "office services" are clearly defined.

Centralization can mean the physical bringing together of the clerks into one main office. Or it can mean the placing of responsibility for all office services of one type in the hands of one manager whilst leaving the clerks physically dispersed. Physical centralization embraces a variety of possibilities. It may involve the bringing together on one floor of a number of elements which would otherwise be scattered; in a small office building containing perhaps one hundred clerks, in a large building containing several thousand clerks, in a number of buildings covering a factory site, or in a number of offices scattered in a district, a town or indeed over the entire country. With such diverse possibilities, it is necessary to have clearly in mind what is meant when the possibilities of centralization are considered. According to the degree of centralization, the advantages and disadvantages will vary and with them the solution to any particular problem.

The term "office service" also has more than one application. Within the office it may be used to mean a service given by one group of clerks to the other clerks. For example, the work of typing, filing, duplicating or calculating may be organized as a service to the remainder of the office. On the other hand "office service" may be taken as embracing the entire clerical function; the service which the office gives to the remainder of the organization. For example, accounting, cost accounting and the provision of statistics are office services provided to the general and departmental management.

This distinction is fundamental and the examples which follow are divided accordingly. The services which are internal to the office are dealt with first. They offer the more straightforward problems and it is, therefore, the easier to draw general conclusions from them. These conclusions, in principle, offer the key to the problems relating to services external to the office which are discussed subsequently.

Typing Services

The typing pool, as the centralized service is often called, is usually formed to meet the needs of a building, a floor or a department. It offers a number of advantages and one of the most important is that the employment of a specialist supervisor enables output and quality to be improved. A supervisor can set standards and see that these standards are maintained. It is not difficult to control the output of typists by some broad measurement such as the dimensions of the typing produced. By these or by other means, a competent typing supervisor can keep a group of typists busily employed. At the same time, expert and full-time supervision can improve and maintain appropriate standards of accuracy and layout.

The presence of an expert supervisor enables the training of junior staff to be undertaken in an organization not large enough to employ a full-time training supervisor. Unproductive time is reduced, since a typist is not left idle while an executive is away or engaged in a series of conferences. The needs of the various sources of work can often be offset one against another so that typists are kept fully employed and it may even be possible to adopt some system of priority, so that urgent work from any department is given preference. This, however, is a process that is easier to describe in theory than to arrange in practice.

Where several typists are employed in a pool, economies can be made in the grade of clerk employed. It is possible so to grade and distribute the work that the expert staff are relieved of simple tasks which can be undertaken by the more junior members. The grading of work also provides obvious channels of promotion which give greater satisfaction to the individual.

At the same time the provision of improved physical surroundings can be achieved at a smaller cost in an office housing a substantial number of typists. It is also possible to make better use of equipment since the use of devices such as automatic typewriters is more likely to be justified in a typing pool where machines are kept more fully employed. Dictating equipment can be used more economically because a smaller number of machines would be employed in a typing pool than under dispersed arrangements.

To summarize the advantages: output and quality can be improved, internal training can be undertaken, idle time can be reduced, economies can be made in the grade of clerk employed, proper working conditions can more easily be assured and better use can be made of equipment. There is little doubt that this formidable list of advantages suggests substantial economies in typing costs, but there are disadvantages, and for these it is necessary to turn to the users of the typing service.

Although by the use of typing pools the time of typists may be saved, it may very well be that time of others is thereby wasted. Where the users are themselves routine workers, as in the case of correspondence clerks, or where only intermittent use is made of the service, this may be no serious objection. But in the case of the executive any time lost may be costly indeed. The dovetailing of the requirements of different officers usually means that someone's work has to take second place. It is not alway convenient to put aside dictation until an allotted hour. Moreover, that delay may in turn lead to other delays not conducive to the general good of the enterprise. What may be even more important, the duties of the private secretary attached to an executive are much better performed if there is continuity of understanding. A good secretary can often, and indeed should, act to some extent as a personal assistant to her chief, thus increasing his effectiveness as an executive.

There remains the disadvantage of divided responsibility. If an executive responsible for a department is dependent upon some source beyond his control for the completion of its work, he is immediately placed at a disadvantage. Worse than that, his superiors can hardly hold him to his responsibility. As long as he can say "I could not complete the job because the typing pool failed to meet my requirements," he has a perfectly reasonable excuse. If, however, the provision of an adequate typing service is a part of his own responsibility he will be able to, and will have to, take steps to see that the service is satisfactory.

In short, whilst centralization may reduce the cost of the typing service, it may increase the costs of the people who use those services, and the problem may be summed up in the following way—

Typing pools are an economical device where there is a large amount of routine correspondence originated by clerks of no very high grade.

Dispersed arrangements are more economical for serving the needs of executives who are able to make better use of their time if provided with a personal service.

Typing pools should not cut across departmental responsibilities and a pool attached to each department is to be preferred to a larger central pool serving the needs of many departments.

Filing Services

The position as regards filing is much the same as for typing. But again it is necessary to be sure what is meant by "centralized filing," since there are many different systems which are described by this name. It can, for example, mean that all the files are kept in one room; it can mean that files of interest to more than one group are kept centrally, whilst those of limited interest are kept by the persons concerned; and it can mean that the files are kept locally but staffed and controlled from a central source. If this matter is to be dealt with briefly, consideration must be confined to the two extremes—complete physical centralization and complete dispersal.

The advantages of complete centralization are many. As in the case of typing, the cost of the clerks can be reduced, output and training can be improved by specialized supervision, the work can be graded and proper working conditions ensured. It is also more economical of equipment and space, a consideration of particular importance in relation to filing. Moreover better methods can be used, since if a number of clerks are engaged on the same job careful planning of method is more easily justified. Centralized filing is often more economical because only one copy of any one document need be filed, and it ensures a more strict control of the records.

But, again, there are disadvantages. If the area served is an extensive one, it may lead to delay in bringing the records to those who use them. If the centralized service is to be operated effectively, rules must be laid down and adhered to, but conforming to such rules may again lead to loss of executive time. It will not always be easy for those responsible for the centralized service to appreciate local needs. The executive may find his very real requirements modified to fit in with some overriding pattern. Finally, there may be disadvantages arising from any division of departmental responsibility.

The resolving of these opposing factors lies in avoiding the extremes of complete centralization and complete departmental autonomy. Again, the problem may be summarized thus—

Centralized filing should be limited to comparatively small areas and should not cut across departmental responsibilities.

Centralized filing is appropriate to routine matters such as sales correspondence, invoices, and other routine forms and to anything which is of a purely repetitive nature, particularly if likely to be used by more than one group of people.

Files should be located so that they are readily available when and where they are wanted. If central filing is likely to provide files more quickly and more easily, it should be established, but not otherwise.

Duplicating and Photo-Copying Services

In the two cases so far examined, the decision to centralize or not must depend largely upon circumstances, and upon whose time is being saved and whose time is being wasted. In the case of duplicating services there is a better general case for centralization.

The principal advantage of centralization is that the greater volume of work justifies the employment of expensive equipment to give greater output and better quality. There is a considerable range of office duplicating equipment available and with it a great deal of subsidiary equipment for preparing the master copies, and for binding, perforating, punching and so on. Designed originally for reproducing documents, etc., duplicators are used increasingly for the preparation of internal forms. With improvements in quality, forms to go outside the organization are also being produced within the office. Once again, expert supervision can be employed; staff can be trained to service machines properly and to make the best use of the equipment; standards of output and quality can be set and maintained.

Under conditions of dispersal, duplicating machines are rarely used to full advantage. Many an executive thinks it convenient to have a duplicating machine somewhere within his immediate control. The cheaper models are fairly simple to operate and the tendency is for them to be installed haphazardly throughout an organization. Apart from the wastefulness of partly idle machines, operation is often left to inadequately trained juniors, and machines suffer through lack of cleaning and maintenance. The poor quality of work which results often leads to forms being produced by outside sources at greatly increased cost.

Duplicating is one of the few office jobs which really lends itself to mass production. It is more akin to a factory job than any other task undertaken by the office. If a hundred copies of a report are to be prepared, or ten thousand copies of a form, all will be precisely alike. Once the master copy has been prepared, the production of the form is a purely mechanical job with appearance the only factor to be watched. Nowhere else in the office do we find these conditions. Nearly every letter which must be dictated is different from every other letter. No two invoices are precisely alike. It follows that, in setting up a duplicating service, the lessons of the factory can more easily be applied in the office than with most other clerical operations.

Two of the disadvantages have been mentioned elsewhere, although in this case they are less likely to be serious: distance may cause delay if the service goes beyond a building or a group of buildings, whilst the exercise of priorities, and the division of responsibility in serving several departments, may also cause delays.

But the most serious disadvantage experienced with centralized duplication services is the bottleneck caused by the preparation of the master copies. If the flow of work is uneven, particularly in regard to such jobs as the production of complicated forms for which the master copies take some time to prepare, it is extremely difficult to provide economical staffing. The problem, however, can be overcome by requiring the departments calling for duplicating services to prepare their own master copies. This can mean that offset litho plates, stencils or spirit hectographic masters are typed or drawn and received ready for processing, or that exact copies on paper are provided from which the master copies can be produced centrally by photographic methods. The only exception to this is forms involving elaborate rulings, which are best produced centrally by trained staff using special equipment.

It may be concluded that since it is largely a mechanical function, the office duplication service can be centralized with economy, subject to reasonable limits as to distance. The preparation of master copies should, where possible, be dispersed.

Photo-copying can be done by a variety of processes. Some machines are relatively cheap and suited to casual use; others are expensive and not justifiable unless the throughput is substantial. Often the same process can be used for taking one or a few copies on paper and also for making duplicator masters. The decision to centralize the photo-copying service must therefore be taken after considering all needs together. Through centralization there may be economy of equipment, one machine serving several departments. More expert operation is possible and a process giving better quality reproduction may be justified by the volume of work handled. On the other hand, there may be inconvenience when urgent service is required.

The ready availability of photo-copiers has led to misuse. Regardless of cost they have been used when carbon copies would have served equally well. This has led to centralization, and even to the deliberate creation of inconvenience, to deter departments from making photo-copies without reasonable cause.

Other Internal Services

There are, of course, many other services internal to the office. Their number precludes dealing with them in the same detail as those above, but brief mention may be made of one or two more.

Communications services, which include telephones, mail and messengers, generally lend themselves to effective centralization. The telephone switchboard service must by its nature be centralized. The postal service also is ordinarily centralized in a postal department with all the incoming and outgoing mail at one address. The mechanical nature of the job and the fact that everything goes to and comes from one Post

Office, suggests centralization as being the normal and sensible arrangement.

In any but the smallest enterprise it is wasteful for each department to deliver its own documents to other departments. An internal messenger service, based on a central point from which messengers go on rounds collecting and delivering at specified times, is usually more economical than any other method. This, of course, does not preclude urgent matters being dealt with by whatever way seems expedient.

The case for centralization is less clear for calculating machine services. In an office where calculating machines of one kind or another are used extensively, it is sometimes the practice to provide a central section to which all jobs requiring calculation are sent. The centralized calculating service is heir to most of the advantages and disadvantages already stated. There are, however, important additional disadvantages.

Extra handling and delays in passing to and fro add considerably to the cost, and savings in actual operation need to be substantial to offset this. The work may also be less accurate; separation from the source of the work precludes continuity of understanding. Clerks have much less opportunity to build up a background knowledge of the matters to which the calculations relate and, since raising a query would involve making contact with another office, errors or ambiguities are likely to go unchallenged. These two are sufficient to suggest that centralization may only be effective in limited circumstances.

There remains a number of other services which are commonly centralized. These include recruitment, training, organization and methods, and internal audit, each of which calls for specialized knowledge. Even in these cases it is most important that centralization should not be overdone; in any arrangement which tends to restrict the responsibility and freedom of action of an executive manager, the losses are likely to exceed the gains.

In all the cases which have been examined so far it will have been seen that only in the case of the purely mechanical and factory-like duplicating service are there clear arguments in favour of centralization.

Accounting and Cost Accounting Services

In turning to the services which the office provides to others—services on behalf of the enterprise—it can be shown that the conclusions are not greatly different from those arrived at in the case of the internal services. The more mechanical the job, the greater is the case for centralization. On the other hand, wherever clerical work is closely linked with the technical operation of the business, the theoretical savings of centralization may be seriously offset by a deterioration in the service. These broad generalizations apply with equal force to the clerical services relating to the three major functions: buying, selling and production.

Buying itself no doubt benefits from a certain amount of decentralization. This is not a clerical function, but it seems reasonable to assume that the buyer needs to be closely associated with the departments he serves. However, wherever the buyer is, he will require immediately at hand those records and clerical services which will enable him to buy. There would not seem to be any case for centralization here.

But when the buyer has ordered and the goods have been delivered, there are grounds for suggesting that the job of sanctioning the invoices for payment may very well be one which can be centralized. It is not difficult to arrange for a central office to be informed of what the buyer has ordered and what the stores have received. This information should be sufficient for bought invoices to be sanctioned for payment. Some invoices, however, require a fair degree of technical knowledge if the information on the records is to be correctly interpreted. If the enterprise served is a large one, dealing with a wide range of activities and commodities, it may well be that centralization of this function is injudicious. The further the clerks are removed from contact with the goods that the records represent and the people who handle these goods, the less will the records mean to them. It is this detachment from reality that causes the type of clerical error which the practical man, with his detailed knowledge of physical events, finds so inexplicable, so stupid and, as he will say, so typical of the clerical mind.

Those who spend their lives in the office must admit that there is some justification for this attitude. It arises because the clerk does not have sufficient opportunity to familiarize himself with the reality which the records are intended to represent. If a job, like that of sanctioning bought invoices, requires technical knowledge, centralization makes it difficult for the clerks to acquire that knowledge. Therefore, the clerks should, if possible, be placed where they are best able to acquire knowledge and interest in the subject of their records. In this case it may, of course, be necessary to take special steps to prevent the possibility of collusion to perpetrate fraud.

The final stage in the process of buying is that of payment; the keeping of the bought ledgers and the drawing of remittances. At this stage the emphasis shifts. Whereas the sanctioning of an invoice for payment involves technical knowledge and familiarity with a range of goods, the keeping of ledger accounts and the making of payments requires no such knowledge. Clerks on this work are concerned only with names and addresses and with sums of money—figures and words with no obscure technical meanings. Here distance from the source of the records proves to be no great disadvantage. On the other hand, the benefits of increased volume by centralization make it worth while to spend more time on the study of method, to install elaborate equipment, and to ensure that the clerks make the full use of both. The keeping of ledgers can be centralized with great advantage and economy.

The position with regard to selling is very much the same as with buying. The salesman and the sales management require certain records to enable them to sell. These, if they are to be effective, must be located as closely as possible to the points from which the salesmen operate. This surely restricts centralization.

The preparation of sales invoices, once the sales have been made, is only a slightly more doubtful case. The handling of the customer's order and the making out of the invoice are processes which are frequently closely associated. The examination of customers' orders and ensuring their execution may require frequent contact with the sales department and with a store or factory. Invoicing and its ancillary operations may involve similar contacts. Both tasks may require not only a knowledge of the goods but of day-to-day conditions regarding supply. Unless the business is compact enough for all the departments concerned to be under one roof, centralization is likely to lead to misunderstanding, delay and inefficiency.

As in the case of the bought ledgers, it seems that the keeping of the sales ledgers and the collection of payment may well be centralized. Once again this is the realm where figures and names and addresses are paramount, and close contact with events of less importance. There is, however, need for the clerks to be aware of sales policy, and to do nothing which may offend customers or otherwise damage goodwill.

In considering the third function—office services relating to production—there is a substantial amount of work for which there is a strong case for dispersal. Unless the cost accountant and his clerks have a thorough knowledge and a lively interest in the work of the factory, their records are likely to be meaningless. Even if the records are correct, and mean something to the clerks themselves, it is possible that they will mean little to the production management for whose use the records presumably are intended. Unless the cost accountant can talk in the language of the production manager and unless the production manager is convinced that the cost accountant knows what he is talking about, the work of the cost office is likely to be largely a waste of time. This requires a considerable degree of specialization. If centralization interferes with specialization and contact with producers and production it is not in the long run likely to prove efficient. Of course, everything depends upon circumstances and size. A small factory in a single building may well find it convenient to centralize all the office services in one place, since their very propinquity will ensure that the server and the served get to learn sufficient of each other's affairs. But if factories are spread about over a large site, or are in different parts of the country, then surely the cost office must follow the factory.

The work which is best dispersed includes stock control in kind, the recording of time spent on operations and its reconciliation with the pay hours, and the preparation of cost accounts and production statistics generally. There are, however, subsequent operations which require a different type of specialized knowledge and different techniques: payroll preparation, the keeping of stock accounts in value, the reconciliation of the cost accounts with the financial accounts. These operations are generally best centralized. The larger the wages department, the more the benefit which can be obtained from mechanical methods and from the skill of clerks having a specialized knowledge of P.A.Y.E. tax, National Insurance and the rules concerning payment in respect of sickness and absence. The ultimate financial accounts must be kept centrally and with them such control and reconciliation accounts as will enable the management to be assured of the reliability of information produced by the dispersed services.

Wherever there is specialization, there is a need for co-ordination. Similarly wherever there is decentralization of clerical work there is need for a strengthening of the central co-ordinating office—usually the office of the chief accountant. Whoever is responsible for the overall accuracy of accounts and statistics, and for the prevention of fraud, must ensure that where office services are dispersed there is adequate control at head office. It is not sufficient for the head office to go its own way, and even delight in discrediting at some later date the figures produced by local or branch offices. Day-to-day controls should ensure that the entire clerical organization works as one team, even though in part dispersed.

Computer Services

The large general purpose computer, by its very nature, makes for the centralization of data processing services. The smaller visible record computer allows of some measure of decentralization dependent upon the size of the organization. Various arrangements can be made, for example—

(*a*) a central computer service using a general purpose machine or, in the smaller organization, a visible record computer;

(*b*) a computer bureau service;

(*c*) one or more visible record computers providing an immediate local information service and at the same time recording data in punched paper tape or other medium to go forward to a larger computer for further processing;

(*d*) a central computer with terminals in those departments requiring immediate information.

The factors which influence the centralization of services include those already discussed under Accounting and Cost Accounting Services. In addition, it must be recognized that the facilities offered by a computer with a large storage capacity and high speed operation are often attractive and even essential. A share in the time available on a large computer is often cheaper and more effective than the full-time availability of a small computer.

The initial collection of data for computer processing must, of necessity, be decentralized. It starts in the factory, stores, showroom, etc., where the practical activities take place. There are various methods whereby data can be recorded immediately, and even passed from a terminal device straight into the computer. If, however, the prime records are handwritten on forms, it may be desirable to bring these to a central office for encoding on punched cards, magnetic tape, etc. This arrangement is second-best in that it involves two stages: handwriting followed by encoding. Factors which may influence the decision to centralize or decentralize include the volume of data (in total and at each collecting point), the number of collecting points and the ability to ensure accuracy without some sort of pre-audit or scrutiny.

Centralized Control

In general, the centralized office service is cheaper to operate and easier to manage. Where, however, rapid service is required for departmental or functional management and distance from the central head office prevents this from being given, decentralization, even at greater cost, may be essential.

But physical decentralization does not necessarily mean that the separate offices must be managed independently. An administrative manager or director may be made responsible for providing office services, however dispersed. He may be responsible for staffing, equipping, designing methods, and controlling operations through local managers or supervisors who, whilst serving local departmental needs, look to him for guidance in clerical matters. He can co-ordinate procedures, avoiding the duplication of work which so often occurs when there are small independent offices. He can also relieve managers, whose principal responsibilities are for production, sales, buying, etc., of the distraction of controlling an office staff.

Whilst such an arrangement offers many advantages, its success will depend much on personalities. The administrative manager must not only provide an efficient service but maintain a good "customer relationship" with managers who may prefer the feeling of independence which comes from controlling their own offices. If there is resistance to centralized control, it must be overcome not only by giving good service but by demonstrating a desire to serve without interfering.

PART II

Control

4 Delegation and Inspection

The question of control comes to the fore immediately an organization of any size is envisaged. Indeed, it may be said that as soon as anyone decides to engage the assistance of another to pursue some objective, a relationship involving some measure of control has been created, although in such an elementary case little more than the obedience of the assistant may be required. Nevertheless the clear intention is that the assistant shall enable his principal to achieve more than he could possibly do by his own unaided efforts.

Where a single individual is carrying out some purpose of his own he is complete within himself. He has his own experience. As the result of that experience, he reaches his decisions. As the result of those decisions, he acts. This cycle of events in that one person is immediate and, it may be assumed, effective. When a second person is introduced, the principal is still seeking to project his mind and will in achieving his purpose, but to do so wholly or in part through the agency of someone else. The ideal is that the assistant should act in any situation as his principal would have acted. Recognition of this will indicate the manner in which sound administration must develop and at the same time the factors which make for limitation to that ideal development. By means of Delegation—the authorizing of someone to act on behalf of management—the original purpose of the organization is capable of indefinite expansion as need arises, but at each successive stage the dangers of perversion and error obviously grow. The greater the number of people working within an organization, the greater the possibility that any one of them may think and act independently rather than as a member of the team. Such independent action (not to be confused with the use of initiative directed towards the common purpose) is undesirable and weakens the collective force of the organization.

These dangers must be recognized and some attempt made to neutralize them. Hand in hand with Delegation must come its correlative Inspection. It is not enough to delegate and assume that the duties passed to another will be carried out adequately. Action must be taken to see at all times that responsibilities are being fulfilled and that the organization is indeed working to a common end. The manager must delegate if he is to keep himself free for his managerial duties: to meet his managerial responsibilities he must inspect. And the same is true, though in diminishing degrees, of each successive level of administration down to the lowest rank of supervision.

Note that authority given to the delegate is "to act," to be, so to speak, the management itself in regard to a particular job or set of circumstances. It is therefore of the greatest importance that both management and subordinates should realize exactly what situation is being created when the assignment of duties is made. It should also be borne in mind that that setting is itself, or should be, an essential part of the general organization. At every level of organization there should be an attempt to balance the requirements and capacities of that level. Balance is not perhaps the right concept as it implies a state in which small differences of emphasis may set up large reactions; a more satisfactory idea is that of the engineer whose materials must be correctly stressed if they are to meet the forces bearing on them and hold a substantial reserve of strength for excessive strains. This analogy may be pursued further. If the materials are in a vehicle on the move then the stresses will be varying widely, there will be constant adjustment of all forces, both as regards internal and external conditions, so that the desired destination be reached, or a given direction followed. Delegation, that is to say, should not be regarded as a complete, decisive and isolated act which happens at one time and thereafter produces a state of inertia; it is a form of continuous adjustment as between principal and subordinate interacting with each other to produce a desired result. Nor is the act of delegation to be regarded as the handing down of a measure of authority, the shedding of tasks, the separation of lesser duties from greater. A moment's thought will show that whatever authority is delegated paradoxically enough still remains part of the original responsibility. The superior does not abdicate when he delegates: he passes over to his subordinates a share of his responsibilities which are now discharged conjointly: the subordinate joins his superior in a task, he does not take it away from him.

If all this seems somewhat philosophical or recondite, let us consider a simple illustration. For example, the one-man business which has become too much for the man in question. He must now delegate, allow somebody else to join in, whose talents and potentialities may be inspired by the same aims and directed in the same manner. If his arrangements are fortunate his capacity has doubled. But what if the reverse is the case? His delegation has added responsibility and risk without a commensurate increase of capacity. Now consider a much later stage in the development of our hypothetical organization. It may be imagined that a large number of integrated groups have been built up whose leaders share a lively understanding of the business and have identified themselves with its objectives but are unable to transmit these attitudes to their subordinates. These latter then become shut off from the sources of drive and progress, their participation becomes meaningless, perfunctory and unsatisfying and their interest limited to such benefits as they can extract from the situation; in short they do not add, but rather withdraw strength from that business. Here is the great danger of size, that it may be all flesh and little spirit. Its symbol and symptom is the supervisor completely absorbed in the formalities of his own desk job, head down, insensitive or indifferent to the real significance of the part he is supposed to be playing in the organization he serves.

The crucial questions in each stage of delegation are: does the subordinate share the same understanding of the purpose of his tasks as his superior and is he capable of applying that understanding in the manner desired? Inspection seeks to provide the answer.

The approach to this matter of delegation may be made quite empirically in any given case, but the successful organization will be found to rest upon certain fundamentals. The first is, knowledge of the scope of the full undivided responsibility, and of the staff who are to discharge it. Then comes decision as to the manner in which the division of that responsibility shall be made, the parts to be delegated, and what may well be the more important decision, those to be retained. Next, there is the selection of the individuals to whom the particular jobs or functions are to be assigned, and the method by which they are to acquire a proper concept of their task. This is of great importance if the real objectives of the organization are not to be lost sight of—there is an ever-present danger of regarding what is being done as a purpose in itself. Finally, there is the actual working of the planned delegation and its maintenance in being.

Knowledge of the full scope of the task before division will supply its principal requirements and indicate the manner in which these may best be separated into distinct functions. It would be idle, however, to do this without taking into account the capacity of those to whom these responsibilities are to be assigned. For the same reason, an organization may well change its form from time to time as individuals are found best fitted to carry out duties in changed combinations. This perhaps may not happen so frequently in the large-scale enterprise, where any particular change which may be desirable in itself is likely to give rise to a number of others which may not be so beneficial. The essential thing is that the requirements of the job should be really met in all respects. Delegation should not be regarded as merely passing work on to someone else; it must be accepted as a natural and necessary process which avoids overloading on the one hand and frustration on the other, thus obviously strengthening the organization.

It should be borne in mind that delegation properly carried out fosters a feeling of responsibility in subordinates and encourages them to progress and expand, as well as giving the more immediate benefits of relieving the supervisor of tasks which the mere limitation of time precludes him from doing himself. Another point is the avoidance of bottlenecks and thus assuring speedier action. Reference to higher levels for decision is avoided where the intelligent supervisor has been delegated to act. It is an axiom of good organization that decision should be taken at the lowest level practicable. It is also good sense.

In a developing concern delegation will probably occur naturally with each stage of expansion of the business. Although it may be salutary to review and check from time to time, as opportunity serves, the manner in which the additional work is assigned, for the most part the scheme of delegation will evolve. A more difficult matter is to apply a complete scheme of delegation to an organization already actively working. Here it is necessary to reconsider the whole range of work and the personnel carrying it out before the plan of delegation can be framed. This, of course, means the consideration of objectives, the study of tasks and procedures, of timing and time-tables where specific performance has to be assured, and careful appraisal of the staff engaged or to be engaged on the work. In practice, naturally, much of this is avoided where some sort of organization exists already. The approach is then more in the nature of an audit to show whether the best dispositions have been made, the soundest form of delegation adopted and the right people assigned to the various jobs. It is only at this latter point that the decision as to what functions should be retained in the hands of the manager can sensibly be made. A scheme of delegation which ignores weaknesses and inadequacies in the agents who carry it out is not merely a mistake: it is a danger in that a false appearance of strength and coherence is lent to something inherently unsound. Better by far, in this connexion, muddling though than just smiling though!

In any plan of delegation it is of the greatest importance that those affected by it should really understand and accept the principles on which it has been based and this applies both from above and below. The importance of delegation may be stated quite shortly—

(1) It is necessary so that no one tries to do more than he can really accomplish.

(2) It enables the manager to free himself for the most significant tasks, thus facilitating treatment of the others in a more economical way.

(3) It spreads the load, giving a more even, continuous and speedier service.

(4) It is not a device merely for passing on work to someone else. It fosters a feeling of responsibility in subordinates and gives them a share in management.

(5) It helps to develop ability.

The appropriate time for the inculcation of this approach to the subject of Delegation is, of course, the training period of new supervisors and this aspect of the matter is dealt with in another chapter. What is most important is that there must be carried over into the mind of the individual to whom a responsibility is being delegated a complete understanding not only of the reasons for the delegation and of the setting in which it is made but of the essential role which the subordinate performs therein. He must himself see how he is helping to achieve the major purposes of the organization and the manner in which his qualities and qualifications are in fact utilized as a direct enlargement of those purposes. It is clear that the process of selecting and training those able to share such a conception requires care. Those selected must have the necessary ability or be capable of acquiring it, must have the time available to undertake the assignment and must not have other duties incompatible with it. If this is not the case it may be necessary to examine the organization and rearrange the work so that such inconsistencies are eliminated. Unless this is done satisfactorily, the whole purpose of the delegation may be defeated. And it clearly will not be done satisfactorily if the supervisors themselves do not hold or share a similar conception of the scheme of delegation, or are constantly tempted to supersede it whenever it appears to be quicker to do the job than train a delegate for the purpose. Nor will it be a satisfactory arrangement unless it is given a chance to work.

At the beginning of this chapter it was asserted that the great value of delegation lies in the speed with which experience and decision leading to action can be preserved and extended throughout an organization, however vast, by appropriate arrangements at different levels. Just as the healthy human organism develops in power and efficiency as it meets the new demands created by growth over a period of time, so it must be accepted that time is an essential factor in the development of group relationships. There must be a measure of follow-up and inspection of the work of individuals and of the manner in which the planned delegation is actually working, but only by experience and judgment of the extent to which the individual subordinate can be relied upon can the exact measure of follow-up and inspection be determined. Too frequent or too meticulous an inspection will produce lack of confidence or irritation rather than competence and initiative. Inadequate inspection may lead to a decline of standard or an easy complacency. There is no rule by which to work—indeed any regular method of inspection will probably fail to achieve its object. Rather, the process should be a continuous one, arising naturally and spontaneously (and preferably unobtrusively) out of the normal course of the work itself. If the situation is such that normal contacts of a suitable nature are not likely to arise, some thought should be given to the possibility of altering the situation so that they do.

This idea carries with it the notion that there is a limit to which the principle of Delegation can be carried as between manager and those he wishes to control and influence directly. The limit may be a very flexible one but it is fairly evident that where the organization is meeting constantly changing conditions, as in competitive business, constant contact between principal and senior subordinates will be a necessity and proper time must be allowed for it. Hence, once again, judgment must be exercised to determine what the situation demands. It may be that as many as fifteen or twenty direct subordinates can work efficiently with one principal, or as few as two or three. The important point is to recognize the existence not only of requirements but also of limitations and to strike a reasonable balance between them at all stages of the organization plan.

Inspection

The corollary of Delegation is Inspection. Inspection can be a very delicate matter. Indeed, it can be so delicate that sometimes men would rather strike than be subject to it, although in such extreme cases one cannot help feeling that this attitude results from something much more than the act of inspection alone. It is, however, most salutary to remember than the object of inspection is to discover things wrong or unsatisfactory. It is just sophistry to argue that inspection can equally demonstrate the converse, namely, what is right and satisfactory. Inevitably the act of inspection will give rise to emotional attitudes and changes on the part of those so examined—possibly of pleasure but much more probably the reverse. The more sensitive and perceptive an individual is, the more pronounced are his reactions likely to be. Furthermore, if sensitivity can be taken to include sense of responsibility, it is clear that the inspection process, whatever it is, will weigh most heavily on those who are already most conscientious. In discharging this duty of inspection, therefore, it is well to remember that for somebody the process will be one of trial in greater or less degree and this consideration should govern all that is done or said.

The manager is called upon to inspect the work, equipment and working conditions of the office, and good delegation will assist him to do this. He is, however, also called upon to do something much more subtle and do it in the subtlest way. This is to inspect, if that is the correct word, the way in which all these things are affecting the development of the individuals concerned, both separately and as a group. The manager may, for example, concern himself with the accuracy of what is being done, and may find cause for dissatisfaction. His chief concern must not be for the past, but for the future. It is the bearing of the matter on the future of that particular section of the work which he must assess. To hold staff rigidly to a code of procedure or a manual of instructions is to chain them to the past. Efficient control is concerned with the inculcation of sound principles and the encouragement of initiative. One of those principles will assuredly be that where initiative is exercised, the resulting action must be co-ordinated throughout its effects. The result of applying such a principle is that initiative is necessarily exercised in an orderly way—a corollary being that any standing instructions cannot be wilfully ignored because to do so would produce disorder for those others who may be working within them. Notice that there is a very considerable difference of approach here. The authoritarian attitude says "no deviations because they lead to disorder!"; the progressive attitude says "co-ordinate your deviations so that a new state of order (presumably an improved state of order) may be attained."

It will be seen that this is just another way of saying what was said in the opening paragraph of this chapter, that the same immediacy of experience, decision and action shall be preserved as are implicit in a single individual carrying out some purpose of his own. An individual who does not co-ordinate his powers to achieve a desired end will miss the objective: a group which does not follow some principles of action will eventually disintegrate, but a group or an individual which does not continuously seek to develop new objectives will certainly become moribund.

In inspecting the work of his subordinates, the manager or supervisor will wish to satisfy himself that proper standards of accuracy, neatness and promptness are maintained.

Accuracy

The supervisor should make sure that he sees a proportion of each branch of the work within a reasonable period. As well as inspecting finished work, he should examine work while it is being done, to see that correct methods are being used. His task is to examine the work critically so as to pick out possible errors and to see that the preceding routine has been correctly carried out. With experience it is possible to develop an ability to spot any item which stands out from the ordinary: this may then be thoroughly checked for accuracy. The scrutiny should aim at revealing not only arithmetical errors, but also errors of omission, errors of principle, departure from agreed systems and absence of proper authorities. Where authorities are necessary, clerks must clearly understand whose signatures they may accept. When errors are found the supervisor should have them corrected and also inform his manager if the matter is sufficiently serious. A record should be kept of clerks' errors, to see whether a particular class of error often recurs, or whether the same clerk is frequently at fault. The supervisor should examine this record and consider how to minimize recurring errors, or try to ascertain the cause of a clerk's inaccuracy.

It is here that skill and understanding must be used so that a situation of tension is not created. Every opportunity should be taken of consulting the clerk concerned with the matter being inspected, and the most successful way of bringing errors home to conscientious people is to put them in the position of checking themselves. It may perhaps be a laborious business, having made certain that an error has occurred, to go to the responsible person and seek his assistance in finding it and it may also be hypocritical. But the trouble is worth taking if the fault can by some ingenuity be separated, as it were, from the rest of the work and dealt with by the individual responsible as though he were re-checking himself. The recording and classification of errors is obviously something of value as giving guidance for further action, but to the clerk it looks like a black book, an indictment which may at any moment be produced with disastrous effects on his career. A wrong attitude may thus be induced, and fear and subterfuge usurp the place which confident, conscientious work should occupy. It should be feasible to arrange for the register or record of errors and their classification to be built up by the clerks themselves so that the atmosphere created is one of open, candid and, it is to be hoped, efficient—which does not of course mean faultless—participation in tasks which may offer traps for the unwary once or twice but should only be perils for the reckless thereafter. By such measures and precautions precisely the same desired ends may be attained, but in ways which are likely to stimulate rather than repress and, too, to be more lasting in their effect.

Neatness

Although some clerks find it difficult to write nearly, the standard can often be improved by explaining to an untidy worker that neatness ensures that records are legible and unlikely to be misinterpreted, and that in itself neatness leads to greater accuracy. Where work is sent outside the office, neatness is especially important; this applies even more strongly to work sent outside the business.

Promptness

There should already be established a time-table of the work, showing at what stage it is required from the various branches of the office. The senior clerks who are in charge of the different groups will need to keep a number of records but, even though the main responsibility lies with them, the supervisor must keep himself aware of the progress of the work. This is done by inspecting the records, by interpreting them, and taking action whenever necessary.

It is a very trite observation that environment has a tremendous influence on the standard of work performed, and the supervisor as well as management are well advised if the best possible conditions are maintained. The subconscious effects of well-planned, agreeable and adequate work-places are probably much more significant than the obvious ones. More and more, with the advance of design in all kinds of office appliances, form, line and colour are being offered to the eye in an almost exciting way. More and more they constitute a challenge to the rest of office paraphernalia. Critical faculties are thereby stimulated and nondescript makeshift arrangements become less tolerable than they were. It is all to the good that standards should be raised in this manner, but their maintenance demands correspondingly increased attention.

The supervisor should keep himself in touch with the working conditions in the office* both from the comments of his clerks and also by personal inspection. Aspects to be considered are—

Layout
Is the arrangement logical for the work of the section? Does it make the best use of the available space and give adequate access to desks, machines, filing racks and telephones?

Lighting
Consider both daylight and artificial lighting. Are there any jobs where bright lighting is of particular importance?

Ventilation
Is it worth while making one person responsible for window-opening?

Cleanness and Tidiness
Do the cleaners do their work satisfactorily? If there is frequent cause for complaint, should the manager be informed? Do clerks keep their desks reasonably tidy?

Decoration and General Maintenance
Is the building and the scheme of decoration in good repair?

Some of these matters may well be the particular concern of maintenance service departments. There is often the fear that the raising of points coming within the province of specialists is to invite rebuff or cause irritation. Such fears may well be groundless. Everyone likes due respect to be paid to the significance of his contribution or position in the scheme of things and it would seem most probable that with the proper approach, the specialist is likely to appreciate reference to him on matters difficult to the non-specialist, and to be very ready to find the solution. In any case it

---

* This subject is seen here from a managerial viewpoint. Legal aspects are dealt with in the Appendix.

would seem to be more sensible to raise the question and learn either the reaction or the answer, than to refrain through timidity and continue with an unsatisfactory situation.

To summarise, delegation stems directly out of the organization plan. The plan should set out the manner in which the common task of accomplishing the objects of the organization is divided up, each position sharing in this common task rather than representing a fragment all on its own. Because the organization is intended to be living and purposeful, care must be taken through training and administration to encourage its members at all levels to make the fullest contribution of which they are capable. This means avoiding rigidity and suppression, encouraging a responsible flexibility and ensuring that the major objectives of the whole enterprise are translated into the individual objective for each partici-pant, through the scheme of delegation safeguarded by an essential but sympathetic policy of inspection.

5 Output Control

The purpose of output controls is to enable the manager and his supervisors to be sure that the office is giving the service it is required to give; that their responsibilities are being fulfilled. These controls must draw attention to any failure to give proper service and, more important, indicate those cases where there is danger that a proper service may not be given in the future. The mere knowledge that work is behindhand is of little help; it may merely be a source of worry. The manager and the supervisor must try to be a step ahead of trouble and use their efforts to prevent it. Output controls should be designed as aids to this end. The control should be over the present and the future; records of the past are of value only in that they enable management to learn the lessons which previous success or failure may have to teach.

Control should be against a fairly detailed plan. It is not sufficient to know in vague terms that work is, or is likely to be, behindhand. The manager must know the position as exactly as possible in terms of man-hours of work of various grades. Armed with this knowledge, he can seek to bring relief clerks from other parts of the office or can plan overtime well in advance to meet the situation. When overtime is necessary, it is of obvious advantage to be able to warn staff some days beforehand rather than interfere with their private arrangements by asking them to stay at short notice. To be able to express the work situation in these more precise terms requires a yardstick—a measure against which the situation can be gauged.

Office work has generally, if not always, to be completed to a schedule. The payroll must be completed by a given time each week; statements of account must be mailed by a certain day of the month; sales invoices must be posted in the ledger within a stipulated period. The administrative manager must try to keep the work to schedule even in the face of fluctuations in the volume to be done. If, for example, there are more employees on the payroll this week than last, that is no reason for the wages to be paid other than at the usual time.

If each major function of the office were self-contained and could be made the responsibility of one clerk, the problems of planning and control would be comparatively simple to solve—albeit still problems.

But the modern office is not organized in this way. Jobs are broken down for various reasons into operations done by different clerks. The simpler tasks are given to the junior clerks, the more complex to the senior clerks. Work which can be mechanized is undertaken by specially trained operators.

It is this environment which makes the control of output more difficult. Specialization calls for co-ordination. Output control is therefore concerned not only with the eventual output, the finished product, but with the control of output at each stage to ensure that the various processes are carried out in concert.

Work Measurement

The purpose of work measurement in relation to output control is to establish how long a job should reasonably be expected to take; or, alternatively, how many clerks are required to do a job in the time available.

Without standards against which to compare the actual performance it is difficult, if not impossible, to judge whether or not a fair day's work is being done. Professor Parkinson drew attention to the fact that work expands to fill the time available for its completion. He stated the obvious to which management had previously been blind. Whether busy or slack, work tends to take exactly the hours that the office is open—and within very wide limits of variation. That clerks sense the varying pressure and react to it is not their fault. They cannot do work that is not there and any failure to provide a reasonable work flow must be the responsibility of the management.

In analysing work for the purposes of measurement, varying degrees of detail can be adopted and it is necessary to understand the meaning given to the following terms*—

Job —the work assigned to a person.

Task —part of a job having a readily recognisable beginning and end and making a substantial contribution to that job or the system of which it forms part.

Operation —part of a task which requires a distinguishable group of movements, for example, setting up and feeding paper into a type-writer as distinct from the operation of typing.

Element —part of an operation which is the smallest usefully distinguishable action, for example, picking up a piece of paper and positioning it on a desk-top.

The most exact method of measurement is that usually referred to as

* Mills and Standingford, *Office Organization and Method* (Pitman).

"time study," involving the breaking down of the work into its elemental parts and the timing of each element by means of a stop-watch. This method has been applied in offices, but by no means widely. Where it has been used, it has usually been associated with some system of payment by results. Time study has not been more generally applied to clerical work because it is not so well suited to the needs of the office as it is to those of the factory.

The exact measurement of work is possible at reasonable cost where operators are doing repetitive work; where, for all practical purposes, each piece of material and each product is the same as any other. In the office, each piece of "material" is usually different. In detail, no two sales invoices in a batch are exactly the same; if they were, printers rather than clerks might be required. In most clerical jobs, the clerks must be discouraged from treating each document the same as any other. One of their duties is to be on the alert for anything out of the ordinary and, on finding it, to take appropriate action. The operations cannot therefore be regarded as strictly repetitive. It is true that the elemental operations are all there and could be timed. But they are not necessarily performed always in the same order, and to record them for purposes of output control might well be a task as long as the job itself.

Let it be said, in passing, that there are simple and highly repetitive tasks in large and highly specialized offices in relation to which time-study methods can be appropriate. But they are the exception rather than the rule, and this chapter is concerned with output control in the average office with its large assortment of jobs and its inevitable exceptions, queries, telephone calls and other interruptions to the smooth flow of work.

Where time-study methods are not appropriate, it is, however, still possible to measure work, and for management to benefit thereby in the more exact control of output, whether it be the output of the office, the section, the group or of the individual clerk.

There are several other methods of establishing standards of output, all of which seek to measure work with varying degrees of accuracy and some of which can be used by a supervisor rather than a specialist. In every case it is, of course, necessary first to prepare job descriptions which define the work which is to be measured.

Pre-determined Motion Time Systems (PMTS)
By the use of advanced time-study methods it has been possible to set standard times (quite small fractions of a minute) for basic physical movements and mental processes. If work is analysed into these fundamentals it is possible, by applying the standard times, to construct a synthetic time for a task or unit of output. Building from these times, the number of clerks necessary to handle a given volume of work, after

allowing for normal queries, interruptions and special jobs, can be established. This technique is often introduced by consultants possessing the necessary time data but some large organizations have developed their own systems, and some data have been published for general use.

Activity Sampling
By this statistical method, it is possible to determine in suitable circumstances how time is spent on the different tasks which make up the work of a clerk or a group of clerks. At random intervals the task being done at a point in time is recorded. When sufficient records have been made (and a large number of observations is necessary) the number of occasions on which each task was seen to be done indicates the proportion of the day which each occupies on average. This method may require a full-time observer to ensure adequate recording and is used particularly in investigations into idle time arising from an uneven work flow. Being concerned with actual happenings, the results are of limited value in setting output standards: the work pace may have been wholly unsatisfactory.

Averaging Actual Performance
Records are kept by the supervisor of the time spent and units of work produced on successive days over an extended period, possibly over some months depending on the frequency with which tasks are performed. Where the work pressure is judged to be low, high or normal, this fact is noted. By examination of these records it is possible to see what can be achieved when the work is available and without putting undue pressure on the clerks. This may be regarded as a reasonable output under normal conditions. Such standards are best applied to the output of a group rather than of an individual.

Simple Timing
As with the averaging of actual performance, simple timing is a method which can be applied by a supervisor in the course of his normal duties. It applies the basic principles of time study in that it seeks to establish what is normally reasonable, but makes use of the office clock rather than a stop-watch.

The techniques in this method may be briefly described as follows—

(1) The first step is to select some unit in terms of which a standard time can be set. This unit should be such as to permit the easy recording of output. In the case of sales invoicing, it might be the invoice; for ledger posting, the individual item posted. The unit of work need not necessarily be directly related to the operation being measured. For example, the

amount of time spent on queries might be expressed in terms of the volume of work from which those queries arise, rather than the actual number of queries settled.

(2) A clerk must then be selected to be the subject of the test. This clerk should be of average skill and experience; to select the highly skilled or the learner may lead to results which, whilst of some interest, will not be suitable as a basis for practical control. Everything necessary must be done to gain the co-operation of the subject. Nervousness alone can spoil the test, resulting in a high output which could not be sustained or in a low output through an abnormal number of mistakes being made. The clerk should be given a full explanation of the test, and should be in sympathy with it. The general working conditions should, of course, be normal in every way.

(3) Representative batches of work should be selected for the test, care being taken to see that they are in no way abnormal. This does not mean that there must be nothing in the work that may cause the clerk to break the even flow to deal with queries. If queries are normal to the job, then the normal batch should include them. How many batches should be included in the test must be a question answered on the merits of each particular case.

(4) The size of each test batch must be such as to be realistic, having regard to the way in which the clerks are expected to work under normal conditions. Something between twenty minutes and an hour is generally suitable. If a shorter period is selected, the time spent in starting and stopping may have a significant effect on the result. In tests of long duration the need for relaxation may also disturb the result. It appears preferable to set standards in the first instance on the basis of sustained effort, and then to add some allowance for necessary relaxation and to cover the inevitable lowering of output towards the end of a day.

(5) The results of a series of tests on a particular job should be examined with care before a standard is adopted. There may be considerable variations between batches; if so the reasons should be sought. It may be more appropriate to select one result from the series as the most truly representative. Whatever method is adopted, the setting of the standard should not be a matter of arithmetic alone; it should be a matter of judgment in the light of experience of the job, the test batches and the clerk.

When the exact time studies are made, a specialist is usually employed. In these less exact studies, a specialist would probably be at some disadvantage. He would lack the experience of the job, its complexities and its exceptions, and he would lack the personal knowledge of the clerks. In view of this, the immediate supervisor is usually the most suitable person to set the standards.

This method is perhaps best described as one of expressing, in terms of time and volume, the output which is known from experience to be reasonable.

Setting Working Standards

Whichever method of measurement is employed, the standard times which result must be adjusted to allow for relaxation and personal needs. For office work this means adding between 10 and 15 per cent according to the pressures of the job.

It is also necessary when arriving at the number of clerks or the number of hours to be allowed for completing a quantity of work to make allowance for queries and other interruptions, and for special jobs (see page 61).

Work Scheduling

Work measurement, in itself, is of no value; its value lies in the application of the results. Time values have many uses, but this chapter is concerned only with their use as a basis for instituting output controls.

The first step towards applying the information gained is to prepare a list of the operations carried out in the office, showing against each—

(a) The normal volume of work in terms of the number of units per day, per week, or as otherwise appropriate.

(b) The standard time per unit.

(c) The total standard time per day, per week, etc.—(a) × (b).

(d) The day and hour by which the operation must be completed.

(e) The day and hour at which the operation can be started.

(f) The number of clerks necessary to complete the operation between the earliest possible starting time (e) and the latest permissible finishing time (d).

This simple list is the basis upon which the detailed plan of work can be established.

In planning the work of the office, the manager must seek to establish a steady flow, reducing to a minimum the effects of peak loads and slack periods. It may well be that the initial schedule shows that more clerks are required on one day than another, even in one hour of the day than another. To plan on the basis of such a schedule is plainly impracticable. Rarely is it possible to do every job just when it is most convenient. Circumstances will demand manipulation and compromise to achieve the best possible results without excessive cost caused by carrying clerks during slack times, and paying for overtime in busy times. The evolution of a workable schedule is no simple process.

Probably the greatest aid to the preparation of a balanced plan is a time chart. If each process is plotted on such a chart, showing in bar form the time available between the earliest possible starting time and the latest permissible finishing time, and carrying a note of the number of clerks required, a picture is obtained of the situation at each hour of the day. The peaks and slack periods are readily apparent and attempts can be made to smooth out the load. At the worst, overtime and time off can be budgeted with some confidence. Important though this process is, there is little that can be said of it in general terms; it is the process of expressing and solving the particular problems of the particular office.

Output Control

The plan devised as the result of work scheduling allows for the production of a budgeted volume of work according to a time-table, with such margins for contingencies as may be judged prudent. This plan is the standard against which actual performance can be measured.

The form in which the actual performance is recorded, and in which the comparison with standard is demonstrated, must depend upon the nature of the job. Some operations lend themselves readily to control on a time chart. Payroll preparation and the making up of wages is one such series of operations. Attendance records and the information on which bonus or commission is calculated are usually available at the same time each week and all processes must be completed in order that payment may be made at the same time each week. The work of payroll clerks, checkers and cashiers must be co-ordinated to ensure a steady flow. A delay on any one process can jeopardize the fulfilment of the programme, and the office manager must be aware of the situation immediately so as to be able to take corrective action before emergency measures become necessary.

A chart such as that illustrated (Fig. 9), if examined every hour or so, can give just that summary of the situation which is required.

It shows, on a time scale, the standard time for commencing and completing each major operation for each department within the payroll. The entry and calculation work should flow steadily over more than two days. A job that lasts so long can, however, fall behind schedule without being noticed. It is therefore important as well as convenient to break the work into departmental units, so that progress can be assessed every few hours. The checking of entry and of calculation does not take so long as the original work, but it must follow closely upon it if the overall schedule is to be maintained. The chart shows gaps which can be filled in with other work.

Below each line on which the standard is expressed is a line on which the actual performance can be shown. As each operation is started or finished a vertical line is drawn at the appropriate point on the time scale. The length of time spent on an operation is indicated by a horizontal line. Wherever an operation has been completed late, a double line has been

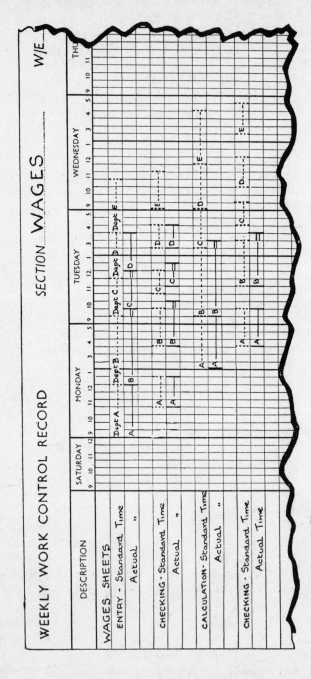

Fig. 9 Work Control Chart
[Reproduced by permission from *Office Organization and Method* by G. Mills & O. Standingford (6th Edn; Pitman, 1977)]

drawn showing the extent to which the work is behind schedule. To make the chart easier to read coloured pencils are often used. For example, the standard may be represented in blue, work completed at or before the scheduled time in green and work completed behind schedule in red. A chart entered in this way can give on a single sheet of paper a digest of the situation of the work of many clerks.

In dealing in terms of time alone it is, of course, assumed that the volume of work has not varied to any great extent from that anticipated when the plan was set. It has been said that one value of such a means of control is that it enables any failure to maintain the programme to be excused most exactly, in so far as increased volume is the cause. That is true; but output controls can scarcely be advocated on such cynical grounds. Control after the event is no control at all. Control must be over the present and the future; it must be a means to prevent difficulties and not to explain them. The control records of the past are of value only to the extent that they teach the lessons of past experience in exact terms and thereby help in the formulation of future plans. The value of the control chart in the face of increased or decreased volume is that it enables the effect in the immediate future to be assessed readily, and in respect of all operations affected.

If it is desired to observe the volume at the same time as the schedule, the scope of the time chart can be extended. The schedule having been based on a given volume of work, the standard number of units (whatever they may be) can be entered above the horizontal line representing the standard time. As the work proceeds the actual number of units completed can be entered above the horizontal line representing the actual time spent. In this way performance can be judged in terms of both the schedule and the volume.

Not every job is suited to control on a time chart. There are those jobs of a continuing nature, where the manager's concern is that the volume handled from day to day is reasonable, and that the work does not pile up until the restoration of the normal state of affairs becomes a major problem. The passing of purchase invoices for payment is an example of such a job. The number of invoices to be handled in a month may be capable of being forecast with some accuracy. But the number and complexity of those received in the post on a particular morning cannot be forecast. It depends upon the state of affairs in the offices of other businesses, as well as on the flow of goods and services received. Two methods of controlling the output of authorized purchase invoices to the bought ledgers are illustrated (Figs. 10 and 11). These are not alternatives and they will be referred to individually below. The chart shows the number of invoices received and cleared and the balance outstanding, this balance including those in query as well as those awaiting attention. This summary of the present situation is set against the balance which the

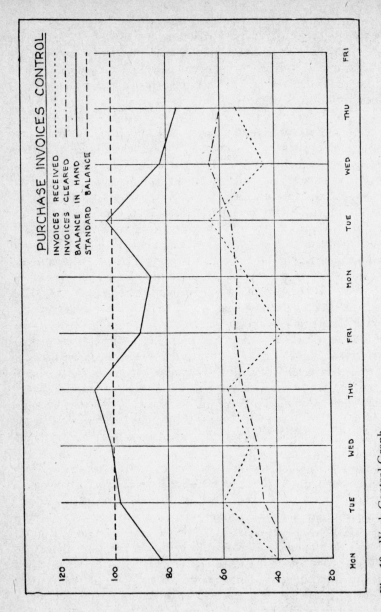

Fig. 10 Work Control Graph

[Reproduced by permission from *Office Organization and Method* by G. Mills & O. Standingford (6th Edn; Pitman, 1977)]

office manager regards as "safe." In Fig. 10, the budgeted balance is shown as a straight line, but in the light of experience this might be set as a curve. It may be known that large numbers of invoices will be received over one period of the month and that the balance will mount, but be

Purchase Invoice Control		Date	
		Actual	Standard
Previous Balance		101	95
Received		52	
Total		153	
Passed for Payment		48	50
Balance Outstanding		105	95
In Query (see below)		60	
Awaiting Attention		45	

Invoices in Query			
	Under 7 days	7–14 days	Over 14 days
Missing Goods-in Entry . . .	6	—	—
Query on Goods-in Entry . .	10	1	1
Goods not Received . . .	34	—	—
Missing Order . . .	5	—	—
Query on Order . . .	2	1	—
Total	57	2	1

Fig. 11

cleared during the ensuing week. Such a known situation can be included in the plan and, as a result, unnecessary emergency action avoided.

Output control charts are but a guide—an indication of the parts of the office which require attention. They do not provide a complete analysis of causes, nor do they provide a solution to the problems which they may reveal. The purchase invoice statement (Fig. 11) is an example of a form of control which provides for more information than can be illustrated in a compact chart. It provides for an analysis of the work outstanding, and enables the manager to follow up on invoices which are not being cleared promptly.

Special Jobs

Hitherto mention has been made only of routine—the jobs which can be measured and planned over a period. In addition, the office has from time to time to undertake special jobs such as the extraction of statistical information. The fact that these jobs may disturb the even flow of output is an additional reason for having a plan into which each special job must be fitted, and a means whereby the effect of the additional work can be judged with some accuracy. All the work of a group should be scheduled, including special jobs as they arise.

Maintenance of Output Controls

Although output controls are of vital interest to the manager of the office, they will not be of the fullest possible value if they are used by him alone.

It is suggested that controls should be maintained as close to the work as possible. Where the office is organized by sections and groups, charts should be maintained by the group leaders, i.e. the level of supervision closest to the clerks doing the job. The overall system of control for the office should be broken down, so that each group leader has an output control record on his desk and is responsible for keeping it up to date from hour to hour. It is scarcely appropriate that the manager should have information and an understanding of the situation better than the immediate supervision. Such a situation would require the manager to take personal action every time the work fell behind schedule or was in danger of so doing. Rather should the manager, by installing a control system, know that his subordinates are in no doubt as to what is actually required of them and that they have the means of judging for themselves how well or badly they are fulfilling those requirements. The group controls should be in terms of the detailed operations. At management level the controls may be less detailed, concerned with the completion of major parts of a job rather than with individual operations.

Whilst these higher level controls may be convenient, they are not essential, except perhaps in those cases where managers have charge of remote groups which they cannot hope to visit regularly. The ideal is that the manager should tour his office, say twice daily, and visit each group, examining the control chart or statement. Any further information required can then be obtained at first hand, and advice and instructions can be given.

In passing it might be mentioned that if the clerks themselves are fully aware of the timetable it may act as a stimulus and provide additional job interest.

Control of output according to a time chart or other similar device does not necessarily give a complete picture of the effectiveness of the office. It may be that the volume of work is below that budgeted, but that no effort is being made to fill the slack periods or to adjust the plan in accordance with the new situation. An overall control of the output of the office can be obtained by taking the units of work produced over a period (say a week) and valuing them at the time standards. This output at standard times can then be compared with the actual time spent on measured work. In calculating the time actually spent on measured work, all time spent on special jobs, on training and on other unscheduled activities must, of course, be deducted from the total hours worked by the clerks.

Once work has been measured in terms permitting of control, and actual output is recorded, it is possible to extend the control to apply to individual clerks. As to whether this should be done as a matter of routine, or as a periodical check, or when occasion demands, is a matter of staff policy.

The Smaller Office

Too often the techniques of scientific management are regarded as applicable to large offices only. In fact, output control is as important in the smaller office as it is in the large. One problem of the small office is lack of flexibility. Two clerks absent out of twenty can present a considerable problem calling for the redisposition of work at short notice. The information which control records afford can be of considerable assistance in determining what that redisposition should be. Furthermore the manager has, in the small business, a wide range of operations to control. Often these operations are of short duration, and for this reason can, in times of pressure, be overlooked until it is too late to complete them by the proper time.

The control chart or other written record may, however, be an unnecessarily elaborate means. It is more important that the principles of output control should be applied, than that any particular means should be employed, provided that the means is appropriate to the circumstances. It is sometimes possible to assess the work position completely and easily by examination of the various documents being handled by the clerks. In a small office, for example, there may be one clerk alone who is normally responsible for passing purchase invoices for payment. If the copy orders, goods-in entries and invoices held by the clerk are kept strictly sorted in folders, a rapid review of the job is possible. Separate folders for the following groups of documents will give the same information as the statement illustrated in Fig. 11.

Invoices Awaiting Attention
Invoices in Query—Missing Goods-in Entry
Invoices in Query—Query on Goods-in entry
Invoices in Query—Goods Not Received
Invoices in Query—Missing Order
Invoices Passed for Payment (i.e. completed work not yet passed over to the Bought Ledger)

Systematic controls of output, in whatever form, enable the administrative manager to ensure that all the jobs for which the office is responsible are done to time; and they enable him to ensure this whilst devoting the minimum of his own time to this aspect of his work.

6 Clerical Cost Control

It is often one of the functions of the office to provide cost information to the general management. The cost accountant provides detailed analyses of production costs, often comparing these with standards set as the result of elaborate work studies. Figures are provided illustrating the cost and efficiency of selling, store-keeping, maintenance and other activities. Statements are issued showing the profitability of departments, activities and products. Whilst it is not always easy to devise the means by which the general management may assess the effectiveness of each facet of the business, the problems which arise have been met and solutions found.

Despite the increasing importance of office costs, the control of them is generally far less rigid than over the costs of other departments. The office is "part of the overhead" and as such its cost is often examined in general terms only. The administrative manager may be criticized for the cost of his office, possibly unjustly—and equally possibly with justice. His critics may be unsure of their ground and be unable to be specific as to their reasons for criticism. He may be unable to justify his costs and policy other than in very general terms. This problem is of equal importance to the administrative manager and to the general management to which he is responsible.

In broad terms it may be said that every cost-control technique which industry employs has been applied to clerical work. But it has often been found necessary to make some modification on the grounds of expense. The exact measurement of work, which is justified in a mass-production factory, may well prove unreasonably expensive in an office where there is a wide variety of operations carried out, many of them not of a highly repetitive nature. This difficulty has, however, been met by making less exact measurements which have nonetheless proved valuable.

The methods of cost control with which this chapter is concerned fall into two classes. Firstly there are those in which the work as done is measured and some standard set with which actual cost may be compared. Into this class fall the detailed standard costing of operations and the less detailed budgetary control. Both are concerned with the cost of clerical work as it is done, but place no emphasis on the cost of service. Secondly there are those methods which seek to relate the cost of the office to the activities of the business; these again can be broad or detailed.

In seeking to control cost it is perhaps not enough to apply either the one method or the other. If the service given is costed, a trend of cost can be observed and conclusions drawn from it. If the weekly cost of the payroll section is expressed as a sum per employee paid, this is useful information. But it offers no guide as to whether that cost is reasonable or capable of being reduced. To complete the picture it is necessary to be able to examine the cost of the operations which the particular system in use demands. Only when the cost of the parts of the system are known and justified can the cost of the system as a whole be judged, unless of course the administrative manager is fortunate enough to have before him the costs of similar systems in operation elsewhere with which he can make comparisons.

The methods which are described below are representative of four types which have been instanced.

Budgetary Control

This method seeks to forecast the cost of the office and subsequently to compare the actual cost with the forecast. If the budget is to be realistic and the subsequent comparisons of actual cost helpful, the forecast must be made in some detail. It is not enough, except perhaps in the smallest office, to budget a total sum for wages, stationery, depreciation, maintenance and other headings of cost.

In the majority of offices wages form the largest single item of cost. The wages budget should be based upon a staff establishment sufficient to carry out the work which has to be done. Where the jobs and the clerks have been graded (for example, according to the I.A.M. scheme described in Chapter 9) the calculation of probable cost is made easier. Each section of the office will have its allotment of A, B, C, D, E, F, G and H grade clerks. Furthermore, if the salary scale is related to these job gradings, a rate of pay can be applied to each grade and the wage cost calculated. According to the anticipated fluctuations in the volume of work, provision must be made for overtime pay and for the cost of temporary staff where these are likely to be employed. A wage budget set in this fashion provides a means whereby fluctuations in cost can be readily associated with some particular job or section of the office.

In addition to basic pay, overtime pay and the cost of temporary staff, provision will need to be made for National Insurance, Pension and other supplementary costs associated with wages. The nature and scope of these will depend upon the personnel policy of the particular business.

Among the remaining costs which the office manager has under his control and should include in his budget are the following—

Stationery and Sundries
Postage
Telephone Rental and Call Fees
Depreciation of Office Machinery and Equipment
Office Machine Hire
Maintenance of Office Machinery and Equipment
Travelling and Sundry Expenses

The estimate of these costs should again be supported by schedules showing the basis of calculation, so that, in the event of significant differences between the actual cost and the budget, the reason can be ascertained.

The scope of the administrative budget will depend in many ways on the general management's policy in assigning responsibility. For example, the cost of space occupied may be regarded as appropriate for inclusion in a departmental budget, or it may be regarded as the concern of the general management and therefore treated as part of the general overhead of the business. If there is a system of budgetary control in operation throughout the organization, then this, too, will have some influence on the scope and form of the office budget.

In establishing a budget such as that envisaged, there must be an assumption of a certain volume of work to be carried out. The schedules supporting the budget must therefore give some indication of the anticipated activity of each section. This can be in relatively broad terms, as for example—

Accounts Section: Number of active accounts in the Bought and Sales Ledgers.
Cashier's Office: Number of cash book entries per week.
Wages Section: Number of employees on the payroll.
Sales Invoicing: Number of invoices prepared per week.

Whilst key figures such as these will not suffice to explain all fluctuations in cost they are a useful addition to the budget and to the actual costs when these are compared.

Operation Costing

Whereas the cost budget deals with the cost of doing work in broad terms, the operation costing provides an estimate in detail. It is a prerequisite of operation costing that each operation shall have been defined and measured in terms of time. This measurement need not be exact in terms of seconds provided that it is realistic and makes due allowance for the vagaries of the job.

Where work has been measured in terms of time for the purposes of output control (see Chapter 5) it is a comparatively short step to extend this into terms of value. The cost of preparing a sales invoice, for instance, could be built up as illustrated in Fig. 12 where each operation has been shortly described and the standard time per 100 units shown. To this has been added the job grade for each operation and the standard cost rate per hour for that grade based on wages plus related costs (overtime, National Insurance, pension, etc.). From this has been calculated the

Operation	Standard time per 100 (mins)	Job grade	Standard rate per hour £	Standard cost per 100 £
1. Receive, control and sort copy dispatch notes	60	A	0.60	0.60
2. Price	120	C	0.95	1.90
3. Check prices	90	D	1.20	1.80
4. Extend and calculate discount	240	B	0.75	3.00
5. Check extension	180	C	0.95	2.85
6. Type invoice	600	C	0.95	9.50
7. Check invoice	300	D	1.20	6.00
8. Prepare for post	100	A	0.60	1.00
				26.65
Stationery				
100 Invoice sets				9.00
100 Envelopes				0.75
100 Postage Stamps (6½p)				6.50
Allowance for Sundries				2.50
Supervision (10% of labour)				2.67
				48.07

Fig. 12 Standard Costing—Sales Invoicing

standard cost per 100 units of each operation and the total cost for all operations. The cost of stationery and postage has been assessed with some allowance for sundries, and finally an arbitrary allowance to cover the supervision has been added. In this way an estimate has been made of the cost of preparing and dispatching an average invoice.

It is possible that a similar estimate in total could have been made more simply by taking the total cost of the Sales Invoicing Section and dividing by the total number of invoices prepared. But such an estimate would not show how the various operations contribute to that cost. With all the factors before him, the manager may well be led to improve his systems and reduce the cost.

Where such detailed standard costings have been introduced, they have sometimes been used as a means of charging other departments of the business for the services which the office performs on their behalf. The cost of sales invoicing can be charged to the Sales Department at a rate per invoice, any fluctuations in the volume of work being then reflected in the accounts of that department rather than in the overall cost of the office service. Similarly if the office charges a fixed rate per employee for calculating wages, this cost is equitably distributed among other departments according to the staff which they employ. Whilst such a method of distributing clerical cost is applicable to routine operations, there are other sections of the office which cannot be dealt with so easily.

The cashier's work and the preparation of financial accounts and statistics for general management are examples of functions which are often properly treated as part of the general overhead. They can, however, still be the subject of a fixed cost allowance within which the administrative manager can endeavour to work.

Every office has the task of undertaking special investigations and preparing special reports for both departmental and general management. Such work cannot, of course, be pre-estimated in detail nor can it be the subject of standard charges. It is nevertheless important that those who make use of these services should be made aware of the cost which they entail. It has in some organizations been found worth while to record the time spent on such work and to assess and make known the cost.

It will be seen that the introduction of the detailed costing of clerical work opens up many possibilities. It can provide merely a measure of cost for the guidance of the administrative manager and to enable the general management to understand how this portion of their overhead arises. Beyond this it can provide a means of allocating clerical cost to other departments and to the various products and activities of the business.

Indices of Cost

Probably the simplest and most widely used methods of judging the efficiency of the clerical service is by relating the cost to some factor indicative of the activity of the business which the office serves. Thus the total cost of the office may be expressed as a percentage of turnover, or as a cost per unit of production or sales. In its simplicity, however, it is often an over-simplification of something which in its nature may be highly complex.

If the office were performing nothing but routine tasks directly related to the volume of business done, a general index might well be adequate. But in every business there is a hard core of clerical work which does not tend to fluctuate with the amount of trade done. The manning of the telephone switchboard and the keeping of the final accounts are random examples of this type of job. Even the routine operations will not necessarily bear a direct relationship to the general activity. In an expanding business it may well be the policy to accept smaller orders so as to obtain more customers, and as a result the invoicing and account-keeping cost per £ of turnover will rise. An increase or decrease in the number of employees on the payroll of a medium-sized business may result in the employment of a wage clerk who cannot be fully occupied.

Where general indices of cost are used it is desirable therefore to supplement them in some way. The simplest is perhaps to break down the total office cost so as to separate the "hard core" of work from the routine which tends to fluctuate with changes in general activity. This latter part of the work may then require further dissection before a reasonable judgment of efficiency can be made by this means.

Costing the Service

A development of the simple index of cost is a series of unit costs each based upon some related factor in the activity of the business.

For example, the cost of calculating and paying wages arises from the employment of people in the various departments of the organization. An acceptable unit is therefore "an employee on the payroll." And a unit cost may be calculated by dividing the total cost of the wages section of the office by the number of employees being paid at any time. Whilst so simple a formula may be adequate for some offices, in others the work of the wages section may include complications such as the calculation of premium bonus. In such a case it might well be considered desirable to dissect the cost of the section as between payroll work as such on the one hand and premium bonus calculation on the other. The section would then have two unit costs—

(a) the cost of payroll work generally, divided by the number of employees paid;

(b) the cost of premium bonus calculation, divided by the number of employees on bonus (presumably a smaller number).

Fig. 13 provides an example of a chart on which the unit cost of calculating premium bonus has been plotted for control purposes. The "standard cost" is expressed as bars, in this case at a level representing 23 pence per employee per week. This standard is not necessarily calculated by any formula; it may merely be the current cost at the time that the unit cost control system is introduced. Once every quarter the actual cost per unit is calculated and plotted as a line graph over the bars. In the figure the first quarter, December quarter, shows an actual cost a little less than the standard. In the March quarter the cost has risen to 24 pence per unit; the reason has been briefly noted on the chart as "Reduction in units."

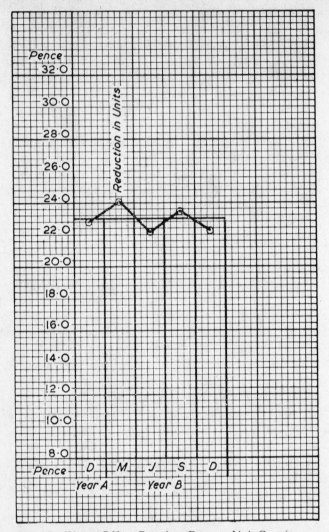

Fig. 13 Wages Office. Premium Bonus—Unit Cost (per Employee per Week)

The total number of employees being paid premium bonus has fallen whilst the office cost has remained the same. Thus a factor outside the control of the manager has influenced his cost per unit of service given. As soon as he can, the manager will presumably reduce his cost in an endeavour to meet the new situation and the actual costs of succeeding quarters suggest that he has some success in this endeavour.

In the office as a whole, there will be a number of different units, each appropriate to some section of the work. In Chapter 2, the organization

of the office of a laundry is described. For this office it might be desirable
to establish the following unit costs—

Section	Unit	Unit cost
Wages	Employee paid	p per employee-week
Premium Bonus	Employee on Bonus	p per employee-week
Laundry Lists	List	p per list
Invoices	Invoice	p per invoice
Accounts and		
other sections	—	£ per week

The number of units has been kept small. In those sections of the office
where the work does not tend to fluctuate with the volume of business the
unit adopted is the pound sterling. In other words, fluctuations in cost will
be observed and commented upon when necessary, but not against the
background of the volume of any particular activity. An examination of
the organization chart of this office (Fig. 6) shows that in some cases the
jobs treated in this way engage one clerk only and for this reason alone it
would be inappropriate to treat them in the same way as the larger routine
sections.

Fig. 14 shows a unit-cost chart for the laundry lists section of this office.
In the December quarter the standard, originally 1·82p per list, has been
reduced to 1·77p per list, the economy being expressed by the shaded
portion of the bar. A note has been made, this time inside the bar, that the
reduction has been possible because an increase in the volume of work
has been absorbed without additional expenditure. In the September
quarter a further increase in volume brings about a further decrease in
unit cost, but the manager, perhaps anticipating a reversal of the trend,
leaves his standard unchanged. In the following quarter, however, the
trend continues and the standard is again reduced, a substantial portion
of the bar being shaded.

Such a chart kept over a period of years provides an interesting and
useful record for the administrative manager and for the top management
to which he is responsible. All significant facts can be recorded. If a rise in
clerical wage-scales occurs the bar representing the standard would be
raised accordingly, even though economies in other directions offset the
cost. The shaded portions of the standard bars represent the results of the
manager's endeavours towards economy and in justice should show the
full result.

An example of the standard being raised and immediately lowered is
given in Fig. 15, a chart of the unit cost of keeping stores records in an
engineering factory office. In the last quarter shown, additional work has
been taken on at the request of the general management and the standard
has risen accordingly.

But during the same quarter some reorganization within the office has

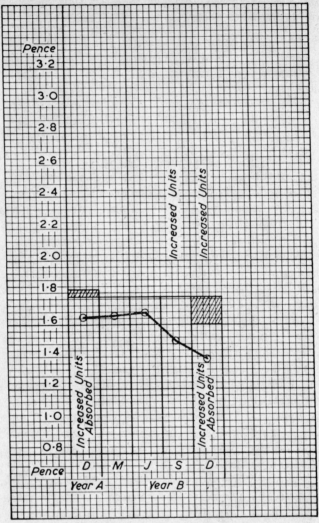

Fig. 14 Laundry Office. Laundry Lists—Unit Cost (per list)

enabled this work to be absorbed without additional staff. The standard has therefore been restored immediately to its previous level, and the portion representing the cost of the additional work shaded in to represent an economy made.

If unit-cost charts of this type are to be accepted by the general management as a true reflection of the office costs and level of efficiency they must, of course, be fully supported by the costing of any changes in standard. There must be a proper distinction between changes in cost

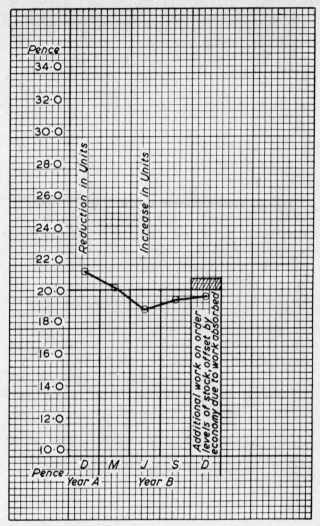

Fig. 15 Engineering Factory Office. Stores records—Unit Cost (per requisition)

which are the responsibility of the office and those which reflect changes in other departments, in company policy or in the scope of the clerical service provided. For example, salary increases given to individual clerks within an approved scale and in respect of promotion on merit must be the administrative manager's responsibility with no change in standard. The cost, on the other hand, of a general revision of salary scales is something outside the manager's control and the full effect could properly be shown as an increase in the standard unit-cost. If the new scale were not fully applied immediately, the level of the bar would show the anticipated effect and an increase in actual cost up to that level could be accepted without comment.

The application of this system in all but the smaller offices will necessarily involve some arbitrary allocation of general costs among the different units. As these items are normally a comparatively small proportion of the total cost, an elaborate analysis is not of importance.

Comparison of Methods

The four methods which have been instanced, whilst not exhaustive of the subject of cost control, are representative solutions of the problem.

Two provide expressions of cost in the form of calculated estimates. The detailed costing of clerical operations indicates what the manager regards as a proper cost for a particular job. And it supports this assessment by a list of the operations which he has authorized as part of the system to be followed, an estimate of stationery and other incidentals necessary, and a reasonable allowance for supervision. Such a costing permits the manager to assure himself that he has eliminated wasted effort and material from his plans, and provides a basis upon which performance may be judged in detail. Whilst there is much to recommend it when designing systems and estimating the effects of proposed changes, maintaining costings up to date for the whole of the work of an office is both laborious and expensive. To control the actual costs against the full detail which they contain also entails elaborate records of each clerk's work and summarization of these records which may well require a special clerk or clerks. In a large office engaged on the mass-processing of documents, the cost of detailed control may well be justified and its possibilities are worthy of examination, but in the general commercial or industrial office with its wide diversity of tasks, some taking but a few hours or even minutes per week, it is seldom justified.

The other method of providing a calculated estimate of cost is budgetary control. This has the comparative advantage of cheapness. It is easy to prepare, in that only broad headings of cost may be used. It is equally simple to collect actual costs for the purpose of comparison. But its cheapness and simplicity of operation are a reflection of its generality, and it provides little guide as to the true efficiency of organization or methods. From the point of view of general management, a budget assists in establishing the general pattern of overhead cost within which the business must operate, and the comparison of actual costs against it enables undesirable trends to be seen and checked.

The remaining two methods are concerned in associating the office cost with the service which it provides. To this extent they provide a more realistic control over cost than those which take no account of true achievement. Indices in broad terms offer a general guide as to whether the office cost is being kept within an amount which the business can afford. If the business can afford ten per cent of its turnover by way of clerical service, it is, of course, of importance to the general management to know when this proportion is exceeded. It may, however, be that the solution to a rising percentage lies in the revival of a shrinking turnover rather than a demand that the manager shall economize. The broad index, therefore, has limited value.

The unit-costing system allows the cost of the office to be observed in relation to the practical services which it is called upon to render. It provides a simple expression of cost which does not demand an elaborate recording system or the collection of cost in great detail. It enables changes in circumstances such as new demands made upon the office to be recorded in terms of cost for the benefit of the administrative manager and those to whom he is responsible.

The decision as to which method or combination of methods is employed must depend upon circumstance. The size of the office, the complexity of its work and the nature of the business which it serves must all be given due weight. One thing, however, is certain; the responsibility of the administrative manager is not fulfilled unless he takes some positive action to control his own costs and account for them at least as adequately as he would for those of other departments.

7 Internal Audit

Among his many administrative responsibilities, the administrative manager has the duties of ensuring accuracy and preventing fraud. These responsibilities cannot be fulfilled in isolation; they arise in every facet of his work. In planning the organization, duties must be so divided that fraud cannot go undetected without collusion. In selecting staff, consideration must be given to trustworthiness. In designing procedures, steps must be included to check and prove the accuracy of work done, and to throw light on those errors which will inevitably occur. Experience shows, however, that these steps alone are not sufficient to assure an administrative manager that all is well. In spite of routine checks, scrutiny and reconciliations, errors in principle and in execution will arise, and even remain undetected unless some independent check is imposed. This independent check is the function of internal audit.

In its broadest terms, the duty of an internal auditor is no different from that of an official auditor appointed in accordance with the law. He must ensure so far as he is able that the books of the business or other organization present a true picture of its affairs. But there is a fundamental difference in approach. The official audit normally takes place after all the clerical work has been done, after all routine checks have been applied and after the most senior accounting staff have examined and proved the result to the best of their ability. Furthermore, the official audit takes place, perhaps, annually only and, at that, some months after the end of the financial year. The internal audit is a continuing process. It includes the inspection of records as they are being made. It is concerned as much with the effectiveness of methods as with the accuracy of the final product.

The functions of an internal auditor can, of course, be performed by an outside agency. A firm of accountants can be engaged to carry out periodic checks of whatever kind may be appropriate. In the small organization this may well be the best arrangement. Where, however, there is sufficient work to justify the employment of a full-time audit clerk or clerks, there are advantages in the internal auditor being on the staff. In the first place it will probably be less expensive to pay the audit clerk's salary than to pay professional fees. Then there are the benefits of continuity; the more the audit clerk becomes familiar with procedures the more effective he can become. When new procedures are installed or minor changes are made, he can be immediately aware of them and, if called upon so to do, can check their effectiveness in the prevention of error and fraud. If the clerks in general know that their work is always subject to audit it will have its effect in encouraging greater care. And if an audit is not a rare, and perhaps even a terrifying experience, the work of the office is not disorganized as a result.

The scope of internal audit is a matter for management to decide. It will usually cover all security measures to ensure the safety of cash, goods and other assets. Beyond this it can be extended to check that all clerical work is being carried out to schedule and that all work done serves some useful purpose. In any office there is an ever-present danger that records are maintained after their usefulness has ended. Statistics may be required to meet a particular circumstance and they may be of great value. As time passes and circumstances change, these statistics may become gradually of less importance, and there must come a time when they should be discontinued or, at least, amended in form. The auditor can be asked to examine the records from this point of view in the course of his work. Indeed his scope can, at the management's discretion, include any aspect of the office.

Audit Responsibility

When an internal auditor is appointed, the question arises: to whom shall he be responsible? The official auditor is responsible to some body beyond the management of the organization, and is for the protection of that body, be it the shareholders, members or the public at large. The internal auditor is working to assist the management in fulfilling their duties. It is, therefore, obvious that he must be responsible to the management, but to whom he should report can be a matter of differing opinion. He can be responsible to the board of directors or its equivalent; he can serve the general management; or he can be a member of the office staff, coming under the senior administrator, by whatever title the latter may be known. If the audit clerk is to report fearlessly on the work of the office as a whole, and have access as of right to the records, he must receive his authority at a high level. He cannot work effectively if his loyalty is divided by being asked, in effect, to report unfavourably on his own chief to someone else.

Whilst the internal auditor must be responsible to some senior member of the management, that member must be able to direct operations. The board of directors can receive reports, but it is unlikely to be able to plan the audits, select and train audit clerks, and see that the work is done. The general manager may be able to fulfil these functions, dependent upon the nature of the undertaking. In banking, insurance or indeed any organization in which the work done is largely of a clerical nature, the internal audit department may quite naturally report to the chief executive. In industry and commerce, it may, on the other hand, be completely inappropriate because the general manager has no particular knowledge of accountancy or clerical work. The responsibility must then fall on the senior administrator, who may be the secretary, the chief accountant or the administrative manager.

The audit clerk's position within the organization needs to be clearly defined and generally understood. Of necessity, he represents the senior management but his personal status is probably equivalent to that of a section supervisor. He is placed in a position in which he must report upon the work of his peers and even on those who stand above him in seniority. It is, therefore, important to establish that he is an agent acting under instructions from a high level, and to remove as far as possible any personal consideration. His relationships with managers, supervisors and clerks must be friendly but formal, and this aspect of his work must be given due weight when the audit clerk is selected.

The Audit Clerk

Dependent upon the size of the office, there may be one audit clerk, or a number forming an audit department under a manager. However few or however many there may be, each audit clerk works largely on his own and must be capable of so doing. In a large audit department, there may be senior clerks and juniors but both will in varying degrees have to face the same problems.

In seeking to analyse the requirements of any job, there is a temptation to describe a paragon of all the virtues. In practice, the ideal person is rarely to be found and it is necessary to look primarily for those characteristics which are vital to the job, accepting second best in other directions. What are the outstanding qualities in a good audit clerk? Technically, he must have a sound knowledge of accounting and possibly cost accounting. He must be quick at figures and be able to write a concise report in good English. He must be neat and methodical, critical in his approach and trustworthy. As a person, the audit clerk must be acceptable to others, pleasant in his manner but not over-friendly. These requirements presuppose a good general education and some training in accountancy. The remaining characteristics are more personal and more important. Technical ability can be achieved by study; the right person for the job must be selected with careful regard for his natural character.

Where there is an audit department comprising a number of clerks, it may be possible to train young men and women with the right potentialities. In the smaller organization, having a few audit clerks, it is usually found more satisfactory to engage those who have already had experience on the staff of a professional accountant. Auditing is an art which is mastered only after extended experience. The skilled auditor can select a sample of work which is adequate but not excessive. He is aware of the common types of error and their causes. He is observant and looks for abnormalities. The mere checking of entries and of arithmetic is not enough. The complete audit demands an appreciation of the purpose of records, and an ability to assess whether that purpose is being adequately fulfilled.

Functions of an Internal Auditor

The auditor inspects and reports on what he finds. He has no executive power; he should give no instructions to supervisors or clerks. He may acquaint them with anything which he discovers to be amiss, and in ordinary circumstances should do so in order that corrective action may be taken immediately. It is the auditor's duty to offer advice and to make suggestions and recommendations in the proper quarters. If he finds errors of principle or of practice it is better that he should report that he has found them, drawn attention to them and seen them corrected, than that he should merely report their existence. The positive approach to auditing seeks firstly to prevent error and fraud and secondly to have errors corrected. This is by far preferable to the approach which is concerned only with detection and reporting.

Whilst the methods adopted by the internal and the official auditor have much in common, their duties should not overlap where this can be avoided. They should be complementary and there should be consultation between them to this end. It must, however, be borne in mind that a statutory auditor has responsibilities which he cannot delegate and that some duplication of effort may arise for this reason.

The existence of an internal auditor does not in any way reduce the responsibilities of managers and supervisors in relation to accuracy or security. If work is subjected to audit, this is no reason for reducing the amount of routine checking or scrutiny. The auditor is not responsible for accuracy; he is there to inspect work which should already be accurate. Because an audit clerk has no set routine, it may seem convenient in times of stress to second him to other duties or to have him act as a routine checker. This is undesirable. The auditor, having himself taken part in doing the work, cannot then audit it. His function must be kept apart or his effectiveness will be considerably weakened.

A competent internal auditor will concern himself as much with the effectiveness of procedures as with the way in which they are being operated. If in his view a system is lacking in security provisions or permits errors to go undetected he must report to that effect. If he sees wasted effort or has ideas whereby a system might be improved, he should say so. In this field, however, he should not assume the responsibilities of an Organization and Methods specialist. Because of his detailed inspection of the work being done, he is often able to draw attention to weaknesses and even to suggest remedies. He should report what he finds, give his comments, but go no farther. If the management decides to follow his recommendations, the responsibility for action will lie with the executive management, with the aid of the Organization and Methods department, where such exists. By collaboration with the Organization and Methods specialists, the auditor can contribute much; by usurping their functions he may cause ill-feeling at the least, and probably waste time.

In the very nature of his work, the internal auditor comes into contact with every activity within the office. He is often in a position in which he, seeing something wrong, could put the matter right. He must resist any temptation to go beyond his function, which is to inspect on behalf of the senior management and report his findings to them and to the local supervision and management where appropriate.

The work of the internal auditor may be regarded as falling into three classes—

Routine Checks
In certain instances the management may require that every transaction of a particular type shall be audited. These are submitted as a matter of routine, but the object is to add further safeguards to accuracy and security rather than to excuse the normal routine checks applied in the office procedure.

Scheduled Inspections
In accordance with the audit programme, different sections of the work are inspected periodically, but at irregular intervals.

Special Investigations
As the management may require, particular aspects of the work are examined. These investigations may result from unexplained discrepancies in accounts, an exceptional number of errors or queries arising, because of abnormalities in statistics or for any other reason. The investigation may, in fact, be the result of the auditor's own findings following a scheduled inspection.

Which work shall fall into each of these classes is a matter for management decision. The following examples should not therefore be regarded as other than typical.

Routine Checks

In their very nature, these involve the audit of every entry as it arises or soon afterwards.

Bank Reconciliation
A weekly check of the bank statement against the cashbook and supporting vouchers.

Payments
The audit of all authorities for payments over a certain amount. As an additional safeguard this may be done before the final authority is given.

Scheduled Inspections

The audit programme must be complete in that it covers all aspects of clerical work and records. At the same time it must ensure that an audit is unexpected. If it is known in advance that work is to be examined, the auditor will not be able to assess the normal accuracy or security because extra care may be taken. There is advantage to be gained from clerks knowing that their work will be audited, but not ordinarily from their knowing when it will be audited.

A complete audit of all entries should not be necessary. The object is not to carry out a routine check but to test the effectiveness of the checks which are already being applied. Rather than a brief examination of all entries, there should be a thorough examination of a proportion. As a general guide, the detailed verification of ten per cent or even five per cent of the work will reveal any significant tendency to depart from the required standards. This sampling technique should reveal any errors of principle, and indicate where errors of practice are occurring. The selection of samples of work is a matter for careful consideration in the light of experience. In checking petty cash accounts it may be found best to examine all payments made in one particular week. In examining the payroll, a thorough check might be made of five per cent of items in each of a number of weeks over the year.

Where work is found to be unsatisfactory, the schedule may need to be changed in order to fit in a further audit quickly. If corrective action is known to be in hand, reasonable time should, of course, be allowed for this to become effective. If the routine has been amended, time should be allowed for this to become established. An examination made when the work is receiving abnormal attention from management and supervision does not give a fair picture of what is likely to occur in the ordinary way.

Within the scheduled inspections fall the following types of work and record—

Cash Balances
Cash held by cashiers and the holders of petty cash floats is checked against the books and vouchers.

Debtors and Creditors
The balances outstanding on accounts in the sales and purchase ledgers are checked and confirmation of them obtained from debtors and creditors respectively.

Purchase Invoices
A sample of invoices is examined to see that they have been properly authorized for payment and that the goods or services which they represent have, in fact, been received.

Payroll
The audit of payments made to see that the correct procedure has been followed in all respects, i.e. recording of time, certification of attendance and overtime, rate of pay, computation, P.A.Y.E. and other deductions, authorization of holiday pay, sick pay, bonuses etc.

Stocks and Stock Valuations
The verification of stock records to test their accuracy and reconciliation with the financial accounts. The audit should cover vouchers relating to receipts and issues, the pricing of issues and stock valuations and comparison of the book stock with the actual stock in hand. In addition, the auditor should ascertain and report on such matters as minimum and maximum stock levels, obsolete and slow-moving stocks, quantities purchased and frequency of stocktaking.

Capital Expenditure
A check to ensure that all capital expenditure has been properly authorized.

Sales Invoices
A sample of invoices examined to see that the quantities agree with those booked out of warehouse stock, that the prices charged and discounts allowed are in accordance with policy and that the amount has been posted to the correct customer's account.

The nature of a scheduled inspection can be varied as well as its frequency. On one occasion an audit may be concerned only with the financial accounts. On another occasion the same entries might be traced also to cost accounts or management control statistics. In these days, the formal accounts of a business are only a part of the records essential to management. The internal audit is concerned with the accuracy of all the information recorded and provided by the office or by other departments. Figures produced by a factory clerk for the use of a foreman cannot properly be ignored because they find no place in the official accounts or in statistics for the higher management. It is to be assumed that these figures are the basis on which the foreman takes decisions, and those decisions have their ultimate effect upon the financial results of the enterprise. For this reason it is important that they should be both accurate and appropriate.

An audit should from time to time cover entire systems or groups of systems from end to end to ensure that there are no weaknesses in principle or practice. For example, material brought into a factory might be traced from the order, through receipt, store and usage to the finished product and its sale. Such a check may well disclose deficiencies in control and also bad estimating or costing of which the management may not be aware.

Special Investigations

From time to time a scheduled audit may reveal inaccuracies which suggest the need for a wider inquiry to establish their true cause. In most cases it is to be hoped that the audit report will suffice to lead the executive management and supervision to trace the trouble and correct it, for this is their function. Sometimes, however, a difficulty may be deep-seated or involve a number of departments and the management may require the internal auditor to carry out a special investigation. In cases of suspected fraud such a step is almost certain to be taken. The auditor's assistance may also be required where there are substantial stock discrepancies or reconciliation differences within the accounts.

Special investigations are quite properly part of the work of internal audit, but they should not be allowed to interfere unreasonably with the routine checks and scheduled inspections. If they do, the whole audit service may be undermined. Because the audit clerk is not tied to a routine operation throughout the day, he may come to be regarded as available to help any department in difficulty with its clerical work. Any such tendency should be resisted. The auditor's task is to inspect and report. If a department is in difficulty with its work, the management of that department must remedy the defect. The auditor may help in diagnosing the problem, but should not ordinarily be used as a relief clerk in the solving of it.

The Audit Plan

It is not possible to forecast exactly how long a particular audit will last. If everything is clearly in order the clerk's work may soon be over. If, on the other hand, inaccuracies are found the examination of the records may be protracted and the report lengthy. This inherent difficulty makes it the more important to plan how the auditor's time shall be spent. If he is allowed to move from job to job without a programme, there is a danger that the various records will not be examined as frequently as is necessary and that this deficiency may be overlooked.

Firstly the routine checks and scheduled inspections should be listed, thus establishing the scope of the auditor's work. Then, against each item should be entered the frequency with which each is to be carried out and some estimate, however rough, of the time to be allowed. From this list, after making some overall allowance for special investigations, a programme can be drawn. At the first attempt, such a programme will be no more than a guide against which progress can be observed. If it is amended as may be necessary in the light of experience, it can become a reliable forecast.

However well established a programme may be it must remain flexible. As each job is completed, the date at which it shall next be undertaken should be reconsidered. If there are reasons for dissatisfaction, it may be desirable to repeat the inspection after a comparatively short interval, or possibly to re-examine some particular record only. In any case, the programme must not become so stereotyped that the office in general is able to forecast when audits can be expected.

The Audit Report

The purpose of the audit clerk's report is primarily to give an assessment of the state of clerical work from the points of view of accuracy and security. Beyond this he must feel free to comment on any other matters which in his opinion are worthy of mention.

It is not usually necessary to report in detail to the higher management every error located. To do so may make for bad feeling within the office and be generally wasteful of time. The auditor should be accorded the right to use some discretion in reporting his findings. If a straightforward clerical error is found, and is capable of immediate correction by the clerk concerned, it may be sufficient to have it corrected, point out its implications and go no farther. A tendency to error on the part of a particular clerk resulting from inexperience or lack of proper instruction should be reported immediately to the responsible supervisor or manager. The auditor who shows a desire to help and advise will probably gain greater co-operation and be more effective than one who feels bound to reveal every minor irregularity at the highest level.

Where, however, there are general departures from the established procedure, he must report the matter to the management since it will probably demand their action. If matters of principle or policy are involved, or dishonesty is revealed, he will certainly be required to take the matter to the highest level. Unless there are special reasons for secrecy, he should make his report known to the local management. When there is unsatisfactory work it is desirable that corrective action should be taken at once. If anyone is to be criticized for bad work it is as well that they should know of it, and have agreed that the criticism is valid.

In these varying situations the audit clerk needs some guidance as to how he shall report and to whom he shall report. In general the auditor's findings are of interest to two people: his immediate superior and the person in charge of the department which has been subjected to audit. In specific cases there may be others concerned, as for example when the audit has been carried out at the instigation of some other member of the management. The audit report should, like any other report, be concise and to the point. If it can conform to some acceptable pattern so much the better; time will be saved in the preparation and in the reading. Reports might, for example, be arranged in sections as follows—

(1) Purpose
The purpose of the audit expressed in practical terms and including any special reasons why the inquiry was undertaken.

(2) Results
A brief summary of the auditor's findings and recommendations.

(3) Scope
An outline of the auditor's work showing what records were examined, what checks imposed and the results of these. Notes should be given in sufficient detail to support the conclusions drawn and any recommendations which may be made.

If such an arrangement is adopted, the higher management may well be content to read the purpose and results only, particularly where the work has been found generally satisfactory. The official responsible for internal audit may wish to read the entire report in order to assess the value of the audit clerk's work. The internal auditor, in referring to his reports at some later date, will be reminded of what was done.

Audit and Management

Although the internal audit is concerned with accounts and other office records, it should not be regarded as a purely clerical function. Management relies to an increasing extent upon statistical information in formulating policy and in exercising control. It relies on the office and on the various clerks attached to non-clerical departments to provide a picture in words and figures of what is occurring. If this picture is distorted by errors of principle or practice, managerial decisions are liable to be incorrect. The importance of clerical accuracy extends therefore beyond the strict province of the accountant.

Whoever assumes the reponsibility for internal audit should include within its scope every record kept in ever department. By systematic examination he should be able to assess the reliability and value of each record to management. By the periodical consideration of procedures and results he should seek to improve the clerical service and eliminate waste.

PART III

Staffing

8 Staffing

The staffing of an office involves, among other things, the following activities—

Recruitment
The activity of bringing candidates for employment to the organization.

Engagement
The activity of selecting from the candidates those suitable for employment, and placing the selected candidates in the most suitable positions.

Transfer
The moving of an employee from one regular job to another of the same level.

Promotion
The activity of selecting from amongst employees those suitable for undertaking work more important than that which they are doing.

Whilst it is convenient to consider each separately, these four activities are closely interrelated. The policy of engagement must depend upon the extent to which vacancies are filled by promotion and transfer within the office. The methods of recruitment must depend on whether a career is being offered with prospects of promotion, or whether the engagement is merely to fill a requirement of the moment.

The staffing of the office is ultimately the responsibility of the administrative manager. He has the task of getting the work done; he must, therefore, select clerks to fill the jobs within his organization. In many organizations, however, the administrative manager has at his command the help of a specialist personnel officer directly responsible to him. Whatever the particular arrangement, the relationship and division of functions between executive and specialist are of some importance.

In this chapter, it is assumed that the administrative manager has the assistance of the personnel officer. Where this is not so all of the functions described will, of course, rest with the manager.

In some offices there is employee representation through a trade union or a staff association. According to the agreements entered into, it may be necessary for the manager and/or personnel officer to consult with an employee representative on matters which influence the prospects of existing staff. Because the arrangements differ from one organization to another, no more specific comments will be made on this point.

Recruitment

In conditions of full employment it may appear that when an office requires additional staff, the only practical recruitment policy is to draw in from every available source every possible applicant; but, in fact, the greater the difficulties of recruitment the more necessary it becomes to approach the whole problem systematically.

The first step in recruitment is to define the job which is vacant and from this, to define the sort of person likely to fill the vacancy satisfactorily. This essential information must be communicated by the administrative manager to the personnel officer. A simple job title such as junior typist, cost clerk or computer programmer is not enough. Often a staff requisition form is used; a helpful device because it serves to remind the manager of the salient points to be made clear, for example—

(a) what are the principal duties to be carried out?

(b) what knowledge or previous experience (if any) is required?

(c) what academic, technical or professional qualifications are essential or might offer a guide as to the suitability of an applicant?

(d) what skills (e.g. typing, calculating, telephone operating) are necessary and to what degree of proficiency?

(e) what age group (if any) is appropriate?

(f) what is the grade of the job or, if there is no grading scale, what salary can be offered?

(g) what eventual promotional prospects are open (if any)?

It may, of course, be assumed that the personnel officer is well aware of the general conditions of employment, staff facilities and the like.

Knowing what is wanted, the personnel officer must go to the appropriate sources. The Department of Employment, through its local offices, may be able to introduce suitable applicants; young people through the youth service, adult clerks through the normal employment exchange and professional and managerial staff through its special register. In addition to the governmental services, there are other bodies which will introduce possible recruits—

(a) the university appointments boards for graduates;

(b) the polytechnics and technical colleges;

(c) professional institutions;

(d) the privately operated employment agencies specializing in the provision of clerical staff.

The private agencies charge fees for successful introductions, but in spite of this, they flourish. They have been criticized for their mode of operation but there can be little doubt that both employer and employee find them worth while.

It is, however, probable that many potential applicants are already in employment and, although considering a change of job, are not actively seeking a new appointment. These can be reached by newspaper advertising. In every town and city there are recognized newspapers to which people turn when they wish to see "situations vacant" notices. It may be a daily paper, evening paper or a weekly paper. When senior posts are to be advertised, there are newspapers and professional journals which carry advertisements of this type. Another method of advertising is through cards placed in the display cases such as are found outside stationers and other shops or, for that matter, cards placed in a ground-floor window of the office where this fronts on to a main street.

In some organizations it is customary to make all vacancies known to the existing staff in the hope that one of them will introduce a friend or member of the family. This method, apart from its cheapness, often results in the introduction of applicants who have some positive reason for wishing to work in that particular office.

Experience will show which of the possible sources are the more fruitful for particular types of recruits. In the larger offices an analysis of the sources of applicants and the proportion of these which proves suitable can be of great assistance. The personnel officer can gather this information by using an engagement interview record which includes the item "source." But further he should, over a period, relate his experience in engagement and promotion and a study of turnover, to his recruitment sources. Using the results of such work he can review his recruitment policy and take steps to keep the cost of obtaining staff at a minimum.

Ideally, the personnel officer wants to interview only those he will engage. The more interviews made for every person engaged the less time the personnal officer will have to devote to other duties which might well be at least as important as those of recruitment and engagement. It is suggested that establishing the cost of each person engaged in terms of recruitment and engagement costs can be instructive.

Engagement

The selection of staff did not wait on the development of modern selection methods. From the early nineteenth century there is, for example, Robert Owen's story, from his autobiography, of how he became a factory manager. He saw a job advertised in a newspaper: he left the small workshop he owned, and went round to see the advertiser— a Mr. Drinkwater. He met objections to his youthfulness in a determined manner and he answered a question on salary with a demand for £360 a year. This, said Mr. Drinkwater, was more than all the other applicants put together had asked for. So Owen took him to see the books of his small workshop, proved a profit rate of £6 a week and got the job and the £360.

Mr. Drinkwater, it can be inferred, must have argued that a man who could make his points as Owen did, and could prove his ability to make on his own the wages he claimed for the vacant post, must be capable of filling it adequately.

Modern methods are essentially refinements of Mr. Drinkwater's technique. Selection is in effect predicting the probable performance of applicants in the work for which they are being considered. Mr. Drinkwater was fortunate in having so relevant a sample of his candidate's work to examine. In the face of an applicant who has not brought a fair sample of his work or who, indeed, may never have done anything like the work he seeks, it is necessary to rely on interviewing and testing.

Adequate experience of the work to be done and specific job-study are necessary to the personnel officer responsible for selection. He should ideally be familiar with every aspect of each vacancy he is trying to fill. Does the vacant job demand predominantly numerical or verbal ability, or ability and experience specific to the job? Are certain scholastic or professional qualifications required, or are certain personal qualities essential? What are the hours, rest and lunch periods, overtime, pay-scale, the training offered, the opportunities for promotion?

The recepton of applicants is important. A comfortable, well-lit room and a pleasant receptionist can give both the necessary good impression of the concern, and a feeling of ease which will assist both the applicants and the personnel officer in the interviews and tests. There should be a supply of topical magazines and daily papers, and with them copies of any staff or social-club handbooks. The receptionist should arrange for each applicant to fill in an application form covering personal details and recent work-history, pass the completed form to the personnel officer, and conduct each applicant, at the personnel officer's signal, to the interview.

Probably most applicants regard the interviewer more as a judge of their suitability than as an informant. If they have any questions in mind they will probably be a general "Could you tell me more about the job?" and various "What are the prospects?—hours of work?—pension arrangements?" and other relatively formal enquiries. The applicant is unlikely to have studied the ways in which employers and jobs differ, and his criteria for what makes a suitable job can probably be met by most "normal arrangements," at least in the larger concerns. In the interviewer he is unlikely to be dealing with a person he will actually work with; the interview is largely a gate through which he will have to pass before seeing and judging for himself an actual job.

The interviewer's approach to the applicant will depend on his own personality and outlook, but he aims at giving an impression of competence to deal with the uncertainties arising when someone applies for a job. He must accept his position as gate-keeper of course; and he should accept some of its implications. For example, here, on the edge of his organization's premises as it were, he should have some knowledge of the outer world, and be able to meet adequately any inquirer. His language should be equal to this—it should be free of jargon peculiar to the concern, and, regardless of his own experience, he should see himself as one of many gate-keepers, each looking after quite attractive, albeit different premises.

He has no favour to confer, and his job extends beyond demanding to see the credentials of callers. People call on him needing to know whether they could expect to work successfully on the premises. To the extent that he must make a decision on this question, he is their judge; but to the extent that he trusts his judgment he serves the caller equally as well by directing him to another gate elsewhere as by asking him to enter.

For the business of the interview lies in the questions "Is there a vacant job which the applicant really wants?" and "Is he likely to be successful in it?" The first question may be answered through taking the obvious points. Is the applicant's travelling time to work reasonable in relation to his normal arrangements, cost and the hours of work for the job? Is the salary offered initially sufficient? Is the job, in outline, what he wants? If the interview continues, it is reasonable here to ask for an outline of the applicant's career, date and place of birth, education, experience, qualifications, last or current job—a simple chronological sequence is most useful, and can be treated with direct questions and such conversation as the answers offer. The interviewer looks for evidence of some success in the activities the applicant has followed. What is he good at? What does he like doing? Do the oddities matter? Does he explain them adequately? What exactly did his recent work involve? Does he understand its purpose or has he a "routine" outlook? (The interviewer may, of course, be seeking a routine clerk.)

The interviewer will cover more ground than can reasonably be detailed here, and he will compare the facts and impressions he gains with his knowledge of the requirements and setting of the vacant job. If he is thinking of opening the gate to the applicant he may well turn to explaining the detail of the job, giving him an opportunity to confirm or withdraw his application for it. He may, at this point, give a test to the applicant where the job clearly calls for a definite skill in arithmetic, book-keeping, correspondence, typing, etc.

With a senior applicant the interview may last an hour. It can take half an hour with any applicant. The interviewer should have finally a record of "career to date" with relevant detail, any test results and some notes on his decision: he should have noted the source of the application, and have recorded the action he has agreed with the applicant. This latter would usually be, with a suitable applicant, "interview with manager."

The authority to engage an applicant is not normally vested in the personnel office. The administrative manager from whom the staff requisition came is going to be responsible for the work of the accepted applicant; therefore he is normally given the authority to engage.

This need not be a rigid arrangement. The administrative manager may well feel that he wishes only to see applicants for senior posts or juniors who are to have lengthy training programmes. He may, of course, delegate his authority to engage to the personnel officer whenever he thinks fit; he will in any case give considerable weight to the personnel officer's recommendations on individual applicants.

However this may be, the personnel officer should pass a report to the manager on each person engaged, together with test results, medical report, a prepared personal history sheet and such other documents as an attendance record card, necessary to open a personal file for the new clerk. Further, he must ensure that the new clerk comes on to the payroll, and that he brings with him when he starts such essential documents as an Income Tax Certificate and National Insurance Card.

Mental tests are given only a passing reference in the procedure outlined above. They can be of great assistance, however, in helping the interviewer to find a substitute for the proof of ability which Robert Owen was able to offer Mr. Drinkwater. Tests can, of course, be designed for a variety of purposes. There are the "trade tests" which are used to establish the applicant's level of skill—tests of typing, shorthand, operation of a particular office machine, payroll calculations, mathematical calculations and so on. These are best used when a vacancy, demanding a particular skill at a known level, has to be filled somewhat urgently; or they may be used to establish the training needs of a particular applicant. In the latter case, they would follow a more normal type of test, such as the Clerical Aptitude Tests, developed by the National Institute of Industrial Psychology. This general type of test is designed to eliminate largely any vocational knowledge factor from the applicant's performance. It assumes only a normal schooling, with the basic abilities thereby developed—the abilities to detect similarities or differences between things, to make simple arithmetical calculations, to use a few facts to arrive at a fact not stated, and to follow simple instructions.

These tests supplement the attempt made by the interviewer to discover how the applicant has been able to use his experience in the field of specific office skills, or the more general field of abilities relevant to office work. If the interviewer finds that the impression he has gained from the interview clashes with the applicant's performance on a test, in either direction, he needs either to extend his interview, or to ask a colleague to interview the applicant to provide a second opinion. He needs then to have closely in mind the requirements of the relevant vacancy, particularly in terms of dealings with people and in terms of desk-work before making a decision.

The selection process can result in accepting an applicant for the specific post he seeks, in his being rejected, or in the interviewer suggesting that he would be suitable for some other vacancy. For the interviewer must be alert to the problem of allocating people to one of a variety of possible vacancies, and in this he faces something similar to the topic of transfer in the manager's field.

Transfer

Perhaps the conventional context of a transfer involves a dissatisfied clerk. There is some difficulty associated with his job, and finally, as it were, he approaches his manager and "asks for a transfer." The conventional reaction on the manager's part is probably, "Why, what's the trouble?"

It is common experience that once a person has settled into a job and has come to regard it as his own, he may well wish to remain undisturbed. He knows what he is doing on the job, he has related himself satisfactorily to the people he works with and he has got to the stage where he recognizes "insiders" and "outsiders" in both tasks and people. Perhaps the one person who, at least for some time, is expected to move from one job to another is the "trainee" and he usually accepts his transfers as having an end in a specific appointment which will be his for some time. And when a manager receives a request for a transfer it may simply be that his clerk wants something of the widening of experience which is offered the "trainee" in order that he, too, may fit himself for a more senior post.

To the manager who finds his immediate "production problems" his main concern, transfers may appear only as a nuisance. When a man is used to what he is doing, he is more valuable than when he is learning, in terms of current production. But such an approach to this topic argues a personnel policy which excludes people as people, and includes them only as means of getting work done. A quite different approach to transfers can also indicate an impersonal personnel policy, as when, for example, a rigid system of "job rotation" is used to force people to change their jobs regardless of their feelings in the matter.

For the manager and the personnel officer transfers are of necessity a recognizable topic when they involve changes in the payroll or personnel records, but transfers can usefully be considered within the same framework as recruitment and engagement. The engagement procedure outlined above has involved seeking agreement with an applicant as to the suitability for him of a certain job. This agreement reached when a clerk is engaged is, obviously, unlikely to last for ever. His ideas concerning what he wants to do may develop or completely change for reasons arising in either his personal or his working life, or the manager himself may need to change the clerk's job. The manager has a continuing responsibility for keeping his agreement with each clerk properly alive. In periods of full employment, the consequence of failing to do so may be a higher staff turnover than is either desirable or necessary; and even when a clerk's mobility is low, the consequence may be the clerk's psychological withdrawal from his job, which in many ways may be worse than his physical departure from the office.

For every clerk there are likely to be times when moving from a job is almost unthinkable, and times when staying in a particular job appears to be almost impossible. An effective personnel policy is based on the recognition of such facts, and its implementation rests on the ability of the manager, his personnel officer, and the office supervisors, to recognize when these times arise in the lives of their clerks. Transfers are the inappropriate tool in meeting the "impossible" times.

Again, the personnel policy must comprehend the idea of development; and this calls for a knowledge of when to offer a broadening of experience, or the chance to see the work of an office from a new angle. And here, too, the manager uses transfers.

Given such an outlook, it might appear that a manager must face an uneconomic situation where there will be far too many learners and a lack of clerks capable of giving a steady high producton. The idea is not to seek to stimulate transfers blindly (note that "job rotation" is a routine stimulation of transfers) as will be apparent when the real situations of real clerks are considered.

Consider a clerk at work; he is on the job because of his initial agreement that it offered suitable employment; he is amongst people in similar work, his job has the air of being normal, and in doing it he is engaged in a normal activity. As he gets into the job he will find from time to time that things arise in the work which bring him annoyance and frustration: the job may be complicated, or become too easy for him; he may find a colleague to be something of a nuisance to him, or he may feel vaguely that he needs to know more of what goes on; he may decide he wants to marry and set up house, he may expect his family to expand, he may set his heart on buying a car; or he may just want to be the boss—a vast variety of feelings and wishes is open to him. But these feelings and wishes will have to become relatively strong before they overcome those forces which bring him daily to work, and take him through his daily routine; he has committed himself to work on this job, he has developed work obligations to those about him, inside and outside the office. He wants a good reputation as an employee, and he avoids behaving like a job-to-job man.

Many of the feelings that would drive him into demanding a transfer, or even as far as leaving his job, would never reach this pitch if some responsible person is in close enough touch with him to help him express and resolve them. But if no one offers to help him with his problem, the vague idea that part of the difficulty may be that he does not fully understand his position may fade, so that only the dissatisfactions of the job remain in his mind.

When the practical case for a transfer appears, there are the inevitable practical difficulties which tend to sustain the conventional "problem" approach to transfers. The manager can best accept that it is an unreal outlook which puts people in a permanently static setting; change is normal, and to be facilitated. Adopting a narrow short-term policy is incompatible with this approach; perhaps the consideration of some everyday facts can make "adopting a broad view" a practical matter. For example, it is obvious that many a senior clerk reached his position through a process of change which began in his becoming an office messenger; his development has been accommodated by the office in which he works. Any manager can probably remember when one of his typists at least was incapable of good layouts, or proper punctuation. It would be difficult to find anywhere a clerk who has always done precisely the same job—even the "old faithfuls" have seen some change of method in the work they do. Against the background of such facts in his own office, no manager should consider transferring a clerk to a different job as in any way outside his normal function of meeting the changing demands of various continuous processes—whether they arise in stock control, production, sales or in employment.

The satisfactory use of transfers is an important accomplishment for the manager to acquire. It demands that he should be able to be effectively in contact with his clerks, his supervisors and his personnel officer.

No emphasis is given here to the manager's own needs in the times when he wishes to transfer clerks purely for work reasons. If the preceding arguments are accepted, however, it should be apparent that an effective personnel policy will best permit a manager to enlist the aid of his clerks in meeting work problems. As the manager transmits a policy of listening to people effectively he can confidently seek the support of the staff when he explains to them the changing needs of the office.

Promotion

A large part of the population of this country must live without thinking of promotion as a topic which concerns themselves; and not everyone in an office will find it important. Many office workers accept an adult clerk's position so long as it provides acceptable working conditions, including salary; and some prefer to find satisfaction in outside activities, rather than spending their energies on striving towards greater responsibility.

But most people will have views on what constitutes "fair" promotion, and on what in practice appears to govern promotion.

As to what constitutes "fair" promotion, it is usually assumed that the people actually employed should be considered first whenever a senior vacancy arises. This in itself is significant in trying to understand people at work. They do not normally act on the idea that they are individually on a specific contractual basis *vis-à-vis* their employer. The contract of employment in itself is quite inadequate to meet the assumptions that employees will make concerning what is right or wrong in the way in which their place of work is managed.

Promotion must be a prerogative of management; but even formally, there is widespread acceptance by managements of the view that wherever possible a policy of "promotion from within" should be followed. Within this broad idea that those in the office should have first consideration, there are generally accepted views on what constitutes unfair discrimination. For example, the idea that a man is not too old at forty has a wide currency and so has the belief that a man should not lose the chance of a better job because his present work is of particular importance to the office.

A sound personnel policy takes such ideas into consideration. The manager needs to know the local colour given to these ideas by his own staff, and before he decides on a promotion he should consider its effect in the office, and particularly upon those of his staff who will be directly involved in the change he makes.

If recruitment and selection have not provided people of the right calibre for promotion, the manager is faced with finding his senior people outside his office when an emergency arises. The importance of timely recruiting can hardly be over-estimated, for a planned "trainee" programme can do much to provide the potential senior with the close contacts he will need with all ranks of the office, and at the same time give him a chance to make a fair claim on a senior vacancy.

If, however, either the emergency or a need for "trainees" arises, the personnel policy implied in this chapter calls for a full discussion, between the manager and his existing senior staff, of the problems giving rise to the need for "new blood." Then, either the problems will be seen in a new light, or a recruitment programme will be agreed. Sometimes the new light may involve a serious attempt to develop ostensibly unsuitable men by means of special training, or a recognition of an individual's development through his private efforts to fit himself for a senior post. No manager should avoid giving every encouragement to his junior staff in their attempts at development on the grounds that he is unlikely to be able to meet their potential needs for senior positions. With either "long-term developers" or "trainees" the manager can justifiably aim at assisting individuals to competence and confidence, even though not to definite vacancies. The world of vacancies is a wide one, and he can aim at helping his unplaceable men to senior posts in other concerns. The effect of such a policy is to make keenness possible where otherwise a secretive and distracted study of vacancy columns might develop.

Conclusion

Recruitment, engagement, transfer, and promotion are terms covering easily recognizable critical events in a clerk's life. Seen from the point of view of the manager, they are essential terms in his conducting the affairs of his office; essential if he considers his principal task of providing an office service to the management of his concern, and essential to him as representative of his concern as an employer. It is suggested that he should see these activities in their personnel policy context. They involve his seeking agreements with individuals, his recognition of their continuing need, as subordinates, for responsible attention, and his acceptance of his duty to recognize their feelings individually in their living and development, and collectively as "his office."

9 Job Evaluation and Grading

The grading of clerical work has a long history: as early as 1836, in a book entitled *The Statesman*, Henry Taylor urged those responsible for Government offices to divide the work into two grades—mechanical and intellectual. Many years passed before this recommendation was fully applied to the Civil Service and, in the meantime, other employers of clerks were attempting to grade their office work. Some of the nineteenth-century railway companies, for example, had grading schemes which classified the work into as many as six or more grades. As clerical work grew during the late nineteenth and twentieth centuries, employers were under greater and greater pressure to introduce grading. It was always expensive to employ highly skilled and experienced clerks, and so employers were under economic pressure to break difficult and complicated clerical work down into simple tasks and have them performed by less-skilled clerks. The introduction of office machinery also led to greater specialization, a process which continues today. The development of grading in clerical work has therefore been closely linked with the growth of the division of labour in offices. The division of labour has been of two kinds: division into *types* of work and division into *grades*. It is the latter with which this chapter is principally concerned.

Throughout recorded history, and in many different kinds of society, it has been accepted that skill and responsibility should be rewarded. The leaders lived better than the led; the craftsman lived better than the labourer. Today, the "differentials" between the wages paid to skilled, semi-skilled and unskilled are as jealously guarded as ever. Job grading seeks to distinguish between the differing *degrees of skill* necessary to do work and between *degrees of responsibility* accepted. The pattern of grading then becomes the basis on which appropriate remuneration is paid; the worker receives the "rate for the job."

In the public sector, it is common for the salary to be related to a job grade regardless of individual efficiency. In industry and commerce, however, it is normal to add something to the basic grade rate in recognition of individual efficiency. A *merit rating* scale is used as the means of recognizing and rewarding effort and proficiency.

Employers may be stimulated to carry out job evaluation, grading and merit rating because of a problem situation. The advantages which can accrue lie among the following—

Economy
Good clerks are scarce because skill is scarce and many other occupations compete for the available supply of persons with the natural abilities necessary to acquire skill. It is therefore common sense not to waste a senior, experienced, skilled clerk on trivial work.

Morale
If people can be in every way suited to the work which they are asked to do, they will be happier than if they are worried by work which is too difficult, or bored by work that is too simple for their capabilities.

Justice
Job evaluation and grading contributes to the just recognition and recompense of skill and effort in both salary and promotion.

Incentive
Realistic job grading, coupled with merit rating, offers continuing incentive to improve salary and status through consistent good work and personal development. The provision of a promotional ladder is, perhaps, more important in offices than elsewhere because of the inherent difficulties in operating bonus schemes based on individual measured output.

Legal
Under the Equal Pay Act 1970, men and women must be paid the same for work which is similar or equivalent. Job evaluation and grading provides a means of determining when one job is similar or equivalent to another.

Job Types

When office work was done mainly by general clerks, there was no great need to recognize types of work. As mechanization has advanced it has become necessary to distinguish between the following—

General Clerical Work
Tasks which are principally mental and manual, although simple machines and devices may be employed, e.g. adding and calculating machines, manifold posting boards.

Typing and Secretarial Work
Tasks which require typing as a principal skill and which may include

teleprinter operation, data encoding, etc., where the machines used are operated through a typewriter keyboard.

Machine Operation
Tasks which require as a principal skill the ability to operate and care for a machine, e.g. accounting machine, offset litho duplicator, micro-filmer, etc.

It will be seen that, in each of these three job types, there are skills employed at varying levels. Those who enter office work doing the simpler jobs within a type can develop their capabilities and progress to more difficult jobs without changing to a different job type.

Where the office services to management have become more sophisticated, it has become necessary in the more senior jobs to distinguish between the following—

Supervision/Management
Tasks which involve accepting responsibility for the work of a number of subordinates.

Technical Work
Tasks requiring a high degree of technical knowledge, e.g. accounting, cost accounting, legal requirements, production processes, export procedures, etc.

Planning
Tasks requiring skill in planning techniques, e.g. O & M, operational research, computer systems analysis, etc.

In these three job types, the level of knowledge and/or responsibility is generally high. Those who do these jobs may have entered them after experience in the first group (general clerical, etc.) or direct from further or higher education in appropriate subjects. Skill is again required at varying levels. Under supervision/management, for example, there are group leaders, section supervisors and managers at various levels of responsibility.

Job Evaluation

In order to place jobs into grades, it is first necessary to establish their relative values. This can be done simply by "ranking": comparing one job with another and judging which of the two demands the higher level of skill, experience, responsibility, etc. If this process is continued, placing job after job in relation to others, every job in the office can be listed in value order. Such a method is rough and does not attempt to assess the extent of any differences.

More refined methods attempt to allot points or scores to jobs. The characteristics which make work more difficult or more responsible are nominated. In the case of office work, these might be summarized as—

Knowledge and skill (45 points)
Responsibility for the work of others (15 points)
Trust—handling valuables or confidential matters (10 points)
Contacts inside or outside the organization (10 points)
Physical effort (10 points)
Mental effort including concentration (10 points)

Such characteristics cannot be regarded as of equal consequence and the number of points allotted to each will vary, as for example the numbers showns in brackets above. To evaluate a job, its nature is considered in relation to each of the characteristics and points out of the maximum allotted are awarded. A supervisor's job is likely to receive high awards for knowledge and skill, and for responsibility. A junior clerk's job will receive low awards in these areas but might be given a high award for physical effort. The total of points for the job is taken as representing its value.

Although points systems may appear to be more exact because the result is expressed as a number, they are no more than a means of arriving at a reliable opinion based on certain evidence. Indeed, some points systems define in words the meanings to be attributed to various point values under each characteristic.

Job Grading

Having evaluated jobs, it is convenient to group them into grades. These grades should be representative of the normal levels of skill which both management and staff can readily recognize. A scheme which is too complex is likely to lead to arguments as to interpretation, and dissatisfaction among clerks who may feel that grading is being used as a weapon against them rather than a basis for just treatment. In any scheme, the number of grades is important. Too many causes difficulty in allocating jobs to grades because the more divisions there are, the more borderline decisions have to be made. Furthermore, when the grading scheme is related to the salary structure, a large number of grades means small differences in salary between one grade and the next, thus reducing one of the clerks' principal incentives for seeking promotion. On the other hand, too few grades may mean that the work is insufficiently divided, with the risk that some clerks are wasting time on tasks which are too trivial for them. An odd number of grades can lead to poor grading because of the temptation to put too many jobs into the middle, or average, grade. For all these reasons the right number of grades is likely to be six, eight or ten depending on the size of the organization: adequate for economy and the recognition of skill, providing sufficient incentive for promotion, and avoiding the risk of the overloaded average grade.

It must be emphasized that it is the *job* which is graded; decision as to grade should not be influenced by the clerk seen to be doing it. The clerk may be highly skilled and very good at the job, but his success may merely reflect the fact that the work is simple and not worthy of his capabilities. Once the work has been objectively graded, a clerk may properly be given the same personal grading as the job he does. If the result reveals discrepancies, work should be reallocated so that the requirements of each job are matched as nearly as possible by the capabilities of the person assigned to it, as diagrammatically illustrated by Fig. 16.

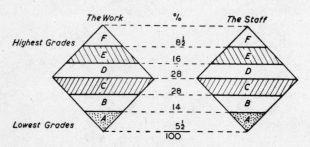

Fig. 16

The percentages quoted in the middle of the diagram show a "normal" or standard disposition of jobs among the six grades. These were arrived at from statistics gathered over many years by the Institute of Administrative Management in terms of its Grades A-F (now expanded to A-H). This standard has become distorted in more recent years as the installation of computers and the introduction of more sophisticated management information services has resulted in a greater proportion of higher grade jobs and less lower grade routine jobs. The standard is still useful, however, as a yardstick against which to explain and justify deviations from it.

I.A.M. Job Grading Scheme

Because the defining of tasks and the evaluation and grading of jobs is laborious, wide use is made of the Institute of Administrative Management's job grading scheme. Developed over many years and up-dated by the co-operative effort of Institute members and their companies, it gives ready-made and generally applicable grade definitions which are quoted below.

"A" Grade

Tasks which require no previous clerical experience; each individual task is allotted and is either very simple or is closely directed. For example—

   (i) messenger work;
   (ii) simple sorting and filing.

"B" Grade

Tasks which, because of their simplicity, are carried out in accordance with a limited number of well-defined rules after a comparatively short period of training; these tasks are closely directed and checked, and are carried out in standard routine with short period control. For example—

   (i) simple copying work;
   (ii) straightforward adding operations using an adding machine.

"C" Grade

Tasks which are of a routine character and follow well-defined rules, but which require either some experience or a special aptitude for the task and which are carried out according to a standard routine and are subject to short period control. For example—

   (i) simple calculating machine operation;
   (ii) preparing invoices according to a prescribed routine where prices are obtained from a straightforward price schedule;
   (iii) shorthand typing including audio-typing of routine work;
   (iv) filing of important documents with a complex alphabetic or numeric classification.

"D" Grade

Tasks which require considerable experience but only a very limited degree of initiative, and which are carried out according to a predetermined procedure. The tasks are carried out according to a standard routine which may vary, but will not vary enough to necessitate any considerable direction. For example—

   (i) shorthand and typing or audio-typing of non-routine work;
   (ii) certifying purchase invoices by reference to orders and receipt documents;
   (iii) routine administration of a group of sales or purchase accounts;
   (iv) calculation of net pay from gross pay.

"E" Grade

Tasks which may require one or more of the following—

(a) a basic level of professional or specialized knowledge, for example Part I or II of the A.C.M.A. (Associate of the Institute of Cost and Management Accountants) examinations;

(b) performance or control of clerical or administrative work requiring mostly routine decisions, but occasional use of discretion and initiative;

(c) work supervision of a range normally of two to six clerical staff. The number supervised may vary according to the complexity or level of the work. For example—

(i) supervision of one section of typists in a central typing office;

(ii) routine computer programming, for example, typically requiring up to one year's experience;

(iii) secretarial service to a director or senior manager;

(iv) leading a section of stores records clerks.

"F" Grade

Tasks which may require one or more of the following—

(a) professional or specialized knowledge equivalent to an intermediate level examination of an appropriate professional association, for example, the Institute of Administrative Management's Certificate in Administrative Management, Part II or III of A.C.M.A. examinations;

(b) performance or control of complex clerical or routine administrative work requiring occasional decisions of a non-routine type, and some use of judgment or initiative on routine matters;

(c) supervision of a range, normally of five to twelve clerical staff, in a section compact enough to enable full personal control to be directly maintained. The number supervised may vary according to the complexity or level of the work, and may include E grade assistants. For example:

(i) supervision of a printing office using a variety of printing, duplicating or reproduction processes;

(ii) conduct of routine O & M or systems analysis surveys;

(iii) complex computer programming, for example typically requiring between one and three years' experience;

(iv) full secretarial service to the managing director or chief executive.

"G" Grade

Tasks which may require one or more of the following—

(a) professional or specialized knowledge equivalent to a university first degree or to an advanced but not necessarily final qualification of an appropriate professional association, for example, final years of A.C.A., the Institute of Administrative Management's Diploma in Administrative Management, or Part III or IV of A.C.M.A.;

(b) performance or control of work of wide complexity or importance requiring regular non-routine decisions and a regular use of judgment and initiative in the execution of predetermined policies;

(c) supervision of a range normally of nine to twenty clerical staff. Control of clerical work may be exercised through two or more grade E or F supervisors; or supervision of a smaller number of grade E or F professional or specialist staff. The numbers supervised may vary according to the complexity or level of the work. For example:

(i) supervision of a large wages office;

(ii) conduct of O & M or systems analysis surveys which may require work control of several assistants;

(iii) computer programming of complex sets of programs which may require work control of several programmers;

(iv) administering and taking part in tutoring and teaching on clerical training courses for staff in grades A to F.

"H" Grade

Tasks which may require one or more of the following—

(a) professional or specialized knowledge equivalent to a university first degree with some experience or a final qualification of an appropriate professional association such as A.C.A., The Institute of Administrative Management's Diploma in Administrative Management, or A.C.M.A.;

(b) performance or control of work of sufficient complexity or importance requiring an extensive measure of judgment or initiative and responsibility for some contribution towards the development of departmental policies as well as for their execution;

(c) supervision of a range normally of twenty or more clerical staff. The numbers supervised may vary according to the complexity or level of the work, but control will normally require a deputy and two or more grade E or F supervisors; or supervision of a smaller number of grade E, F or G specialist staff. For example:

(i) supervision of a customer accounts office with responsibility for control of credit according to a predetermined policy;

(ii) leading complex O & M or systems analysis projects requiring supervision of other specialist staff;

(iii) computer programming controlling complex projects, with responsibility for a programming section, and possibly other systems staff.

The I.A.M. scheme also provides nearly 1,000 task definitions with appropriate grading, sufficient to cover all but the most unusual office work. That it has been called the "lazy man's method" of job evaluation and grading may be taken as praise rather than criticism.

Merit Rating

Any scheme of job grading needs to be supplemented by a system of merit rating of the clerks. At any one time the clerks employed on work of any particular grade will include efficient and less efficient clerks; experienced clerks and those still learning the job; and some doing the work exceptionally well and who really deserve promotion to work of a higher grade, but for whom a job in a higher grade is not for the moment available.

In industry and commerce almost every employer tries to relate clerical salaries in some way to merit. This may mean no more than reviewing each clerk's performance once a year and assessing the amount to be paid to him, in between a minimum and maximum for the job grade. Such loose methods are not altogether desirable. A clerk who has recently done some special task well may be unduly rewarded. A clerk who, after a year of good work, has recently made a bad error may be unduly penalized. In many offices, therefore, the merit rating follows a procedure which seeks to ensure that clerks are judged on all pertinent aspects of performance. There may be a form to be filled in, on which the supervisor or manager awards points for such factors as regular attendance, punctuality, willingness, accuracy, pace of working, and ability to settle queries without help.

The Institute of Administrative Management publishes with its job grading scheme a merit rating scheme which recognizes five situations as follows:

"Starter"

This rating is assigned when the clerk has started in a grade, either as a newcomer or as a result of promotion and has the ability to tackle the new job. It represents the degree of efficiency which can reasonably be expected during the period that the job holder is learning the work.

"Qualified" (or "satisfactory" or "average")

This rating is assigned when the holder has completed the learning period and is qualified to perform satisfactorily all the normal aspects of a job in the grade without further instruction.

"Experienced" (or "more than satisfactory", or "above average")

This rating is assigned when the job holder has been in the grade for some time and has not only mastered the normal aspects of a job in the grade but also acquired a sufficient knowledge and understanding of its implications to be able to deal reliably with all the circumstances likely to arise.

"Superior" (or "plus one")

This rating is only assigned when a job holder, in addition to the acquisition of knowledge and experience, continually demonstrates an ability to perform work in the grade in a noticeably superior manner.

"Outstanding" (or "superlative", or "plus two")

This rating is confined to those of outstanding ability in the job grade. Generally speaking, it is only used for those who are fully capable of doing higher grade work or for those who have performed their jobs in a consistently superior manner with accumulating experience for a number of years, or are very versatile in other work of the same grade, or recognised as leaders among other staff of the same grade.

The essence of the I.A.M. scheme is that it stimulates management to identify the overall performance of a clerk. It asks questions: does this clerk do his job in the manner expected of a qualified person?—or with the uncertainty of a starter?—or with the confidence and capability of an experienced person?—and so on. Ordinarily a clerk, on entering a grade, would be rated as a starter. As time passed and the clerk improved he would progress to become qualified and eventually experienced. The next step would be promotion to the next highest grade, again being rated as a starter, and so on. The fourth and fifth ratings, superior and outstanding, are ordinarily reserved for—

(*a*) those who deserve promotion but for whom no opportunity is immediately available;

(*b*) those who, for lack of natural ability, are unlikely to be promoted further and may stay in the one grade for the remainder of their service—and in so doing develop a performance which justifies some additional reward.

Installing and Maintaining Schemes

As the Institute of Administrative Management scheme is widely used in industry and commerce, and because it is one of the few which covers the whole range of clerical work, it is here used as a general example. To begin with, the clerical work should be broken down into *tasks*, i.e. until no further division of labour is possible. A task is a piece of work which would not normally be divided between two or more clerks. The tasks can then be graded by reference to the grade definitions given on pages 105–7 or by identifying each with the published I.A.M. task definitions. The work of any one clerk, i.e. a clerical *job*, is made up of a number of tasks. Theoretically, all the tasks comprised in any one clerk's job should be of the same grade. For practical reasons this ideal may not be capable of achievement, especially in small offices, but something is wrong if a job is found to be made up of, say, four grade B tasks, two grade C tasks and three grade E tasks. Such a clerk, if he is highly skilled, will be inadequately employed for six out of the nine tasks he performs; or, if he is only of average ability, he will be inefficient at performing three of the most important tasks in his job and inadequately employed on four others. The work of the office may, therefore, need to be re-organized so as to provide the maximum of grade homogeneity in each job.

Where it is not possible to achieve complete homogeneity in grouping tasks into jobs the grading of the latter calls for good judgment. For example, extra supervision can be employed in respect of a few tasks of a higher grade than the rest. A job can then be graded as D in spite of the fact that some grade E work is included. Sometimes it will be found that the bulk of the tasks included in a job are all of one grade, but the range of work is unavoidably very wide. To compensate for this abnormal range a higher grading might be allowed for the job; for example a job with a very wide range of grade D tasks might be graded as E.

The actual installation of a job grading scheme needs to be handled carefully. It hardly needs saying that the grading must be done honestly and sincerely. Any attempt at favouritism and any prejudice will be apparent and will be bitterly resented. Finality must not be expected: it may take a year or two to get rid of initial anomalies; grading must be reviewed every few years in the light of changed circumstances.

Any scheme must be acceptable to both management and staff; they must have confidence in it. In some organizations the relation between staff and management may be such that the scheme would have to be the subject of joint consultation, even going to the lengths of union and management representatives sitting down together to do the actual grading. In other offices the clerks will be willing to leave the grading to management and merely wish to discuss grievances and anomalies should any be experienced. No hard-and-fast rules can be laid down.

A well-designed job grading scheme in clerical work does more than put the right clerks in the right jobs and provide the basis for an office salary structure. It also gives the administrative manager the information he needs for recruiting, training and promoting staff. The analysis of clerical procedures into tasks and jobs indicates the training needs of the staff and the main lines of promotion. From the information so gleaned the manager is able to plan the recruitment and training of staff. With his knowledge of probable staff wastage, plus any advance information about future developments likely to affect the staff requirements of the office, he can prepare replacement tables and relate his staff recruitment and training programmes to these forecasts of future requirements. If this is done with care, there need be no lack of suitable clerks ready for promotion when the need arises, and at the same time clerks prepared for promotion need not be frustrated by being kept back for unduly long periods. Office work has in recent years acquired a reputation for dullness and frustration which has made recruitment difficult: it is not too much to claim that a sound job grading scheme is the first step towards remedying this unhappy state of affairs.

10 Salary Scales

In chapter 9 job grading and merit rating were examined as means whereby there can be economy and also the just recognition of each individual's skill and performance. Having put the right clerks into the right jobs, the next stage is to relate the salaries to those jobs and thence to the clerks who do them.

The simplest way in which this could be done would be to have a salary structure in which there would be a rate for each grade of job. If there were six grades, then six rates could be decided on in accordance with current salary rates*. For example—

Grade	Per week
Highest	£70
Senior	£60
Above average	£50
Below average	£40
Junior	£30
Lowest	£20

But in practice a salary structure as simple as this is not used. There is no tradition of set rates for particular jobs in clerical work as there is in many kinds of manual work. Furthermore, this simple salary structure takes no account of individual differences in the efficiency of clerks, the tradition of annual increases in clerical salaries, local variation in conditions in the clerical labour market, different market rates for the same work, or the possibility that market conditions may vary within a grade for different types of clerical work. These five complications will be examined in turn. In discussing the first it will be impossible to avoid bringing in the second, as the two are related.

Allowing for Individual Differences in Efficiency

The simplest way in which this can be done is by relating salaries within each job grade to the merit ratings. If, for example, there are eight job

---

* The salary rates quoted in this chapter are illustrations only.

grades, A to H, and five merit ratings, 1 to 5, the salary structure would be something like this—

Grade of Job	*1*	*2*	*3*	*4*	*5*
H	£94	£99	£104	£109	£114
G	81	85	89	94	99
F	69	73	77	81	85
E	57	61	65	69	73
D	45	49	53	57	61
C	35	38	41	45	49
B	26	29	32	35	38
A	17	20	23	26	29

With an efficient system of staff-reporting and salary-review a salary structure of this kind will work well: efficiency is fairly rewarded, staff are encouraged to become efficient, and there is no extravagance. Also, if the job grades used are those of The Institute of Administrative Management, it is simple to compare salaries with those of other employers using the same grading system. It will be noticed that the scales for the different grades overlap. This is done deliberately because clerks who have reached a high merit rating in any particular grade are usually worthy of promotion to the next grade. They may have to wait for a suitable vacancy to arise, but in the meantime they ought not be penalized financially. Furthermore, a highly efficient clerk in one grade is probably as valuable to the employer as a starter in the next higher grade.

In practice some employers vary this structure in several ways. Job grades A to C might be combined and the salaries linked with age on the assumption that efficiency in this routine work increases automatically with age. Provided that clerks who do not come up to this expectation after fair warning are told to find other employment, such a salary structure need not lead to inefficiency or extravagance. The employer would, however, have to rely on non-financial incentives as the spur to efficiency. A salary structure of this kind would also probably relate the steps in the salaries for the higher grades to the length of service instead of making individual assessments of each clerk's merit rating. This practice is based on the assumption that efficiency automatically improves with the length of time spent on this kind of work. The system has practical advantages in offices where clerks are likely to be transferred fairly frequently from one kind of work to another within the same grade, making precise assessments of their merit difficult at any particular time. Salary scales which overlap for different grades are not liked by some employers, who prefer to see promotion from one grade to another marked by a transfer to a new salary scale. Thus a salary structure in the common form set out below is arrived at—

Senior Clerical Grade A	£62 rising in two years to £70
Senior Clerical Grade B	£52 rising in two years to £60
Clerical Grade	£45 rising in two years to £50
Junior Clerks	£17 at 16 rising to £43 at 25

This kind of salary structure can be varied considerably. The extreme example is when the employer uses an age scale throughout, for example—

£17 at 16 rising to £65 at 35

An element of merit rating might be introduced simply by providing for an efficiency bar on this scale at, say, £50. The employer might go a little farther and have three merit scales at the upper end of the scale, thus—

Clerks in Merit Grade A	£60 at 30 rising to £70 at 35
Clerks in Merit Grade B	£55 at 30 rising to £65 at 35
Clerks in Merit Grade C	£50 at 30 rising to £60 at 41
all Clerks 16 to 29	£17 rising to £45

Another indirect method of assessing the merit of individual clerks is to relate salary scales to educational qualifications, e.g. membership of a quasi-professional institute or possession of a certificate of proficiency in a special clerical skill such as are awarded by the Royal Society of Arts and similar bodies. Thus in the fictitious example quoted above, merit grade A might be open only to clerks who had passed the intermediate examination of an appropriate professional body. Similarly, a scale for audio-typists might embody a higher maximum for someone holding the designated certificate of skill.

As one of the objects of relating salary scales to the efficiency of individual clerks is to encourage improvements in efficiency it follows that salaries must be systematically reviewed. Many employers do this on clerks' birthdays; others (risking a peak load of work) do so on a fixed date each year, e.g. 1st January. No hard-and-fast rule can be laid down about this.

Annual Increases in Clerical Salaries
Linking salaries to the age or length of service of a clerk is based, as has been seen, on the assumption that a higher age (or longer service) means that the clerk is more experienced and is therefore more efficient. Age and length of service have the merit of being completely objective and easily ascertained and for this reason are liked by managements who have to face critical staff associations or trade unions representing clerical staffs. Furthermore, there is a long tradition behind this type of salary

structure: it goes back to the eighteenth century, and in 1808 a committee which studied the salaries of clerks in government offices reported—

> The principle of gradually increasing salaries after certain periods of service, and at fixed intervals, if they are not made too short, is highly to be approved, as holding out a due encouragement to diligence and fidelity.

In spite of this hallowed tradition there are dangers in the system. Generally speaking it will be successful only when certain conditions are fulfilled. They are—

(1) That there is careful initial selection to ensure that recruits are all potentially capable of filling jobs in the higher grades, combined with some probationary period in which mistakes in recruitment can be rectified.

(2) That recruitment on these scales is limited to the number of jobs in the highest grades likely to be available for the clerks by the time they are reaching the maximum of the scales, after allowing for normal wastage.

(3) That their training and experience are such as to fit them for the jobs in the highest grades by the time they are approaching the early thirties.

(4) That a constant check is kept to ensure that clerks are given jobs in the higher grades as their salaries increase, and that they are not retained in the lower grades.

(5) That enough clerks are available on lower rates of pay to fill the jobs in the lower grades. These clerks may be: (*a*) younger men and women well below the maxima of these age scales; (*b*) married women who, of choice, require a routine job with convenient working hours and are not seeking career prospects.

A clerical salary structure of this kind is generally justified only when the employer restricts the mobility of the clerk, expecting him to make his whole career with the same employer and not seek opportunities of promotion elsewhere. This state of affairs can arise when the employer is very large, such as the British Civil Service; or if the work is specialized, such as railway clerical work. Difficulties can arise if management mis-calculates: the discontent culminating in the strike of frustrated Irish bank clerks in the 1950s is an example of the kind of trouble that can arise if a salary structure is not properly geared to the job structure of an organization. On that occasion the Dublin Labour Court observed—

> . . . what is wanted is obviously a staff structure giving a pyramid standing on its base and not on its apex, so as to ensure a proper relationship between the number of responsible posts to be filled and the flow of staff rising to the points at which they can be promoted to fill those posts.

Local Variations in Clerical Salary Rates

Successive surveys of clerical salaries by The Institute of Administrative Management show that local variations in clerical salaries exist. Firms who have offices in different parts of the country therefore have to take these local variations into account in setting up their salary structures.

Clerical salaries are higher in London than elsewhere, and organizations having offices in London and in the provinces usually have a two-tier salary structure with a higher rate for London. Some go further and have a three-tier salary structure providing separate scales for (1) Inner London, (2) Outer London and large provincial towns and (3) all other areas.

These differences are often thought to be related to local differences in the cost of living. In fact, differences in the cost of living have very little to do with the question. Differences in the cost of living depend on whether clerks are single or married, the number of their dependants, and whether they happen to live close to their offices. The differences in clerical salaries arise from local variations in the demand for a supply of clerical labour. In London the demand is great for clerks to staff the offices of the Government, of the City, of the headquarters of industrial concerns, of the Law Courts, etc. The supply of clerks is limited in the centre of London by the lack of housing accommodation, so employers have to attract clerks from distant residential areas. To do this they must offer higher salaries (and often luncheon vouchers and shorter hours) to compensate the clerks for the time, cost and fatigue of travelling and the cost of meals out in restaurants. A similar but less acute situation can arise in other large towns. If an employer can provide offsetting advantages, such as free travel to and from work, the amount of the London allowance can be less: the railways have a relatively small differential for their clerks for this reason: the glamour of a job in London's West End may attract clerks from a distance without a very high salary differential, especially when it is combined with an entitlement to a "house discount" at a well-known store. Thus the cost of living has only an indirect influence on regional variations in clerical salaries; on the other hand, local differences in the clerical labour market cannot be ignored in drawing up salary scales. Employers are under constant pressure to transfer clerical work from high-cost to low-cost areas; and movements from traditional city centres to suburbs and new towns have proved beneficial to many.

Different Rates for the Same Work

Changes in the pattern of office employment have disturbed some of the traditional types of salary scale. Clerical work was almost wholly a career job. Clerks expected to start with simple routine and progress through grades, improving status and earnings. For young men, the career was for life; for most young women the career was until marriage or the birth of the first child. The lower grade work (I.A.M. Grades A, B and C) was done by young people and the higher grade work by the more mature people. During the 1960s, revolutionary changes took place. The increased availability of higher and further education and competition from other occupations reduced drastically the number of young people entering office careers at school-leaving age. The gap was filled by married women aged 30 and over, and by men and women nearing or over normal retirement age. Grade A work came to be done by pensioners; Grade B and C work predominantly by married women.

Whilst the lower grade work was done by teenagers, the rate for the job grade and the grade differentials were acceptable. The adult doing routine work now requires an "adult" rate of pay. The effect has been to disturb the career pattern, even to the extent of seriously reducing the differential between adults doing C and D grade work. In this situation, the employer is led more and more to give weight to age rather than the rate for the job.

Different Scales for Different Types of Clerical Work

In the British Civil Service and in the public sector generally, different salary scales are applied to different types of work.

The types are usually those mentioned in Chapter 9: general clerical work, typing and secretarial work, machine operating. Sometimes the divisions are more detailed. The fundamental reason for separating the types of work is that each type has its own labour market. If the demand for typists exceeds the supply, salary rates for typists will tend to rise. But this is no reason for increasing the rates for general clerks and machine operators at the same time.

In industry and commerce, some employers adopt a similar practice, although the differences may be expressed as differentials from a basic general scale.

Salary Rates for Part-time Work

Where part-time clerks are employed salaries are usually at hourly rates proportional to the full-time salaries for full-time work of the same grade. Some employers, however, find it necessary to offer slightly above the full-time hourly rate. This is in order to allow for the clerk's expenses in travelling and buying meals out, which may be the same as those of a full-time clerk, but representing a much higher proportion of earnings.

Temporary clerks working the normal week are usually paid at a rate per day. This rate is often higher than that for the regular clerk, but on the other hand the temporary clerk may not receive either sick pay or holiday pay.

Overtime Pay

Practice in respect of overtime varies considerably. Some employers pay by the hour for overtime worked, with or without an increment. In other offices the understanding is that a reasonable amount of overtime is covered by the salary paid. Where there are known peak loads of work and slack periods it is sometimes customary to grant time off as recompense for overtime worked. This may be an informal arrangement, or a record may be kept for each clerk ensuring that each hour worked is in due course repaid.

The long-established custom of allowing "tea and supper money" when overtime is worked still persists in some offices. When overtime is worked it is recognized that the clerk may have to buy meals out instead of having them at home, and an expense allowance is granted accordingly.

Bonuses

Output bonuses of any sort are rare in offices, mainly because of the inherent difficulties in obtaining accurate measurements (see Chapter 5).

There is a tradition in many offices of giving an annual bonus at Christmas time as a fixed amount for all, a percentage of annual salary or as a gift in kind.

Long-service Increment

Where employees of long standing have reached the limit of promotion within their capabilities, service increments are sometimes paid. These permit the recognition of loyalty and of the kind of experience which such clerks alone can bring to their work, without disturbing the general salary structure.

Alternatively long service may be recognized by a bonus at Christmas or at the annual holiday.

Other Remuneration

In seeking to compare one salary scale with another it is often necessary to take into account the benefits which an employee may obtain through canteen facilities, luncheon vouchers, pension schemes, life assurance, etc.

General Level of Clerical Salaries

Inflation made it necessary for employers to make fairly frequent upward revisions of clerical salaries. Failure to keep pace with the upward trend in wages and salaries resulted in a high labour turnover and a disgruntled staff. On the other hand, few employers were so opulent that they could afford to pay more than the prevailing market rate. It was, therefore, essential that conditions in the clerical labour market should be kept constantly under review. Many employers find it easier to do this if they (1) have their salary structure on The Institute of Administrative Management Job Grading Scheme and (2) take part in and make use of the Institute's survey and analysis of clerical salaries. The economic forces at work in the clerical labour market are complicated and can change rapidly in response to technical developments and changes in other sections of the labour market. Employers have to go to some trouble to see that their own salary scales are in harmony with what other employers are paying: the least troublesome way of doing this is participation in The Institute of Administrative Management national survey of clerical salaries, the results of which are analysed to relate salaries to the job grades of the clerks, place of employment, industry, and other factors.

Conclusions

In spite of the manifold variations between one employer and another, there is a recognizable pattern in the determining of clerical salary rates and scales. In other occupations the worker may reach his maximum basic wage at about the age of 21 and earn no more unless he gains promotion to a supervisory position. In office work, however, it is usual to take into account that a clerk is capable of a continued widening of experience and increasing of skill. Consequently it is normal to provide for increases in salary far beyond the age of 21 and often up to within a few years of retirement.

Within the framework of this concept there are various types of scale giving emphasis to age, years of service, service within a grade or merit within a grade. And beyond the general scale lie various provisions for overtime pay, bonuses, service increments, pensions, etc.

The general aims are economy, morale and the just recognition of skill and effort. In the achievement of these, the existence of a ladder of promotion is of paramount importance. The individual needs to be able to develop his potentialities, to see how he may pass to more responsible work and to see that he may reap the reward for his efforts. A salary structure based upon the job type and grade and the merit of the clerk within that job is perhaps the most practical method of gaining these objectives.

11 Personnel Practices

Good management stems largely from good personal relations between managers, supervisors and clerks. The importance of good relations between employer and employee is universally recognized. But who is the employer? The Civil Servant or worker in a nationalized industry is employed by the State, the citizens of the nation as a corporate body. The person employed in industry or commerce is often the servant of a large and impersonal company. Whilst the State or the company is regarded as an object of loyalty, the way in which a person reacts in his work is conditioned more by those people with whom he comes into daily contact. The employee's opinion of his employer is often his opinion of his immediate supervisor and manager.

It is not usual for supervisors and managers to have complete freedom in matters of personnel policy. On the other hand they have, of necessity, some freedom in the interpretation of that policy in practice. In exercising this freedom they must, above all, see that individuals are treated fairly and without favour. There is probably nothing which lowers the morale of employees so much as the feeling that one is favoured more than another. What is wanted is the just interpretation of a policy which is in itself just and continuing. A policy which is constantly changing produces a feeling of insecurity in people and this in turn lowers the sense of loyalty and of belonging to the organization.

In certain matters, for example hours of work, sick pay, holidays and pensions, the law requires that the employee shall be given precise written notice of his entitlements. In many other matters rules can be published to ensure as far as possible that all managers and supervisors, whilst inevitably using some discretion, interpret the policy in the same way. The legal aspects of employment are summarized in an Appendix (see page 227); this chapter is concerned with managerial aspects.

In formulating policy and the rules by which it is to be interpreted there are two principal guiding factors. Firstly there must be regard for policy in industry, commerce and the services generally. Conditions of employment are part of a nation's standard of living. Whilst it is difficult, if not impossible, to express this standard in exact terms, it is there as an impression in the minds of employers and employees alike. At any time there are certain conditions which are about normal and others recognizably above or below that normal. Conditions which are noticeably below normal may prove adequate because of some compensating factor such as a special interest in the job, some "glamour" surrounding it, or particularly good social relations. In the long run, however, those employers who do not conform with the general standard will tend to suffer a high labour turnover and be unable to attract the better types of clerk.

Secondly, there must be regard for policy in other departments of the organization. Working conditions and terms of employment differ as between clerks and other workers, sometimes for traditional reasons but often for quite logical reasons. It is obviously desirable that all clerks within the organization should be treated according to a common policy, in order to ensure uniformity of treatment as between one person and another. It is equally desirable that there should be uniformity of treatment as between every person in the organization, subject only to those differences which are generally accepted as reasonable. In establishing rules, care should be taken to state them in simple language. They should be positive and not riddled with exceptions. Rules, however well designed, will need to be broken from time to time in the interests of fair dealing and humanity. The management must therefore reserve the right to vary them in particular circumstances and make this intention known. Such variations should, of course, never be made lightly or for reasons of expediency. If a rule is broken, the exception should be capable of justification and of being seen by all to be just.

The scope of personnel practices is wide and is here taken to include working conditions, terms of employment other than salary, welfare and social amenities and the stimulation of interest in the organization and the job. In each of these fields there are practices which are generally followed and others which have been adopted in some organizations with success and may well indicate the current trend of development. As to which of these practices, outlined below, should be adopted by any administrative manager must depend upon local conditions and circumstances. It appears evident, however, that the operation of a liberal policy incorporating the best of these can bring lasting benefit.

Trade Unions

Except in the public sector, trade union representation of office staff was rare and clerks traditionally showed little interest in unionization. From the late 1960s, however, there has been some change of attitude, not only among employees but among the larger employers who may feel that it is more convenient to negotiate with a union than with individuals.

Although the *rate* of growth in trade union membership in industrial and commercial offices has been sufficient to excite comment, it started from small beginnings. It is difficult to establish how many clerks in the private sector are trade union members; the so-called "white-collar" unions embrace also non-clerical staff. From such figures as are available it would seem that by 1975 less than 20% of the total potential membership had been enrolled.

The personnel practices dealt with in this chapter are considered in terms of the majority of offices which are not unionized. Where office staff are represented by a union, relationships may tend to become more formal and policies more the result of bargaining than of unilateral managerial decision.

Working Conditions
In certain respects, working conditions are governed by the Offices, Shops and Railway Premises Act, 1963. Legislation is always concerned with the prevention of really bad conditions; mere conformity with the law is not good management. In considering the physical working conditions, local as well as general practices must be borne in mind. The office is not just a department in isolation to be compared with its counterparts in other organizations. It is a member of a team which includes all the other departments of the organization which it serves: the factory, the laboratory, the warehouse, the shop. It is therefore of importance that conditions throughout the organization should accord with some general policy. Elaborately decorated and equipped offices serving a factory in which conditions, perhaps of necessity because of the nature of the work done, are hard, can only cause ill-feeling and a lack of co-operation between departments. On the other hand, the offices attached to a sales department dealing in luxury goods may themselves have to provide a background of luxury, against which the potential customer may be received.

The office accommodation provided must be governed to some extent by the buildings available. Whilst some clerks may be housed in modern buildings with large open floors, many have still to work in offices not ideally suited to their purpose. Whatever the basic accommodation, however, much can be done to ensure acceptable conditions. Attention can be given to decoration, lighting, heating and ventilation without incurring great expense. The space can be allotted so that each clerk has a reasonable working area and can feel that the employer regards his work as of sufficient importance to warrant proper attention.

Office Rules
Whilst some rules are necessary to the smooth running of any organization, a multiplicity of rules may be regarded as irksome and even unreasonably restrictive. Rules should be few in number and such as will

receive the natural support of ordinary people. Each rule should be prefaced by an explanation of its purpose.

Hours of Work

The length of the working day and of the working week are often of outstanding importance to the clerk, and can be the factor which determines whether or not the most suitable staff can be recruited.

The five-day week is normal. In some organizations, the office must be open on Saturdays and, in a few, on Sundays too. For some computer staff and those doing work directly connected with round-the-clock productive processes or services, shift working is necessary. Clerks working an abnormal week have usually to be compensated by a higher basic salary, by overtime increment, or by time off during normal working hours. Where a skeleton staff is required on Saturdays, this duty may be spread among the clerks so that all share in the overtime earnings and in enjoying the two-day weekend break.

About one-third of the office work-force consists of married women who have two jobs, one in the office and one in the home. Employers cannot ignore this situation and behave as though the normal working hours will suit the entire staff. The married woman requires time for household shopping; the mother may have to take her children to school before starting work. The various alternative arrangements made include—

(a) a shorter day, starting late and finishing early;

(b) a three or four day week, which may be convenient where work-loads fluctuate;

(c) flexible hours, when the clerk is free to arrive and depart as convenient within certain prescribed limits, and is paid by the hour.

Office hours must be those during which business is transacted with the public, with other traders, or with other departments within the organization. They therefore vary according to local and trade custom. Most offices start between 8.30 a.m. and 9 a.m.; most finish between 5 p.m. and 5.30 p.m. The length of the normal working week (excluding lunch breaks) is predominantly between 35 and 38 hours. In central London, the working week tends to be shorter, predominantly about 35 hours. This may be assumed to reflect the difficulties of travelling and the time spent in getting to and from work.

Lunch breaks of up to an hour and mid-morning and afternoon breaks of up to a quarter of an hour are usual, although where there is a canteen it is considered reasonable for the lunch break to be shorter. In small provincial towns, where it is possible for clerks to go home at midday, more than one hour may be allowed for lunch. Where mid-morning or afternoon tea or coffee is brought into the office, or is available from a vending machine, a formal break may be unnecessary.

Timekeeping
Whatever is done to encourage good timekeeping, there must, in the interests of just treatment, be precise records of lateness. Various timekeeping records can be maintained, ranging from clock-cards and other mechanical means to the use of a signature book or records kept by supervisors.

The means of converting persistent offenders are few. In some offices it may be possible to withhold all or part of a bonus; in others, the time lost may be deducted from any overtime which might otherwise be paid during the month. In both of these cases, however, the amount of money withheld is not likely to be large, and may have little effect on the offender. Example and persuasion are likely to have at least as good an effect as loss of pay. The only real sanction possible, other than dismissal, is to show that continued lateness must have a deterrent effect on the clerk's progress. It is impossible to promote to senior jobs, involving the supervision of others, someone who is not there to see that work is started at the proper time. If this point is made clear it can be effective in those cases where promotion and the possibility of substantially increased earnings carry weight.

Holidays
The need for an annual holiday is generally recognized, but there are variations in the length of holiday granted. The established Civil Service enjoys long holidays and this has always been recognized as one of its attractions. In industry and commerce the normal allowance is three or four weeks, with additional time for supervisors and other senior staff. Whilst additional holiday time may be related to a person's grade or job, it is also in some organizations related to length of service. In these latter cases it is usual to grant additional days or weeks after, say, ten, twenty-five and forty years' service have been completed. In order that no one shall be away for too long at any one time, the annual summer holiday is often restricted to two weeks. Any additions to this are to be taken at other times and outside the peak holiday months.

Where holidays are staggered, the arranging of holiday dates is often a difficult matter. Each clerk has probably a very good reason for wanting a holiday at some particular time. A married woman may need a holiday which coincides with that dictated by her husband's job. A married man with young children must go away during school holiday times. Others may wish to join friends. If all these requirements can be met every year without dislocating the work of the office, the manager is indeed fortunate. Because of these inherent problems, it is usually found necessary to plan according to some reasonable but impersonal rule which all will accept.

The problem is to some extent reduced where the organization provides small working units. If, for example, the office is divided into groups of about six clerks engaged on similar or related work, the group can be asked to settle their own holidays provided not more than one is away at a time. There will still be difficulties, but those which call for a managerial decision will be reduced in number. In some offices holidays may be chosen strictly according to seniority and length of service. This system is usually accepted as being just; the more junior have at least the prospect of a better choice as time elapses. Whatever basic system is employed, however, there must be some elasticity. The annual holiday is an important event and it is unwise to deal with the problems which arise without the greatest possible consideration being given to individual needs.

Extra leave may be requested by married women during the school holidays. This is undesirable, since it throws extra work on the remaining clerks at one of the busiest periods, when they themselves might also have wished for extra leave. It is therefore desirable to make certain at the time of engagement what arrangements the clerk has made for the care of her children during such times. It should be made clear that she should not expect other than the normal holidays unless there is specific agreement to the contrary.

It is usually convenient to regard holidays as accruing month by month up to a set date, say 31st March in any year. This means that a decision must be made as to the holiday entitlement of clerks who join a concern in the first few months of the year, or who leave before taking their holidays. In the first case consideration must be given to the purpose of the holiday, which is to provide a break from work in the interests of health. A clerk starting work in January will clearly need a holiday before the summer of the following year. On the other hand a clerk who starts in the early summer might be supposed to have taken a holiday before starting work. In marginal cases, it may prove a satisfactory compromise to grant a week's holiday in the late summer or autumn. In the second case, a clerk who leaves in the early summer without having taken a holiday has in effect earned it month by month during the preceding year and may therefore be considered entitled either to take the holidays or to receive pay in lieu, since he will not expect to be granted a holiday at his new job.

Other Leave
From time to time clerks may request leave of absence for personal reasons. Whilst each case must be decided on its merits, it is as well to have some guiding policy in the matter. In some offices, time off is given as compensation for overtime worked. An account is kept of overtime

worked and corresponding leave granted at times mutually convenient. In others, there is an understood allowance over the year which is not exceeded except for very special reasons. Such systems provide for the normal requirements. It is, however, necessary to guard against an arrangement designed to meet personal emergencies becoming so formalized as to be regarded as an extension of the holiday allowance.

Sick Pay

Some scale of sick pay is usually advisable if only as a general guide. This may vary according to the length of service from, say, a fortnight for people of a year's service, ranging up to perhaps three months in the case of clerks who have been with the organization for five years or more. This does not mean that payment should be automatic on the one hand, or cease automatically on the other. In the first place it should ordinarily be subject to the production of a doctor's certificate and withheld at the management's discretion in extreme cases where there is reason to believe that the system is being abused. On the other hand, a schedule of payment, however generous, may still be insufficient in the case of an employee who has fallen into misfortune. Here the personal circumstances of the clerk must be given consideration, and such matters as the hardship which he or she may be suffering, the length of service, and the loyalty of the employee are all factors to be taken into account.

Help and advice may also be needed in arranging for convalescence or in other matters. The manager may need to keep in touch with the family, visit the hospital, and indeed offer all the sympathy and encouragement which would seem natural in the case of a personal friend. It may also be necessary to arrange for the clerk to work shorter hours during the first few weeks back at work.

Long-service Privileges

There is a general recognition that it is appropriate for extra privileges to be granted to staff of long service, particularly in those concerns where it is a tradition handed almost from father to son that members in one family make their entire career there. Difficulty arises, however, in trying to formalize and make automatic what is intended to be personal and individual. If it is common knowledge that "you get a gold watch after forty years" the ceremony of presentation becomes routine and some of the sense of recognition is thereby lost. A hard-and-fast scale of awards should therefore be avoided.

Long before an event such as forty years of service is reached, it is common practice for staff of appreciable service (perhaps five to ten years) to receive special privileges of some kind or another. Extra holidays are the most usual, but this may also be accompanied by an annual cash bonus or by privileges such as a staff account or the entitlement to buy at a discount. The rewarding of service and loyalty, however it may be done, is of value in making known that a clerk or supervisor is recognized as having established a permanent place in the organization.

Pensions

Pension policy must be considered against the background of the basic state schemes and legal requirements as to other schemes. In most organizations, private schemes (which may be contributory or non-contributory) are designed to supplement these basic provisions. They may be restricted to certain grades of staff, to those above a minimum age, or to those with more than a minimum length of service. The objective is to ensure a reasonable income in retirement for those who have given loyal service, and for their widows. What is reasonable will depend on the general standard of living of the employee, as represented by salary rate on retirement.

There are various ways of conducting such a scheme, the more common being to set up a trust fund through an insurance company or to set up a private trust fund. These two methods are common in large companies, but small concerns may find it more convenient to take out deferred annuity policies. Eligibility for entry may depend upon an age or service qualification, or both. A retiring age of 65 for men and 60 for women is usual, but in private businesses, at least, retirement is not necessarily obligatory. It may, however, be necessary for lighter duties to be found for the clerk concerned, with possibly some reduction of hours and pay. In some cases the agreed pension is paid as from the operative date, regardless of whether or not a salary is still being earned, either in the old job or some more suitable alternative. In others, the pension is proportionately increased according to the length of time by which retirement is delayed.

Life Assurance

It is common for employers to provide some life assurance for staff during their working lives, or alternatively widows' pensions. The amount of benefit assured is usually related to earnings, say one to three years' salary. The number of years' salary may be fixed or may be increased with length of service or according to grade.

Canteens

Businesses employing a substantial number of staff usually provide a canteen service, which can be of considerable value. Where there is no canteen, luncheon vouchers may be issued for taking a meal at a restaurant.

The majority of canteens are subsidized and it is as well for this fact to be generally known to the staff, even to the extent of publishing the running expenses of the canteen and disclosing the amount of the subsidy.

However well the canteen may be run, and however highly it may be subsidized, it is liable to be the subject of complaints from those using it. Sometimes the compaints may be justified; at other times a canteen complaint may be the reflection of dissatisfaction arising from another, quite dissociated cause. In some organizations there is a canteen committee comprising representatives of the staff and canteen management under the chairmanship of a senior executive. This committee has the duty of receiving and discussing all complaints and seeking to remedy them.

Welfare

Having considered the precise conditions of work in relation to the day-to-day requirements of the job, it is necessary to consider what steps shall be taken to meet the human requirements of the employee in the job. Here again a general body of opinion has grown up as to what is acceptable and reasonable. In a small office, consisting of some half-dozen clerks perhaps, it seems obvious to deal with human problems on a "family basis." If a clerk, an old and trusted assistant, needs time off to look after a sick mother, it seems quite natural that she should be given as long as she needs without any further question. Multiply this, however, into an office of fifty or sixty, or much larger, where there will inevitably be a small proportion of the more unscrupulous type of person, and difficulties arise. On the one hand there may be absence which is not justified. On the other hand rules designed to prevent this may result in the unsympathetic treatment of loyal members of the staff who are more scrupulous about their attendance.

The word "welfare" in connexion with employees has, perhaps, lost some of its true meaning. It has sometimes come to be associated more with the provision of certain specific services than with its wider intention, namely than an employer is concerned with the general well-being of his staff. A good welfare service is perhaps more an attitude of mind of the part of management than any particular acts. If the employer feels responsibility for his employees as people, this will be reflected in the understanding and assistance which is given.

In the larger organization there may be a medical officer or nursing sister available in case of sudden illness. In the smaller concern the intention behind this service may find expression in sending a clerk home in a motor-car or taxi-cab. With a large staff it is perhaps possible to provide complete sporting and social facilities. In the smaller office it is still possible to provide some social life. Space can usually be found for table tennis and a dart board; a small committee can organize motor-coach trips or theatre parties.

Whilst the management must play a leading part in organizing health, social and recreational activities it is important that the clerks play an active part also. If welfare services appear as merely part of the remuneration for the job, or as acts of charity, they will be treated as such and the family spirit lost. The ideal is that management should recognize the needs as they arise, and by help and encouragement see that they are fulfilled.

Communication

Each member of the staff must, of necessity, have sufficient knowledge of the affairs of the organization to do his particular job. A sales clerk must know the names of products and possibly their catalogue code numbers. Armed with these the clerk can at least do the job mechanically. If the clerk has in addition seen all the products in their final state, has seen them made and understands their purpose, he can bring a much greater interest to his work. He is no longer dealing with paper work; he is truly a vital link in the chain of manufacturing and producing something which fulfils a worth-while purpose. How far his outlook is broadened by this additional knowledge will depend on his imaginative ability and the extent to which this is stimulated. This is but one example of the fields in which knowledge can be extended to enable clerks to lead a more interesting and effective working life.

No one likes to be a pawn in the game, dictated to as though his understanding of the game as a whole is of no consequence. No one likes to feel that others are planning his life in the background without either his knowledge or consent. People like to know what is going on and, if any changes are impending which affect their lives, to be able to prepare to meet them. Certain knowledge can be obtained by a clerk in the course of his job and by observation of what is going on around him. But this will be incomplete and may for this reason be misconstrued. There is a need for the staff to be kept informed, through someone in authority, of changes and developments which will affect them in their work. Conversely there should be opportunity for the staff to ask questions about such matters.

In the narrow field of the clerk's own job there are such matters as changes in system, changes in the volume of work or extensions of business. Changes in system will impinge directly on the lives of certain clerks. Long before the management has settled its plans these clerks will be aware that something is afoot. From what little they can glean, rumours will arise. At the best there will be an atmosphere of uncertainty; at the worst, a severe lowering of morale. An increase in the volume of work may demand overtime, again affecting the working and social lives of the clerks. Forewarned they can plan accordingly. Extensions of business, such as the opening of a new branch, will involve more clerical work and possibly more clerks. Again, some of the existing staff are involved and they should be informed as soon as is reasonable rather than be faced with the new situation at the last moment.

In the broader field of the organization as a whole there is also a need to give information. The task of the office is to produce a clerical reflection in words and figures of what goes on in other departments. If the clerks are to do this intelligently they must understand what these other departments do, what their problems are and how the smooth working of the office is likely to be affected by them.

Much of this passing of information can and should be done by the administrative manager or supervisor. This is not, however, always the easiest or most effective method. For example, a verbal description of a factory is no substitute for a visit to it. Some of the more commonly used methods of communication with the staff are described below.

Staff Handbook

There is certain basic information which should be imparted to new staff. Whilst much of it can be given by word of mouth, the newcomer who is meeting so much that is new cannot be expected to absorb everything in this way. A handbook or leaflet to be read at leisure and consulted in the early days of employment helps to establish a new clerk more quickly. Such a handbook or leaflet can deal with such matters as the history and activities of the concern, its organization, conditions of employment, office rules, training and promotion schemes, welfare services and so on. It should be written informally but precisely. A staff handbook, once issued, must be kept up to date as changes take place. The copies which are issued to new staff must, of course, be amended. Those in the hands of existing staff are probably rarely, if ever, consulted, and it may be sufficient if an amended copy is available to them for reference.

Visits to Other Departments

Visits to departments outside the office are an essential part of the induction training of new employees. At this stage, they are a form of introduction to the organization as a whole. A visit may also be a vital part of training for a particular job connected with the work of a particular department. In this case it is no longer concerned merely with stimulating general interest. The clerk should meet those people with whom he will speak and correspond in the course of business, and know something of their problems which may react on the work of the office.

In some concerns it is arranged that representatives of other departments shall visit the office. The factory foreman and his equivalent rarely understand the problems which they can create in the office by rendering returns late, badly written or inaccurate. The exchange of visits and of viewpoints usually produces only good.

Staff Committees

From the basic information needed by each one of the clerks, it is appropriate to turn to the more general spread of information, for which some form of staff representation is needed. The term "Joint Consultation" is a familiar one, although various interpretations may be applied to it. Whatever meaning is accepted, however, all have at least one feature in common: that representatives of the staff should be able to meet representatives of the management to discuss matters of mutual concern. How such representatives are selected, when and where they meet, and what matters are of mutual concern, are subjects on which there are differing opinions. For instance, in a small office the arrangements may be quite informal, in fact almost unconscious, and if a new development occurs it would be natural for the manager to discuss it with the office at large. As the numbers grow larger, it becomes necessary to confine discussion to the heads of sections, or to representatives of the groups of clerks mainly affected. As the concern gets even bigger, such meetings may become fairly regular and thus, in effect, a Staff Committee has come into being.

Even in the smallest office, however, there is every advantage to be gained from formalizing these arrangements to some extent, since it is well for the staff to be aware what means are open to them for discussing difficulties, even if they are rarely used.

Representatives can be appointed by the management calling together the heads of sections, or they can be chosen by members of the staff either by mutual agreement or by election. In the latter case, the electoral groups should be arranged in such a way that the office as a whole is represented. This might be by groups, or by grades of clerks or by types of job. Discussion should be as free as possible and the staff should feel that any information they may need is open to them. Matters discussed in committee are likely to be of a fairly general nature, i.e. a difficulty affecting a group of people as a whole rather than one particular person, since individual grievances or personal difficulties are more usefully discussed at a private interview.

As the office gets bigger and becomes possibly a group of offices, the committee and all its arrangements will tend to become more formal, and efforts may need to be made to prevent this. It may be, for instance, that the smaller office committees will need to be reintroduced, leaving the main staff committee to meet less frequently and to deal only with matters of general significance.

House Journals

In a large organization, a house magazine of some kind is a useful means of spreading information about the concern and the people in it. Personal matters are always of particular interest to almost all members of the staff, and such things as service anniversaries, marriages and retirements are worth including. The scope can be extended to articles on holidays, hobbies and letters from staff who have left and taken up some activity of special interest. The more serious minded will study the articles about the working side of the concern but these must always be presented in as attractive a form as possible, and the more they are illustrated the better. The type of production may vary from a duplicated news sheet to a lavishly produced magazine of the kind prepared as publicity.

Some businesses regularly publish the company accounts to their staff. The "piece of cake" illustration is a typical method of demonstration, whereby the whole cake represents the gross profit of the firm or possibly the turnover, and slices of cake are cut off as the various expenses are set aside.

Pattern of Communication

No one of the methods described above is sufficient in itself to enable management to have complete understanding with the staff. Whichever of them are used, they serve only to supplement and not to replace personal conversation. The administrative manager must make an effort to know his clerks and afford them the opportunity to know him as a person. In the larger office this may be difficult to do informally. The number of clerks may make it impossible for the manager to get to know other than his supervisors and senior clerks really well. In the same way as he passes information to the clerks through the supervisors, he must obtain information about the clerks through the same channel. Supervisors should regard it as a duty to report to the administrative manager matters of interest about their clerks so that he may speak to them as the occasion warrants. The manager will then be able to commend good work or work carried out under difficulties, offer congratulations or sympathy in family matters, welcome those returning from sickness and generally demonstrate his interest in the individual.

Whatever other opportunities he may take for conversation with his clerks, the manager must at regular intervals discuss their work and progress. At every review of grade and salary each clerk receiving an increase should be interviewed. The clerk's progress should be discussed, the path of future progress outlined and criticism offered as may be necessary. Where a clerk is not regarded as worthy of an increase in salary it is probably more important that an interview should take place. Those who are not progressing may not understand why this is so. They may in self-defence assume that others are favoured for no good reason, but whatever their reactions these will have adverse effect upon morale generally.

Any organization must operate as a team. An effective team must have unity of purpose and unity of understanding. These, when achieved, are not the outcome of chance, but of positive and sustained efforts on the part of the leader, the administrative manager.

12 The Training of Clerks

Clerical work is basically concerned with reading, writing and arithmetic, subjects which come within the scope of general education. In addition some schools provide tuition in commercial subjects and in shorthand and typewriting. From this it might be assumed that young people leaving school are already fitted to a large extent to become clerks; that all that remains is for them to gain experience. But the knowledge which they have gained is little more than a glimpse of the background to a clerk's work, valuable though this is. If a junior clerk starts knowing the meaning of such terms as invoice, credit note and delivery note that is indeed a help, but there is much more than that to be learnt. Commerce has almost a language of its own, and each business has its own terminology. The public services also have their own terms of special meaning. A clerk has not only to learn the routine of his own particular job, but something of the general pattern of clerical work and of the industry or service in which he works.

The acquiring of this knowledge can be left to the individual; indeed this was at one time the accepted method of training. The new junior clerk was given simple tasks probably under the instruction of the existing junior clerk about to be promoted to some more difficult job. As the clerk progressed he learnt from those clerks immediately above him and passed on his knowledge to those who succeeded him. The more highly organized offices have become, the more work has been mechanized, the more has this method become inadequate.

Training should always have some definite object in view. Ordinarily this object is that a particular clerk shall be able to perform some specific job efficiently. Sometimes the training may be wider in its purpose and directed towards the development of a clerk in preparation for promotion to a more senior job as yet unspecified. In either case it is important that neither the trainer nor the trainee should be vague as to the intention. In its simplest terms, training is the process of changing a person from what he is now to what he needs to be in order to do his job. If this process is to be carried out without wasting time and effort, it requires the active co-operation of both parties.

The effort spent in teaching a clerk will obviously bear greater fruit if the clerk is naturally suited to the job. Training can only add to and build upon the foundations of existing knowledge and experience. If a particular job demands facility in arithmetic, it will be easier to teach someone who is already "quick at figures." If a job calls for a command of the English language, it will be easier to teach someone well-read and able to speak grammatically in ordinary conversation. It has been said that there are as many kinds of people as there are people. Each person has his own natural aptitudes, his own fund of knowledge and experience. The ease with which he learns, and his subsequent working efficiency, depend in some considerable measure on these factors. It is therefore important that training should follow on careful selection of the trainee in relation to the job.

The knowledge which a clerk needs to bring to his job can be divided into four categories, each of which presents its own training problems. Firstly, there is what may be termed "background" knowledge; the general understanding of industrial, commercial or Governmental practices and terminology. Because of its general nature, the clerk can learn much at college classes and by reading. Secondly, there are certain fundamental skills such as book-keeping, shorthand, typewriting and the operation of various other office machines. These can be regarded as falling within a separate category because they are not directly connected with any one particular office or job. A calculator operator, for example, is armed with a skill which can be applied in many jobs, but must still be taught a particular job in which that skill is to be used. Thirdly, there is the general background knowledge about the particular organization and office in which the clerk is to work. Into this category fall such matters as the functions of departments, the goods they handle and the duties and responsibilities of individuals. Lastly, there is the knowledge necessary to the clerk's particular job. This is vital and for that reason receives the greatest emphasis. But it must also be emphasized that knowledge of the job is only fully effective if the groundwork of a more general nature has preceded it.

Training is but one of the administrative manager's responsibilities, and it is natural that he should seek every assistance possible, whether from his subordinates or from outside sources. The four categories cited above are important in this connexion. In background knowledge and in fundamental skills the manager has the facilities offered by colleges of further education and schools run by machine manufacturers. If clerks are released during office hours to attend appropriate courses of instruction, the burden of training within the organization will be considerably reduced. Training in the affairs of a particular organization and for a particular job must, of necessity, be dealt with internally. The methods employed within the office are, therefore, of prime importance. It is generally accepted that the office systems are of importance. But these systems cannot be more effective than the clerks can make them. If the systematic planning of procedures is worth-while, so also is the systematic planning of training, and the selection of the most effective teaching methods.

Most of the training activity within the office will naturally be directed towards enabling clerks to do their immediate jobs. Clerking is, however, a calling in which the individual can and does develop in capacity over many years, if not over his entire career. It is not, therefore, sufficient to deal with the requirements of the moment in isolation. The job which a clerk does today can and should make use of the knowledge and experience gained in previous jobs. It can equally serve as preparation for other more exacting jobs which may follow as the years go by.

Organization and Selection

It is undesirable to consider training entirely in isolation; it is one of a sequence of events. First comes the establishing of the job as part of the organizational structure. According to how the work of the office is divided, so will the jobs be simple or complex. In the ideal organization the jobs will have been created so that each is suited to a clerk of a certain level of experience. This enables a pattern of development and promotion to be established. Junior clerks, having experienced the simple tasks, can move to jobs in which that experience serves as a basis upon which to build new knowledge. As the years go by, a clerk can move from job to job, each in succession demanding more knowledge. In this way, the task of training is reduced; each job is in itself a contribution to the needs of some more senior job. The progression from junior clerk, through the various grades to supervision, becomes a natural process; the training necessary to any particular job becomes a contribution to the development of the person.

There are inevitably a number of channels through which a clerk may progress. A junior typist does not ordinarily become a senior wages clerk, but will probably become a private secretary, having passed through various stages of responsibility. A junior punch operator may become a senior computer operator before becoming a supervisor. The organizational structure should therefore provide for development and promotion for clerks, in no matter what basic skills they have specialized.

The initial selection of clerks will guide them into one of these channels, and much will depend on the decisions taken at that stage. In the first five years of a clerk's working life, for example, he will be trained to do a number of jobs. This training will cost time and money; the time of those who train and of those who are trained. At each move from one job to another, there will be a period during which the clerk is inefficient because he is a learner. Care taken in selecting and directing young people into the type of clerical work to which they are particularly suited brings not only immediate, but lasting benefits.

Background Education

It is generally accepted that young clerks should be actively encouraged to continue their education after leaving school, and that this education should include vocational subjects. Colleges of further education provide courses leading to the following:

Certificate in Office Studies (BEC General Certificate)
This is suitable for students aged 16 and over with no specific academic qualifications; subjects include English, Clerical Duties, and two chosen subjects which might, for example, be Typewriting and Storekeeping.

Ordinary National Certificate in Business Studies (BEC National Certificate)
This is suitable for students aged 16 and over with four or more GCE "O" level passes in suitable subjects. Subjects for the certificate course might be Structure of Commerce, Economics, and English, plus a selection from Accounting, Statistics, Principles of Law, Modern Languages, Economic Geography, Economic History, etc.

Clerks are ordinarily required to be released from work to attend college classes for one day a week for up to two years. Day-time study is sometimes supplemented by evening classes.

Those who are seen to have technical, supervisory or managerial potential can continue thereafter to take a Higher National Certificate in Business Studies (BEC Higher National Certificate) followed perhaps by a professional or managerial qualification.

Training in Basic Skills

Reading, writing and arithmetic are no longer the only clerical skills, important though they still are. Offices are equipped with machines and other devices which clerks should be able to use effectively. Office systems and services make use of techniques which clerks should be able to employ with understanding. It is always possible to acquire skill by trial and error whilst doing a job. It is usually more efficient and more effective if skills of a general nature are developed by intensive training away from the job. The need for such training may arise from either one of two situations which will be examined separately.

With mechanization and the growth in size of offices has come a greater degree of specialization. It has long been accepted that the typist should learn to type, and that the accounts clerk should master the elements of book-keeping before starting work. The same principle is now applied to the operation of accounting machines, visible record computers, duplicators, calculators and other types of equipment. In some cases instruction is available as part of the background educational courses at colleges of further education; in others the employer must make use of the training facilities offered by machine manufacturers.

In the smaller offices, and in some sections of large offices, a high degree of specialization may not be possible or economic. The situation may demand that clerks can be moved from task to task, exercising a variety of skills. In some European countries, young clerks generally are trained to be able to type, keep books manually or mechanically, and operate all of the machines and other devices normally found in an office. They are given the basic skills necessary to perform a wide range of jobs with the minimum of training on the job. To them, it is unthinkable that a separate "specialist" must be asked to type their letters. In Britain, through the advice of the Industrial Training Boards and with the co-operation of the educational authorities, a movement is being made in the same direction. Colleges are equipped with a representative range of the more common machines and expect to teach students how to operate and care for them. Internal training schemes provide for young clerks to be attached to different sections of the office, perhaps only for a few days or hours, in order to learn to operate adding machines, calculators, duplicators, photo-copiers, etc., and to understand the correct procedures for handling mail, sorting papers, filing, using the telephone, receiving visitors, etc.

The basic office skills may be needed at any time during a clerk's career. They are best acquired when young, not by picking them up by chance, but under proper instruction. The competent carpenter is expected to be able to use any of the tools of his trade when called upon to do so; why should not the competent clerk be equally versatile?

Induction Training

When a clerk joins the staff of an office for the first time, there is inevitably a loss of efficiency whilst he becomes familiar with his surroundings. It is to be presumed that he was told something of the organization and its activities at the engagement interview, but this cannot serve as more than a brief introduction. If he is left to learn gradually as opportunity affords, the period of settling in may well last for weeks, especially in the case of a shy person.

Most organizations meet this problem by deliberate induction training. However familiar the organization may be to those already in it, the newcomer has a lot to learn, and he is unlikely to absorb it all at once. The programme may therefore be spread over perhaps three days. After the initial formalities of engagement the new clerk is brought into the office, allotted his desk and introduced to his immediate colleagues. Most people find it difficult to remember new faces and names, and it is best if the initial introductions are few. They must, however, include one person of about the same grade to whom he can look for general information.

At some convenient time during the day, the clerk can be taken on a brief tour of other departments. If it is an industrial organization, he can be shown the factory at work, and introduced to one or two people with whom he may later have business. Such a tour should be conducted by a supervisor able to give some explanation of what is seen, and to answer questions. On the following day, an hour might be spent in describing the organization, and particularly the part which the clerk's own department plays in it. Questions should be encouraged and answered fully. On the third day, some time can be given to an outline of the history of the organization and of its achievements. An organization is a living thing, with practices and traditions derived from its past. Some knowledge of what has gone before, imparted with authority and enthusiasm, can help to inspire newcomers to accept and carry forward those traditions.

Training on the Job

However thoroughly a clerk may have been trained in clerical work in general, this is no more than preparation leading up to the learning of a particular job. Training in specific procedures is a continuing process. It is necessary as each new clerk joins the office, as each promotion or change of job takes place and as any change of system is introduced. It is a fundamental function of supervision and management. Because job training is commonplace and often a matter of some urgency, it has been the practice to delegate this duty to the clerks themselves. A new clerk is seated beside an experienced one, who is expected to hand on his knowledge and experience. Whilst this method may be effective in the end, it is not usually the most efficient.

Much depends upon how well a clerk is taught his job. Training is costly. Some time must inevitably elapse before a learner is fully effective. If this period can be reduced the dislocation of work resulting from inefficient clerks will be reduced. The clerk who has inadequate knowledge of his job is liable to error and his mistakes may well upset and delay the work of others as well as his own. It is important that training should be as immediately effective as possible; that the beginner should be changed into a competent and confident clerk in the shortest possible time. It is therefore worth-while spending some time and effort to ensure that the best methods are used.

The proficient clerk is not necessarily the best teacher. Teaching is an art in itself. Anyone can show another what is being done. Not everyone can show what should be done, or explain why it should be done. One outstanding deficiency in permitting one clerk to teach another is that bad habits are likely to be perpetuated. A clerk may have instituted minor changes of procedure which have gone unnoticed and unchecked, and these are passed on as being the correct method. The cumulative effect of such changes can, in time, lead to serious inefficiencies. The training of a new clerk is an opportunity for ensuring that the job is done correctly. But that opportunity is only taken if the instruction is given by someone who knows what should be done and who understands the purpose underlying it. That person is usually a supervisor or senior clerk.

Training should be directed in the first instance to teaching the normal procedure and ensuring that this is thoroughly understood. In any procedure there will be exceptions to the normal, and the instructor may be tempted to lay emphasis on these. If, however, they are introduced too soon, the learner may become confused and even disheartened at the apparent complexities of the job. It is better that the basic routine should be fully absorbed initially, and the exceptions passed to an experienced clerk or to the supervisor. When the clerk has become practised in dealing with the normal, he can be progressively instructed in how to deal with the more difficult aspects of the job.

The training of clerks often presents a difficult problem because it is dealt with in conditions of emergency. A clerk may leave unexpectedly and a replacement must be brought in. A clerk is absent on holiday or through sickness and someone must fill his place for the time being. These situations can be met more easily if training is planned in advance as a continuing operation. In some offices there is always a training programme in being, and time being devoted to its fulfilment. The object of such schemes is to ensure that at least one other clerk has been trained to do each job, and can move into it at short notice. The clerk trained as a reserve is normally one of the same or a lower grade, so that replacement when necessary is by transfer or promotion. A situation in which an emergency vacancy is covered by a clerk of a higher grade is obviously undesirable. Systematic training along these lines is not easily introduced, but where it has been established as part of the normal responsibility of supervision, considerable benefits have accrued.

The task of training can be much simplified by means of the T.W.I. (Training Within Industry) Job Instruction method. This is sponsored by the Department of Employment, which provides instruction in its use. In essence it provides for complete preparation by the person teaching and for the trainee to learn by doing.

Unless a job is very simple and highly repetitive it is unlikely that a clerk can learn to do it in one lesson. The first stage of preparation is, therefore, to break the job down into suitable units of instruction. These units must be such that each can be self-contained and each can follow naturally on what has been taught previously. Each unit should comprise work which can be taught in about twenty minutes. If too much is included in a unit of instruction, the learner is likely to become confused and fail to remember. If too little is included, the instruction may appear disjointed and the work uninteresting.

Each unit of instruction is then planned on a "breakdown" sheet. The operations are broken down into steps, each of which calls for some positive action by the clerk, and these steps are listed in sequence. A step should achieve something and the breakdown states what is done rather than how it is done. Against each step are noted any points which are important to the efficient performance of that step, and any hints which may assist the clerk. It is not sufficient to prepare notes on the job as it is understood by someone already familiar with it. The instructor must endeavour to see the work as through the eyes of a beginner and attempt to anticipate the learner's difficulties. Furthermore, he must prepare to assist the learner to link the units of instruction so as finally to produce a clear conception of the job as a whole, and to relate the job to other jobs associated with it.

Before commencing to teach, the instructor must be completely prepared. If he is to gain the learner's confidence, he must show that he has no doubts as to what is to be done. The desk at which the clerk is to be taught must be properly set out with all the necessary equipment, forms and specimens. If dummy forms are being provided for practice purposes, these should be available.

The actual instruction itself is in four logical steps—

(1) Prepare the clerk.
(2) Present the operation.
(3) Try out performance.
(4) Follow up.

Each of these steps is of equal importance and their objective is to teach the clerk to do a job quickly, correctly and conscientiously.

Prepare the Clerk

The object of this step is to stimulate interest in the instruction which is to follow. Learning requires effort, and the desire to make this effort must be created. The best instruction can fail unless interest is aroused to a point where the learner feels that he wants to learn. The approach is essentially a personal one and the instructor must know something of the trainee's background, experience and interests. If he can, in conversation, find some existing interest to which the work can be related, the instructor's task will be the easier.

Part of the preparation is to establish a relationship between the job and its environment. Firstly, the purpose of the job must be made clear.

A learner cannot be expected to show enthusiasm over a job which may seem by itself pointless. Secondly, it must be shown how it links with the work which comes before and after.

Present the Operation
Making use of the earlier preparation, the instructor should demonstrate and explain the operation in clearly defined steps following logically one upon another. At each step, he should stress the points vital to effective performance and give reasons why they are important. The training should proceed only as quickly as the learner can absorb it, and great patience may be necessary. It is useless to pass to a second step until the first is understood. Patience and thoroughness will be well rewarded. Half an hour spent in effective training can well save days in turning the learner into a proficient clerk.

Try Out Performance
No instruction can be regarded as complete until it has been tested. The learner should now do the job under the guidance of the instructor who should immediately correct any errors. When the learner appears to be able to do the job, he should be asked to explain what he is doing and why—giving those reasons which were given to him. Many mental operations cannot be checked by visual observation and the learner's understanding must be tested by questions. These should always be framed in such a way as to preclude the answer of a mere "Yes" or "No." Questions beginning with words such as Why, What, Where, When and How are the most effective in producing a revealing answer.

Follow Up
The learner, having mastered an operation, must be given an immediate opportunity to practise. However well the work may be understood initially, repetition is necessary to ensure that everything that has been taught is remembered. The clerk should be left to continue working alone. From time to time the instructor should return to check what has been done, to correct any errors and to give encouragement. As the clerk becomes more familiar with the work doubts may arise regarding points of detail and variations from the normal. He should be encouraged to ask questions and these should be answered fully and seriously. The apparently stupid question may reflect inadequate instruction rather than any shortcomings on the part of the learner. The instructor's observation and assistance should continue until he is satisfied that the clerk can work satisfactorily under normal supervision.

Centralized Training

In the larger organizations there are advantages to be gained from the establishment of a central training school. The most important of these is the employment of one or more specialist teachers. However interested a supervisor may be in the training of his clerks, it is but one of his functions and he cannot expect to achieve results as quickly as one who has no other duties to perform. In addition, it becomes possible to develop and make use of training material such as film-strip, charts and diagrams. Clerks who are trained as members of a class often make better progress than when given tuition alone. There is an atmosphere of competition where progress and achievement can be compared with that of others, and the standards demanded can be higher.

Where there are numbers of clerks doing similar work, a training school can develop the clerk to the extent of teaching the actual job to be done. Otherwise the scope of centralized training must be limited to background subjects, induction and basic skills. Training for a specific job must remain in the hands of the supervisor responsible for the work. Whatever the scope of the central school, however, the teachers must not lose touch with the realities of work in the offices which they are serving. There must be continual liaison with these offices, and it is as much the duty of management and supervision to keep the teachers informed as it is the duty of the teachers to seek up-to-date information. Facilities must be provided for teachers to visit the clerks they have trained in order to assess the effectiveness of training and to assist in correcting any faults in operation which may have developed.

In the smaller organization it has been found worth-while to employ a specialist training supervisor. This supervisor, usually a highly skilled machine operator, assists the executive supervision in training matters generally. He can deal with certain parts of the induction course, give basic instruction in machine operation and may also train clerks in routine jobs. There are natural limitations to the work of a training supervisor. He cannot undertake all the training in the office; to do so would require mastery of every job, and a knowledge equal to that of every supervisor. It is therefore important to establish limits within which he shall work, and above all to leave no doubt that his function is to assist and not to relieve the executive supervision of one of their more important responsibilities.

Developing the Clerk

It is convenient to consider training in stages: the provision of general knowledge, the establishing of basic skills and the training in how to do a specific job. But it is desirable also to consider these stages as part of the development of the general capacity of the clerk. Clerical work provides a career. However important it may be to train a person quickly and effectively to fulfil some immediate need, it is equally important to recognize that training as part of a more sustained process. Each job that a clerk learns and undertakes is developing his future potentialities. If the fullest possible use is to be made of each clerk's capacity, there must be no artificial barriers to his progress. When a job has been mastered and the clerk has become fully experienced in it, thought should be given to the next, more difficult job, to which he should be transferred when the need arises.

The clerk who is left too long in one job when he is capable of more senior work will become bored and frustrated. And boredom and frustration are signs that energy, which could be better used, is going to waste. It is not always possible to offer promotion as soon as a clerk is deserving of it. There is, however, generally the possibility of a change of job within the same grade. From one point of view, it may be easier to leave proficient clerks where they are. From the broader viewpoint it is better to continue their development by teaching them other jobs so as to increase their knowledge and experience.

The progression from junior clerk to supervisor and even administrative manager, should not be a matter of chance. If every clerk is given an equal opportunity to develop his capacity to the full, the selection of those to fill the higher posts will be the easier. Opportunity for development should not be regarded as passive. Management has the duty of making the opportunity and of encouraging the clerks to take it to the full.

PART IV

Supervision

13 The Duties of a Supervisor

The supervisor holds an intermediate position between the manager and the clerks. He has a definite field of responsibility for a part of the office, which it is here convenient to refer to as a section, and will normally, but not necessarily, have group leaders or senior clerks between himself and the clerks. He will have fellow supervisors within the office, contacts with productive, selling or other departments outside the office, and in all probability contacts with customers, suppliers and others outside the organization which he serves.

His duties and responsibilities reflect this position and exist in respect of each of these relationships—towards his superior, the administrative manager; towards his equals, his fellow supervisors; towards his subordinates, his group leaders and clerks; towards his contacts elsewhere in the concern; and towards people outside the organization. These responsibilities arise from a single source, the office work for which he is responsible.

If a supervisor is to be fully effective it is important that his duties and responsibilities should be clearly defined. He should feel free to act with confidence within the scope of his authority, and not be left in any doubt as to where this freedom begins and ends. And it goes without saying that his authority must be equivalent to his responsibility. The definition of a supervisor's responsiblity must rest with his own manager, by whom it is delegated, and the detail in which it is defined in any particular case is a matter for the manager's judgment. It will depend not only on the nature and complexity of the section, but on the capacity and experience of the supervisor.

As with any matter in which there must be no room for doubt, the authority and responsibility of a supervisor is best put down in a written summary. The organization chart provides a guide to the division of duties within the organization, but so concise a record must of necessity need some amplification. The manager will want to keep his definition as short as possible; to define in too great detail is inevitably to place restrictions on authority rather than to guide its use. One aim is to prevent an overlapping of duties as between one supervisor and another, and conversely to ensure that every function is covered. Another aim is to ensure that a supervisor will refer back to his manager for guidance and decision when circumstances beyond the bounds of his delegated authority arise. What is wanted in essence is a unity of understanding between the manager and his subordinate.

The written mandate can, of course, be prepared by the manager in isolation, but, this having been done, there remains the problem of ensuring that its implications are fully understood. It is perhaps better that manager and supervisor should prepare a statement jointly, discussing each facet of the supervisor's job and reducing its essence to writing. In this way an understanding is reached first and the definition of responsibility is restricted to concise notes of those points which both parties are agreed warrant inclusion.

The Work of the Section

The first prerequisite to the proper discharge of a supervisor's duties is evidently to have a clear appreciation of his *raison d'être*. It is the work of the section which is of paramount significance; without it there would be no need for clerks and therefore no supervisor.

The supervisor must understand and sympathize with the objects to be achieved by his section. This understanding must be more than a deep knowledge of the system and its operation; it must include an appreciation of how the work of his clerks contributes to the productivity of the organization as a whole. Without this understanding, a supervisor cannot be expected to deal intelligently with abnormalities when they arise; he would not comprehend their true significance. Without this understanding, a supervisor cannot be expected to sustain his own enthusiasm in his job or to stimulate the interest of the clerks in their work.

The objective having been mastered, there must follow a detailed study of the work; of each operation carried out by each clerk and the part which it plays in serving the common purpose. He must gain familiarity with all the forms and documents used, their sources, their treatment, and their destination.

All the clerks on his section will be working to some kind of method, if only based on their individual ideas of how the work should be done. His job is to co-ordinate these activities and seek better ways of achieving the same results. Minor adjustments and improvements in method he should be able to apply himself, after making all necessary arrangements with those concerned, including, if necessary, other supervisors. If the need for a substantial change is apparent he must consult with his manager, and, possibly, with an Organization and Methods specialist. In the matter of development and improvement the problem is rarely that of knowing what to do, but of deciding what to do first. The danger is that of doing nothing until the opportunity arises or the time is available to have a "major overhaul"; that way lies stagnation.

Inspection of Work

However well planned the work may be, the supervisor needs to take continuing action to see that it is efficiently done. He must ensure that it is done economically without wasted time or effort, and that quality is maintained. Clerical work well done is neat, accurate and delivered to time. To ensure that the work of his section conforms with these standards the supervisor must inspect it whilst it is being done and when it has been completed.

It is obviously not possible for everything to be inspected and checked in detail; to do so would take almost as much time as the work itself. There is an art in selecting samples of work for scrutiny and in scrutiny itself. The supervisor must develop this art and apply it systematically to each clerk's work. The inspection of the end-products of a section's work is often the easiest way of ensuring that the work generally has been satisfactorily done, although this cannot be regarded as removing the need for examining samples of work whilst it is in progress. The supervisor should see and approve all key figures such as control totals, and all letters, statistics, accounts and other information issued from his section.

Control of Work

To control the efficiency of the section he must satisfy himself that the section as a whole, and indeed each member of it, is producing a satisfactory day's work. In this connexion a great deal can be done by observation—just seeing that each clerk appears to be working reasonably. This, however, is the crudest of techniques because the aim is to see not merely that the clerks are doing some work but that they are doing enough work, and that the procedures which they follow give the best result from the effort they expend. To measure a clerk's work fairly some standard must be established and some routine records kept such as are described in Chapter 5.

Equipment

Whilst the supervisor has probably no direct responsibility for the selection and provision of equipment, he has other duties in relation to it. Furniture, machinery, stationery and other items are in his care, and for the use of his clerks in the course of their work. He must, therefore, take an active interest in them and make recommendations when he feels some change is desirable.

Furniture should be kept clean, machines regularly cleaned and maintained, and stationery stored so as to prevent loss or damage. If the furniture provided is no longer appropriate for the work, the supervisor should recommend its replacement. If machines are underutilized he should recommend the mechanization of other work; if they are overloaded he should state his case for the purchase of additional machines.

Changing circumstances and the modification of systems can cause forms to become obsolescent without their being completely inadequate. They should, therefore, be systematically reviewed before re-ordering. The supervisor should examine forms in their completed state rather than as blanks. It can then be seen whether they do, in fact, meet the requirements of the job, as it is currently done.

To those who are closest to the job, the need for change is usually the least obvious. People are adaptable and will often suffer inconvenience as a matter of habit. The supervisor needs occasionally to make time to consider things objectively. Is the furniture right for the work? Is the layout the most convenient? Are telephones sited in the best positions? Is the lighting sufficient at each desk, machine and filing cabinet? Are files becoming cluttered with papers no longer required? Are desk drawers filled with papers that should be filed?

The Section as Part of the Organization

The supervisor and the clerks do not work in isolation but form part of an office which, in turn, forms a part of the organization which the office serves. It is appropriate, therefore, to examine the responsibilities of the supervisor in relation to others both inside and outside the organization.

The Supervisor and the Manager

From the business point of view the section supervisor's relationship with his manager is the most important. The supervisor has already been shown to have wide and diverse responsiblities for the work and efficiency of his section. In its discharge he will need the full support of his manager, and a spirit of mutual confidence must exist between them. The supervisor contributes to this by keeping his manager fully informed as to the state of the work, and particularly of any adverse tendencies such as work falling behind schedule or defective in any other way. There is no reason why this habit of regular reporting should prove burdensome to either party and without it the supervisor is liable to find himself at a disadvantage when a real emergency arises.

In this context the term "manager" is intended to imply the supervisor's immediate superior, and it is with him that this exchange of information and views should take place. One advantage of the establishment of a close understanding is, however, that where it is convenient to do so, the supervisor may deal direct with a more remote senior official without upsetting the line of control—making it, in fact, the servant of the organization and not the master.

Apart from dealing with the work, the discussions should cover the field of staff relationships—the proficiency and suitability of each individual clerk, any shortcomings which exist and the steps proposed to remedy them, the merits of those suitable for promotion either inside or outside the section, and indeed the general condition of the section as a social unit. Try how he may, the manager cannot expect to maintain close contact with each individual clerk in an office of any considerable size and he must rely upon the supervisor to keep him acquainted with their qualities and potentialities. This is the more important since the manager will from time to time be called upon to deal with the human problems which inevitably arise within a working unit, when the possession of such information is fundamental to an effective solution to the problem.

Service to Departments

The supervisor must at all times be conscious of the need to provide efficient service to the departments for which his section's work is performed, and must communicate this feeling to his entire staff. Understanding of, and sympathy for, the needs of the "practical" people in the factory, warehouse or shop is a necessary foundation for good clerical work. In dealing with these departments he and his staff should show courtesy, speed and efficiency. In general he should have know-ledge and authority to deal with the majority of requests and inquiries by himself, but, as always, he should consult with his manager whenever anything unusual or difficult is called for. In the same way he should be ready and able to meet criticism and eradicate its cause; where he cannot, he should seek the guidance and support of his manager.

The supervisor's sense of responsibility should guide him in these matters and enable him to distinguish between demands for work which is properly his concern, and those affecting others with whom he should communicate either for action or for information.

In all this field of activity there is no substitute for personal acquain-tanceship and understanding with the people involved. In a small or medium-sized undertaking where the office is closely associated with other departments this state may well exist quite naturally and with no conscious action on anyone's part. In the larger organization, however, positive action is necessary. If an exchange of visits can be arranged, well and good; at least he should visit related offices and departments and meet his associates in their places of work. Moreover, he should seek to arrange such visits for his senior clerks and indeed as many of his staff as are directly concerned with the work which gives rise to the relationship.

Representing the Organization

Where his work brings him into contact with concerns and individuals outside, it must be remembered that to them the supervisor represents the organization. Conscious of this responsibility, he must conduct the affair with proper courtesy with whomever the business may be. He should know clearly to what service he or his caller is entitled and what information may or may not be imparted, and act accordingly. Again, it is not sufficient that the supervisor himself should observe these standards; he must see to it that his subordinates act in an equally responsible manner. He must see that any communication, whether personal, verbal or written, is business-like in content and creditable in presentation.

Co-operation
The effectiveness of an organization depends upon full co-operation between its related units. This is nowhere more true than in the office. Co-operation rather than competition should be the keynote of the relationship between the supervisor and his fellows; while it is to be expected that he will develop a proper pride in the running of his own section, this must not be allowed to colour his association with others.

Work is likely to be exchanged and shared and it is up to the supervisor to see that no shortcoming on the part of his section is allowed to impede the work of another. Many common or related problems will be experienced, and by regular interchange of views and experiences with his colleagues, both formally and informally, he will be able to strengthen the effectiveness of the supervisory body and contribute to the creation and maintenance of a responsible supervisory outlook within the office.

The Supervisor and His Subordinates

The staff of the section are going to make the greatest single demand upon the supervisor's time and energies. Of all factors affecting the work of the section, the human one is the most complex, and, at the same time the most delicate. It permeates all other aspects of his work that have been considered; organization and allocation of work; method, machinery and system; location and layout, and relations with people outside, all affect and are affected by the feelings of the staff of the section.

The tone of these relationships should reflect his purpose to "guide" the clerks to the proper discharge of their duties and whilst he is in the first instance responsible for discipline, this consideration should rarely need to arise if he interprets his responsibility in this way and sets out to achieve it in that spirit.

At the outset he must try to know his clerks personally and seek to understand them and be understood by them as human beings. He should seek to acquaint himself with their domestic backgrounds and personal interests so far as can be achieved without appearing to pry into their private affairs. In this way he will be better able to treat them as individuals with differing emotions, aspirations, reactions and scales of value. He will also demonstrate that he is an approachable, sympathetic and sensible man, capable of advising his clerks not only on matters concerning their work but on personal affairs which they bring with them as worries to their work, and so help to create an atmosphere of mutual respect.

This is a position which cannot be achieved in a day nor, having been achieved, is it ever secured. It can only stem from a deliberate and conscious effort on his part to study the clerks as individuals and adjust his approach to each one accordingly. The situation itself makes the opportunity for the contacts which he needs, as he will first appear to the clerks as an authority on the work, as a leader in allocating the work and as an instructor in explaining the work.

He will be concerned in ensuring not only that proper provision is made to execute the work at any time but that necessary training is given to insure against breakdown in time of sickness or holidays. In the manoeuvres which always attend such arrangements he will have every need and ample opportunity to study the merits and characteristics of the individuals and discuss with them the plans which emerge. With this foundation for a basis of easy communication on work matters the supervisor should have no difficulty in gaining the confidence of his clerks sufficiently for them to be ready not only to discuss freely and frankly their reactions to the work and its environment but also to ask for his help in more personal matters. In such interviews his original role must be that of a listener, and the exercise of a little patience in hearing what is in the clerk's mind may itself put the clerk at ease and reduce what seems a formidable human problem to quite manageable proportions.

On no account must any sign of unrest or discontent be ignored, for that is the sure way to a major upset. By tact, patience and judgment the supervisor should seek to ensure that problems and grievances are ventilated and remedies sought or explanations given.

Communication with the Staff

The necessary communication with the staff has been discussed—the giving of training, the allocation of work, the issue of instructions and the personal conversations between supervisor and subordinate. There is another important type of communication which might be called "voluntary," only to stress that it is easily overlooked and certainly not to imply that it is unnecessary. This is the explanation to the staff of significant changes in the volume or character of the work, or of the routine employed, covering not only the cause of the changes but also the steps that are being taken. Clerks should be encouraged to express their views on the plan and these views should be considered before bringing it to finality—given only that the situation is neither created nor implied where decisions may be taken on the strength of a popular vote.

From keeping the staff fully informed as to the purpose, requirements and handling of the work it is a short step to soliciting their continuing help in developing and improving the situation. As they are closest to the work they have the greatest opportunity for constructive criticism on points of detail and this is greatly to be encouraged. The existence of a formalized suggestions scheme, with special stationery and tangible rewards, is a help towards overcoming any diffidence on the part of the clerks, who may feel that a suggestion is tantamount to a criticism of the supervisor. Suggestions should not only be encouraged, they should be seen to be encouraged.

Development of the Clerk

The supervisor will for most of the time be dealing with a constantly changing situation, particularly amongst the staff of his section. He must seek to develop each clerk according to his individual abilities and limitations, seeking to extend the former and eradicate the latter. These characteristics should be discussed frankly with the clerk and an indication given of the likely range and speed of progress (if any) and what further effort is needed to achieve it.

The clerk must know how he is getting on and, especially in the early stages, the supervisor must discuss his view of the clerk's work and conduct. Good work should be praised and bad work criticized, but whilst praise may be public, censure must be private, and given moreover in the spirit of seeking to help rather than condemn.

Development should be recorded by the writing of a personal report on each clerk from time to time, principally for the guidance of the management in determining how best to use the services of each clerk. It may be that some of these reports, the more laudatory, will result in the transfer away of some of the best members of the section. This is not only feasible, it is even desirable, since a steady movement towards promotion is an important factor in morale. The supervisor must throughout make it clear that he will not stand in the light of his clerks' progress.

The Supervisor and His Assistants

Hitherto the supervisor has been assumed to be in immediate contact with the staff. In practice this may not be so and quite likely there will be group leaders in direct control of work units smaller than the section (see Chapter 2).

In dealing with his group leaders, the supervisor has only to draw from his experience of the manager-supervisor relationship, which should reproduce itself one stage lower in the hierarchy at the supervisor-group-leader level.

The group leader will normally be immediately responsible for getting the work done, and it is particularly important that there should be mutual confidence and understanding between the supervisor and his senior assistants. The tone of their relationship should be similar in all respects to that between supervisor and manager, whilst all that has been said on the relationship between the supervisor and his clerks should apply equally to group leaders and their subordinates.

14 The Training of a Supervisor

Increasing emphasis is nowadays being placed upon the need for proper vocational training, and the purpose of this chapter is to establish its place in the development of clerical supervision and to suggest methods and procedures which can be applied to its fulfilment.

Vocational training is nothing new—the particular need for it at this present time arises only from the era of rapid development and change through which mankind is passing. The training of craftsmen has been developed since at least the Middle Ages through the craft guilds and the apprenticeship system. Crafts were handed on by skilled men to their successors, who themselves were precluded from practising their art until they had satisfied the standards of their forerunners, thus ensuring a continuing high level of output and workmanship.

In the same way, training for the professions has a long history of closely guarded regulation by the heads of the professional bodies, who lay down not only standards of competence and performance but, in many cases, codes of conduct and ethics. This is true, for example, of the legal and medical professions and, more recently and more closely related to clerical work, that of accountancy.

Training in Industry

Twentieth-century developments in industry and commerce have introduced an entirely new field of specialization—the organization of working groups to serve and develop modern mass-production methods. As advances take place in the design and scope of machinery and equipment, so emphasis falls increasingly on the need for corresponding advances in industrial and commercial organization, and so the development of planned schedules and procedures supersedes in importance the encouragement of the individual personal skill.

Developments in industrial methods call for parallel improvements in clerical procedures, and lead to the highly mechanized office and complex clerical systems which are today commonplace. The very existence of these features implies a need for a specialized knowledge in the field of office management, and their development and improvement depend upon adequate training in this field, so as to equip the supervisors of clerical work adequately for their task.

The need for improved productivity is widely stated and universally accepted. That it depends at the outset on efficient and effective training is no less apparent. And these axioms apply to administrative management and supervision as much as to coal-mining or cotton-spinning.

Moreover, the need is an immediate one; time spent in leaving the supervisor to learn by trial and error (a euphemism for bitter experience) is time wasted and time lost. In so far as a supervisor comes to his job deficient in fundamental training, he will inevitably carry out that job at a lower level of proficiency than might otherwise have been achieved. He is the vital link between management and staff, and on him rests the day-to-day responsibility for getting the work done. At the point where the actual work must be done he is the key to efficiency.

The Need for Training

The duties of a supervisor have been summarized in the previous chapter. Whilst they are concerned with clerical work, they are not the duties of a clerk. The good clerk cannot therefore be expected to become a good supervisor without a much wider knowledge and experience which cannot be gained merely by being a clerk.

A supervisor is a member of the management team and as such he must understand part at least of the policy of the organization which he serves. This understanding can be gained only by contact with higher levels of management, by being present when decisions are taken and having the opportunity to see why they are taken. In his contacts with other departments he must understand something of their work and problems, so that he may co-operate fully and enable his section to give effective service to the organization as a whole. In his dealings with other sections of the office he must understand how his work fits into the general pattern and how any action on his part is likely to affect the work of others.

The step from clerk to supervisor is a major step. The proficient clerk needs to understand his own job. The supervisor must understand many jobs, and from a wider viewpoint.

Finally and perhaps most important of all the supervisor is a leader. He must know how to train and instruct others; how to assess the volume of work which he asks others to do; how to ensure that work is carried out correctly and to time. He must be able to judge the capabilities of his clerks, to develop their potentialities and, knowing them as people, maintain them as a contented and effective team.

As in any other job, supervision can be learnt by observation, trial and error. This method is, however, of long duration and costly. With systematic training the clerk can be made into an effective supervisor in months rather than years and without the organization suffering unduly from a beginner's mistakes.

The Development of the Individual

The pattern of organization within the office will in large measure determine the stages through which clerks will pass in their development into supervisors of various grades and in some cases into managers. In the various organizations described in Chapter 2 a span of control of about six is employed. Group leaders act as working supervisors in charge of small groups of clerks. Supervisors are responsible for sections comprising about six groups. Managers control offices of about six sections. With such an organizational pattern it is natural that the potential supervisor should first be trained as a group leader and have the opportunity of gaining experience at that level. The group leader who is judged to be capable of wider responsibility can in due course receive further training before appointment as a supervisor. Similarly the supervisor who is a potential office manager can be developed to that end.

If the division of responsibility at different levels within the organization is logical, the pattern of training and development for the individual will be readily apparent.

The Training Programme

If training is to be systematic is must be planned in advance as a whole. There must be a programme which states, however briefly, when instruction is to be given, on what subjects and by whom. The programme should be complete having regard to the trainee's existing knowledge and experience, and the knowledge and experience necessary to his job. From this it follows that the latter must be known in fairly precise terms. It is impossible to define what is to be learnt without first defining the job and the demands which it makes upon the person doing it.

As in the general development of the individual, training for any specific job should be planned in progressive stages. The order in which subjects are presented is of vital importance because knowledge and understanding cannot be acquired except in relation to that which is already known. To take a simple example, the significance of a sales accounting procedure will only be fully understood if there is a previous knowledge of sales policy and procedure. The sales accounting procedure can be learnt in isolation, but this will not provide that depth of understanding which will enable a supervisor to deal with the queries raised by his clerks. Nor will it enable him to know when matters of detail should be referred to the sales management for information or for decision.

The sequence of training should in broad terms proceed from the general to the particular. In an industrial undertaking a trainee will require a general knowledge of the industry and its products. This should be given first, and against this background he should proceed to learn about the particular business in which he is employed. From a general knowledge of the business and its organization, he should proceed to gain a more detailed knowledge of the departments with which his section of the office is primarily concerned. Finally the trainee must study the section as a whole and the work of each clerk within it. This approach from the general to the particular should be employed in relation to every aspect of his job, be it concerned with procedure or with the art of supervision.

The training programme is not to be regarded as a secret document seen only by those responsible for training. If the trainee is to co-operate to the full he must know from the commencement the course which he is to take. He should have a copy of the programme and should understand in broad terms the significance of each stage and the reasons underlying the order of events.

Vocational Education

It is not usually easy for an administrative manager, busy with his day-to-day executive duties, to spend more than a few hours each week in training potential supervisors. That training is one of a manager's responsiblities is true; it is equally true that without some assistance he may not be able to fulfil it as conscientiously as he would wish.

Whilst there are subjects in which the manager alone can instruct, there are others in which outside assistance is available. There are numerous professional and general courses available at technical and commercial colleges or from correspondence schools, and there is a wide selection of books which can be studied. From study the trainee can gain must of the general background knowledge which he requires. He can learn the arts of accounting, cost accounting and secretarial practice, and he can perfect his command of the English language. It is unlikely, however, that he can choose without some guidance the courses of study which he should follow.

If the office manager is to benefit from this outside assistance he should endeavour to select his potential supervisors as early as possible. Whilst young people can and should find time for study, those who are older and have assumed the responsibilities of a family may find it difficult or impossible to take part in courses lasting for, perhaps, as long as five years. The older trainee can, of course, be encouraged to take short courses or to study isolated subjects, and can undertake prescribed reading.

In recommending courses of study it is advisable to make some assessment of the natural abilities of the individual. Many have embarked on ambitious courses, only to fail because they required a greater aptitude for academic study or a higher level of intelligence than they possessed. Whilst they undoubtedly will have gained some benefit in spite of their failure at examinations, they would probably have benefited more had they taken a more suitable course. For those unlikely to succeed in qualifying in accountancy, cost accountancy, company secretarial or administrative management professional examinations there are alternatives. Education authorities provide courses of a general vocational nature, leading to the Ordinary and Higher National Certificates in Business Studies (BEC National and Higher National Certificates). As the individual's path of development is seen to lead towards supervision, courses preparing for the examinations for the N.E.B.S.S. Certificate in Office Supervision and/or the Institute of Administrative Management's Certificate in Administrative Management are appropriate. Those who aspire to progress from supervision to management can continue to take the examinations for the Institute's Diploma.

For the older person there are the short intensive courses in supervision and management held at residential colleges in some parts of the country. These courses, usually lasting for a week or two, are of particular value in broadening the outlook of one who is to be promoted after long experience as a clerk.

In selecting potential supervisors for training it is necessary to have in mind some minimum standards of academic knowledge. Any supervisor at whatever level must be capable of clear self-expression, whether writing letters which are to go outside the organization or memoranda and reports to other departments. In the higher posts it may be necessary to have ability in public speaking. A supervisor is a leader and a leader cannot be inarticulate. In clerical work, expression is as often in figures as in words. However routine his section's work may be, the supervisor is likely to be providing figures which ultimately form part of the accounts of the business or other organization. He must, therefore, have some fundamental knowledge of book-keeping in order that he may appreciate the significance of any action he may take. That a supervisor should have studied the art of supervision goes without saying.

Beyond these minima will inevitably lie other requirements, dependent upon the peculiarities of the job.

Background Training

The supervisor requires a sound knowledge of the practical affairs with which his clerical work is concerned. Most office work is concerned with providing a reflection in words or figures of events which have occurred or policy which has been determined elsewhere. Whilst procedures will have been established with this in view, a true reflection cannot be obtained unless those operating these procedures have a full understanding of their purpose and significance. The supervisor needs sufficient knowledge to be able to deal not only with routine but with any exceptional circumstances which may arise.

As an early stage in training, the trainee should be taught about the organization, its history and its functions. The history of the organization is the source of its good traditions, and every supervisor has a duty to perpetuate these traditions so long as they remain appropriate. He should not conform blindly with what has been done before, but enter into the spirit that lies behind it. It may well be that a short talk on this subject is given by a senior member of the management rather than departmentally.

It is usually convenient to provide the trainee with an organization chart and to explain the functions and inter-relationships of departments by reference to this. Wherever appropriate he should visit departments to see the work which they do and to meet the people with whom he will have dealings in the course of his work. A full understanding of the work and problems of other departments will come only after experience, but a systematic survey in the course of training will enable this understanding to ripen the sooner.

In addition to learning in general terms about other departments, a supervisor needs to know more particularly about the work of other sections of the office. Whilst the various sections and offices within the organization may specialize, they form part of one clerical service and their functions are inevitably related. The supervisor of each section must know what the responsibilities of his colleagues are and how their work is co-ordinated with his own.

The object of this stage of training is to bring to the trainee an understanding of his environment. It should enable him to see the work of his section in relation to the other parts of the office. It should enable him to relate his work with that of other departments outside the office and with the organization as a whole. Armed with this knowledge he should be able to work intelligently and make wise decisions within the scope of his authority.

Training on the Job

Whilst it is convenient that background training should be given away from the section which the trainee is to supervise, there comes a point at which instruction must relate specifically to that section and its work.

The trainee has to gain detailed knowledge of each clerk's work, and learn how to supervise it. He must be given full opportunity to criticize and question what he sees, because he must understand and sympathize with what he finds. If he is in any way dissatisfied with what he finds he must be convinced that what is done is right or, if his criticism is valid, be given an opportunity to change it. The main objective is training and not reorganization. The trainee should not therefore be encouraged to carry out a review in the way of an Organization and Methods specialist. On the other hand, the new supervisor cannot be expected to put his whole heart into his job of leading others unless he believes fully in what he is asking of them.

The scope of training on the job can be divided under the following heads.

The Work of the Clerks

The trainee must understand what is being produced by the clerks and how the work should be done. As a supervisor he will not do the clerks' work himself, and there is no reason why he should seek to be as proficient as they in matters of routine, e.g. machine operation. As a supervisor he will, however, be responsible for the training and instructing of the clerks and for judging whether their work is correct. His standard of knowledge must be at least sufficient for these purposes.

Control of Output

The trainee must know what is required in terms of volume, promptness and economy of cost. He must arm himself with some assessment of how long each job should take to do, and with a time-table showing when each job should be started and completed. He should learn how to keep in touch with each clerk's work so as to know when there is any danger of work falling in arrear, and how to report to his superiors on the state of his section.

Inspection of Work

It will be impossible for the new supervisor to check the work of all his clerks. He must therefore learn how to scrutinize and carry out spot checks so as to ensure that standards of accuracy and appearance are maintained.

Forms and Equipment

The trainee must examine and understand all forms in use and be satisfied as to their purpose and suitability. He must become familiar with all machines and equipment in use and satisfy himself that they are appropriate and properly used and maintained.

Records

The trainee must examine and understand the purpose of all records maintained by the section.

Staff

If the staff of the section are not already known to the trainee, the study of the work of the section provides an opportunity for him to make their acquaintance.

Whilst the field of training can be divided in this way, the trainee will, in practice, study each clerk's job in turn as a whole. Provided that every aspect of each job is covered, this method offers an advantage. It is desired to impress upon the trainee the scope of his responsibilities as a supervisor, and the repeated examination of jobs from all angles helps to this end.

Training in Supervision

Much of the art of supervision and its problems must of necessity be learnt by experience. It is, of course, undesirable that every newly appointed supervisor should learn only by his own mistakes, particularly as in so doing the work may suffer and the staff become upset. Every endeavour must be made to forewarn and forearm the trainee so that he shall not unwittingly act against the general policy, particularly in the fields of working conditions and discipline.

In some respects the work of the supervisor as such will probably have been formalized. Attendance records, lateness records, personal reports on clerks and salary recommendations are among these. Where a procedure exists the trainee should be instructed in it. If there is a staff handbook or published office rules, the trainee must be told in detail how the contents are to be interpreted. If there is a job grading and merit rating system in operation he must understand how it is to be applied.

The advent of a new supervisor without experience can, of itself, cause a disturbance in the working climate of the section. No two clerks will react in the same way, perhaps, but all will react. Much will depend on how the supervisor acts in the early days and weeks of his appointment. Whilst he may have been thoroughly schooled in the work, his leadership is the leadership of people. This is the most important aspect of his job and at the same time the most difficult to teach. The fact that it is both important and difficult is, of course, no reason for leaving the human aspects of supervisory training to chance; on the contrary they must be given special attention.

All possible steps must be taken in the training prior to the new supervisor taking over his responsibilities. But to the trainee who has never experienced responsibility and authority over others, this cannot be more than theory, important though that is. The training must therefore continue after appointment, and the programme should provide for this. From day to day, as new experiences are felt and new problems met, they must be discussed fully. After a lapse of, say, two months, the theory taught in early stages should be reviewed and related to the experience which has by then been gained.

The scope of training in supervision will naturally depend on the responsibilities to be undertaken. A group leader's supervisory functions are probably restricted to training, the giving out and scrutiny of work, and the control of output as to volume and time of completion. The emphasis in such a case is on the more formal aspects. The supervisor on the other hand has a greater concern with matters of morale, discipline, promotion and with the human aspects generally. Even where there is a highly organized welfare service, he is the one who will first see the need for its help in particular cases. He must be able to talk sympathetically with his staff when they are in trouble, assist them if he can or seek assistance on their behalf.

Training Methods

The methods employed in training will depend to some extent on circumstances. In the large organization there may be a central training school which can relieve managers of the more general portions of the training programme. In the small organization, the entire burden may of necessity fall on the management. Whatever the situation, however, it is worth while giving careful consideration to each item of the programme to decide which method should best be employed.

There are advantages (where numbers permit) in training potential supervisors in groups rather than individually. Management time is saved in explaining subjects to more than one person at once. More important still, the trainees gain much in knowledge, experience and confidence if they can work together and discuss their common problems.

Whichever method is selected, it should serve as many as possible of the following purposes—

(1) To give the trainee some definite task to perform which will lead him to gain some specific knowledge or experience.

(2) To produce positive and concise evidence of what has been learnt.

(3) To ensure that what has been learnt is firmly impressed on the trainee's mind and is not likely to be forgotten as further stages of training are undertaken.

(4) To provide, in addition to theoretical understanding, a positive lead as to the action to be taken in given circumstances.

It is wasteful of time for the trainee to try to learn as a passive observer. Watching a clerk work is not of itself stimulating, and in the case of repetitive work may even becoming boring. A report that a clerk's work has been studied is no guarantee that it is understood unless the trainee is closely questioned about it. The method whereby a trainee is merely given an opportunity to visit each clerk and learn by observation is not adequate. It offers no evidence of having learnt, and it certainly does not help to develop supervisory ability.

The methods which are briefly described below are not alternatives in the general sense, although there may be more than one which could equally well be employed in particular circumstances.

Talks

It is natural that much of the instruction is by word of mouth. Managers and others will tell the trainee about the organization, its activities, policies and procedures. Such talks must be prepared. A spontaneous discourse on some topic or other may be interesting and informative, but it may equally be incomplete and fail to drive home the key points. Those who undertake to give trainees instruction should prepare at least a note of the points they wish to make, so as to ensure that what they say is complete and not liable to confuse or mislead.

A talk by itself does not ensure that the trainee has understood or that he will remember. Ordinarily no one remembers, other than for a short time, that which they have heard once only. Repetition is essential to memory. A talk should therefore be followed by some other activity. For example, if the work of a department is explained verbally, it could be followed by a visit to that department. The trainee could then be asked to write a brief account of what he has learnt, this being checked and discussed with him. This sequence involves hearing, seeing, writing and discussion, thus impressing the matter firmly in his mind. Furthermore he has demonstrated his knowledge and understanding in his report and in the subsequent discussion.

Visits

Visits to departments serve a two-fold purpose. They stimulate interest and provide a knowledge of practical matters which will assist in the proper performance of clerical work. In addition they enable the trainee to meet and talk with other members of the organization on their own ground. These personal contacts can subsequently be of great value when the trainee comes to take on his responsibilities and must co-operate with people who might otherwise be known only as a voice on the telephone.

Discussion

Where it is possible to train potential supervisors in groups, discussion is often of more value than listening to a lecture. Such discussions should be led by a chairman who knows the subject, has decided the points which he wants discussed and can stimulate the group in their work. Vague discussion without coming to specific conclusions is of little value. The exercise of the trainee's mind in arriving at the right conclusions in concert with others leaves a lasting impression.

Tasks

Learning by doing involves the active exercise of the mind. This method is of particular value when the trainee is learning about the work for which he is to be responsible. In studying the work of a clerk, he can be given a number of tasks, each of which will produce evidence of what has been learnt and also provide the trainee with aids to supervision. For example, he could be asked to survey the work of a clerk and produce some or all of the following—

(1) T.W.I. Job Instruction breakdown from which a new clerk could be trained in that job.

(2) A time-table covering a typical week.

(3) A list of the points which he would particularly look at when scrutinizing the clerk's work.

(4) An assessment of the grading of the job.

(5) An analysis of the queries which arise with suggestions as to how they might be prevented.

(6) An assessment of the time which the various parts of the job should occupy.

Such evidence assists the manager responsible for training to know quickly whether the necessary knowledge has been gained, and how far the trainee has progressed in acquiring the outlook of a supervisor.

Other tasks might include the preparation of a procedure statement, an inquiry and report on some aspect of the work which is unsatisfactory or the charting of the flow of documents. Whatever task is chosen it should exercise the trainee's mind, give him a positive purpose to achieve and produce concise evidence of the results of his work.

Questionnaires

The questionnaire provides a simple method of guiding the trainee to find information for himself. A list of questions is provided and the trainee in the course of studying any part of the work is required to find the answers to them. An example of such a list is given in Fig. 17. A general questionnaire may be designed to cover any clerk's job or a specific job; or it may cover supervisory duties.

The Mentor

The trainee should throughout his training be able to look to one person as his mentor. This person, ideally the manager to whom he will be

---

SUPERVISORY TRAINING QUESTIONNAIRE

Purpose
  1. What does the section produce as a result of its work?
  2. What is the ultimate purpose of this result?
  3. In what ways does the work of the section contribute to the company's final accounts?

Control of Work
  4. (*a*) On what standing authorities does the section act? Prepare a list of these.
    (*b*) What schedule of authorities is kept and how often is it reviewed and confirmed?
    (*c*) In what circumstances is special authority obtained and from whom?
  5. How should the supervisor of this section inspect the work done—
    (*a*) to satisfy himself that it is to the required standards of quality?
    (*b*) to ensure that it is being produced to time?
    (*c*) to ensure that the volume produced is reasonable having regard to the number of clerks?
  6. What key information must the supervisor always scrutinize personally?
  7. On what matters must the supervisor report regularly to his manager and at what intervals?

Fig. 17

responsible on appointment as a supervisor, should approve the programme, watch over its progress and check its effectiveness. Instruction may be given by many people: the managers of various departments, supervisors of different sections of the office and even by an outside source such as a technical college. It is perhaps best that this should be so, in order that the trainee's outlook shall be broadened. But the co-ordinating of this training and the development of the individual should be in the hands of one person, the mentor.

However short or protracted the training period, the mentor should meet the trainee regularly, say once weekly. At these meetings progress should be reviewed and discussed and the next stage prepared. The trainee should ventilate his problems and the mentor should criticize and advise. In particular the mentor should endeavour to give the training continuity, relating one subject to another and ensuring that the various stages of training follow in natural sequence.

The Final Task

The ultimate test of the effectiveness of training lies in how well the new supervisor does his job. It is likely that he will enter upon it with enthusiasm and it is likely that some of this enthusiasm will be misdirected. Until he has gained experience, he may well underestimate some part of his responsibility or overstep some part of his authority. If he does, this is the measure of the extent to which those who have trained him have failed in their endeavours.

It is no easy task for a manager to ensure that someone new to supervision fully understands when to act on his own discretion and when to seek advice or decision. In the final stages of training the question of authority and responsibility should be fully discussed and defined. The trainee and his mentor should, at a series of meetings, review every aspect of the job. As a result of these meetings, the trainee can be given the task of preparing a short statement summing up such key matters as—

(1) The purpose of his job.
(2) The work which he may not delegate.
(3) The information which he must report to his superior.
(4) The decisions which he may and may not make.
(5) The scope of his disciplinary authority.

Such a statement, representing a basic understanding between manager and supervisor, can do much to ensure a successful start and to give the beginner the confidence that comes from being sure of what is required of him.

Continued Development

Carefully planned training, such as that advocated above, can ensure that the new supervisor becomes effective quickly. But as the years pass, some form of "refresher course" becomes repeatedly necessary if a high level of efficiency is to be maintained. The mere doing of the job day after day will not keep the supervisor's mind alert and receptive to new ideas. The resistance to new techniques and methods which management so often meets, can be attributed to a large extent to failure to continue the education and development of senior staff.

Among the means of continuing the development of supervision are—

(1) Providing books and journals on administrative management,
(2) Sending supervisors to conferences and courses at which they will meet and discuss problems with people from other organizations,
(3) Encouraging suitably qualified supervisors to join The Institute of Administrative Management and to take an active part in its affairs.

PART V

Planning

15 The Organization and Methods Function

One of the most significant developments in administrative management has been the introduction of the specialist Organization and Methods function. This has occurred because, with the increase in the size of the office, with the extension of the office services performed and with the introduction of more complicated methods and machines, it has become increasingly difficult for the administrative manager to give the time necessary to reorganization and to designing office methods. Some far-sighted concerns introduced this specialization as early as the late 1920s, but only in more recent years has it become general practice.

Reasons for Specialization in Methods

The argument for this specialist function has been partly stated, but it may be helpful to restate it more fully. The time element is of fundamental importance. The first duty of an executive is to get the work done. His primary concern is smoothness of operation, particularly within his own sphere of control. Before everything else he has to make sure that the work of the day is carried out according to programme and in an adequate manner, and at all times he must be available to deal with any problems raised by his superiors and by his subordinates. In short, the greater part of an office executive's time is likely to be devoted to current matters, so that although he must be expected to give some attention to planning for the future and to designing better methods, this attention can rarely be detailed.

It has been mentioned that the primary concern of the executive is smoothness of operation, particularly within his own sphere of control. This also is significant. Very few office procedures fall completely within the sphere of control of the one manager only; in many large organizations systems extend from one office to another. In any organization, large or small, systems extend beyond the office into other departments. An office executive cannot be expected, when studying a problem, to take into full consideration the requirements of other parts of the organization and, even if he should attempt to do so, there is always the possibility that he may allow bias towards his own departmental interests to sway his judgment. A specialist, on the other hand, should be free to examine the whole field of inquiry regardless of departmental responsibilities or considerations.

For the reasons given in the previous paragraph, it may, in a large business, take weeks or months to study and design a single procedure. In a smaller organization it may not take so long, but still it can take more time than the average executive can give. He cannot afford to try to shut out the day-to-day problems while he is engaged in long-term planning. This is one of the principal justifications for the specialist.

Problems of organization and methods are becoming increasingly complex. New machines and devices are constantly being developed for use in the office, from the simple manifolding device to the electronic computer. Anyone who starts to reorganize an office system will want to have a working knowledge of the range of equipment available, or at least a knowledge of that part of the range which is applicable to the size and type of office with which he is concerned. With new machines and devices coming on to the market so frequently, it is as much as a busy executive can do to keep in touch with the general classes of machines available, still less to be aware of the uses to which they can be put. The specialist on the other hand can be expected to acquire and maintain this knowledge.

Specialization carries with it other advantages. A specialist not only requires a knowledge of equipment and devices; he also requires a knowledge of the even more diverse methods, ideas and short cuts which can be applied to the various functions performed by the office. He must have a wide knowledge of office methods, not merely as applied in his own concern, but those applied generally. This is not to suggest he should have, as it were, a standard solution for every situation, for that would be the antithesis of his approach, but he should have a wide body of experience upon which to draw. Moreover, he should have a profound knowledge of the organization which he serves. He must know its people, because it is they who will operate the procedures, and he must also be acceptable to them. He must know its policies and practices and its probable lines of development, for he has to integrate his systems into a living organization.

What is more important than all the arguments that have already been put forward, the specialist acquires a knowledge of the technique of designing office systems and an attitude towards economy. The technique itself is described in succeeding chapters. Concerning the attitude towards economy it is necessary to contrast this with that of the office executive upon whom there is constant pressure to provide a service to management rather than to provide this service at a lower cost. The office executive may be forgiven if, when preparing his organization, he allows caution to be the predominating influence. In deciding between alternatives, he will probably choose the method which looks safest rather than that which is the most economical. Even so his judgment may be misguided, since usually the simplest and most economical method is also the most accurate. The specialist on the other hand will constantly be seeking simplicity and economy. He, too, may be led into error, and somewhere between his approach and the more cautious approach of the executive a reasonable compromise may be found.

Responsibilities of the Specialist

Having established the need for, and the advantages of an O & M specialist, it is necessary to look a little more closely at the function itself. It is foremost an advisory function. However experienced the specialist may be, he can only offer advice. When a decision is taken the methods adopted must be those which are acceptable to the executive management. If a manager does not agree with a method which has been proposed he cannot be expected to accept it against the dictates of his judgment and be responsible for running it. Either a new method must be devised which is acceptable to him or someone else who is in sympathy with the proposed method must be made responsible for its operation. In practice it rarely, if ever, comes to this, and the method which is adopted is a resolution of the needs of the situation as seen by all concerned.

The specialist then is an adviser and he is an adviser on organization and on methods. Organization deals with such matters as the general duties and responsibilities of people and their relationships in carrying out the work of the business. The methods are concerned with the actual procedures laid down to deal with the various tasks allotted to the individuals. Organization refers to the "who" and methods to the "how." In practice the two are indivisible and it is not possible to say whether one comes before the other in considering any particular job. Generally it is necessary to start with some kind of organizational structure and then to plan the methods against the background of this structure. But as the methods develop some modification of the organizational structure may be seen to be desirable, and so there will be interplay between the two aspects as long as changes are taking place.

In the main the specialist will be concerned with designing new procedures, either to find better ways of dealing with existing tasks or adequate ways of dealing with new tasks. Ideally he might hope to survey the whole of the work of an office over a period of, say, five or ten years, but this rarely obtains in practice. In most live businesses changes are constantly taking place which call for the design of new methods. He may find he has to spend most of his time dealing with the problems which arise rather than in designing an ideal organization in its widest sense.

In addition to designing new methods he will be concerned with office layout, design of forms, making recommendations on a variety of matters relating to office organization and in helping other people, the executives in particular, to deal with any reorganization which they have themselves undertaken.

The appointment of a specialist should in no way suggest that the line executives are thereby absolved from any responsibilities in regard to the improvement of methods and organization. They will continue to exercise this responsibility, and it is only in those cases where the employment of a specialist is justified that he should be called in. To suggest that changes should only be made with his agreement would be the negation of good organization.

Setting up an O & M Service

Ideally the head of the O & M service should report to the senior administrator responsible for the offices of the enterprise. It is difficult to be specific, for the pattern of the organization varies from one concern to another. The senior administrator may be the financial director, the company secretary, the chief accountant, the comptroller or the office manager, but essentially he must be someone who has a real interest in adding to the efficiency and reducing the cost of the clerical organization. Unless the specialist reports to someone who regards these matters as of importance he cannot fulfil his function successfully.

The idea of setting up an O & M service is not always acceptable to the executives of the offices to be covered by the service. In addition to the natural inclination to distrust specialists of whatever kind, there is the not unreasonable feeling on the part of the manager that he is himself an expert who does not require help from anyone else. The reasons why he may find this help is useful have already been stated.

Generally it is preferable for a start to be made with as little outward show as possible. This is not to suggest that the project should be kept secret, but rather that the unit should be a small one and that the area of activity should at first be limited. Expansion and a widening of activities will be more appropriate if this follows several successful installations. Generally the specialist must expect to be somewhat unwelcome at first, but if he proves his worth he will find that his services are not merely tolerated but will be sought. Much will depend upon the way he goes about his job.

It can on occasion happen that the wrong use is made of the O & M service. A tendency can develop to call in the specialist too frequently on trivial matters which might be settled more economically by the local management and supervision. Sometimes this is coupled with a tendency for the manager to retain to himself the larger and more important items of reorganization which he finds of particular interest. This last difficulty can only be overcome if in the long run it is shown that the service given by the O & M specialist gives better results than that from other sources.

Those concerned with the setting up of an O & M service should not expect spectacular and quick results. The service is a tool of the management. Not only has the specialist to learn his technique, but the management have to learn how to make use of the specialist.

The Operation of the Service

The selection of suitable assignments is a problem at all times and not only when an O & M service has been newly inaugurated. Generally the most profitable jobs to start on are those parts of the work which are known to give trouble or those which employ the greatest number of clerks. If the purchase of new equipment is being considered this also should provide an obvious task for the specialist.

The specialist will do best where he is most welcome and if a departmental manager is willing to make use of the service, it is likely that investigation in his department will be more profitable than elsewhere.

Often the specialist must wait until he is called in by the executive management to deal with particular problems. This need not necessarily be so. He can always suggest to the management particular tasks on which he thinks he can be of assistance. Nevertheless, as an adviser he can only effectively deal with those problems which the management are willing that he should handle.

It is important to keep a control on the costs of the O & M service. In some concerns the cost of each assignment is calculated and charged to the department benefiting from the work carried out. This kind of arrangement is rarely practicable until the service has become well established, so that in a newly established O & M service the control must be that put on the time spent on each assignment.

A record should be kept of each assignment, including the terms of reference, the time spent on the job, the day-to-day or week-to-week progress and the results achieved.

A programme should be drawn up for each job and agreed with the management concerned. As far as is possible an attempt should be made to draw up a budget of how the time is to be spent before any action is to be taken. On a large and complex assignment it is probably not possible to give with any accuracy an estimate of the time that the whole job will take; it is impossible to foresee what difficulties will be encountered or how long it will take to reach an agreement between the various parties concerned.

But it should always be possible to estimate the cost of one step at a time, and before any investigation work is undertaken the head of the O & M service and the executive who is principally concerned should agree on what the first step is to be and how long this is expected to take.

This step should be no more than one or two weeks' work for an investigator and, as the first step, might be limited to making an initial survey and obtaining a general appreciation of the problem. When this first step has been completed, the next one can be dealt with in the same way, so that everyone concerned is in agreement on what is being done and knows how much it is costing. Agreement on costs and action is reached more easily in advance than after the event.

If several specialists are employed the question of the organization within the O & M service needs to be considered. One possibility is that different members of the service should specialize in different types of work (for example, one in sales records, another in production records and so on) or in different types of equipment (visible record computers, communications equipment, reprographic machines). It may also be helpful to have a specialist in form design.

On the other hand there are advantages if members of the service specialize in different departments, since they then become familiar with the background of the jobs they deal with and are able to tackle each assignment with greater speed. A further advantage of specializing in different departments occurs if extensive use is made of the service; if it is necessary to exercise priorities this is more easily arranged with the executives concerned where they have certain investigators allotted to their own sphere of activity.

Sometimes a compromise between the foregoing alternatives may prove satisfactory. Thus an investigator allotted a particular department may build up a special knowledge of a particular class of equipment used extensively in that department and he may at the same time be available to give advice on the equipment to those working in other departments.

Selection for O & M

Moderation is necessary when drawing up a list of the qualities required to fulfil a particular job, otherwise a long list is produced which, though ideal, is unobtainable. The list of the qualities required by an O & M specialist is particularly prone to this disadvantage and in what follows only the most important attributes have been mentioned.

Perhaps the most important pair of qualities is an inquiring mind coupled with tenacity of purpose. An investigator must take nothing for granted. He must have a critical mind and a real desire to make improvements. He must have an independence of mind that permits him to accept his own ignorance unashamedly, and demands that he must understand each of the problems he meets fully and precisely. He must have the ability to keep his mind on a problem until a satisfactory solution has been reached. He must be energetic, so that he provides his own motive power since there is no pressure of routine work to keep him going. Originality or inventiveness is a great asset, but this follows naturally from the other qualities which have been mentioned and from a deep interest in the work.

He must be tactful and persuasive, since he can only work through others. He has to draw much of the material for each investigation from other people and in particular from routine workers who may be disturbed by the idea of having their routine upset. Once his solution has been propounded he has to convince others that his ideas are practical.

Finally he must have the ability to express himself both orally and in writing, since all his ideas have to be conveyed to other people before action can be taken.

The foregoing are the basic important qualities. He needs much else besides, but this can be learned and is dealt with under training.

Although a practical and broad experience of clerical work is obviously an advantage, it is important that newcomers to this work should be recruited before their minds have become set. Authorities differ as to the ideal age. Adequate training can often make up, in part at least, for lack of experience, whereas flexibility of mind is all-important. Generally the necessary maturity of mind is not attained before the age of 25 and it is usually considered that newcomers to the work should not exceed the age of 35. It is however unwise to be dogmatic in the matter of age, for there have been many excellent exceptions to these rules.

Training for O & M

Formal education for this new profession can be obtained at many technical and commercial colleges, which offer courses leading to The Institute of Administrative Management's Diploma in Administrative Management with options in Organization and Methods. Short full-time courses of from one to four weeks' duration are also available and are of particular value to those starting an O & M service for the first time. Much, however, must be learnt on the job.

Background

The trainee requires to learn the object and policy of the undertaking, the products made or the services provided and the general methods by which the concern operates. He requires a general knowledge of the organizational structure and he should get to know such of the senior officials as he is likely to meet in the course of his work. This kind of requirement is necessary for trainees for any senior post, and most organizations are able to give such training, either formally or informally. If there is no central training school, the trainee must obtain his information by tours of the establishment supplemented by talks with members of the management.

The Office Organization

As with other departments, the trainee needs a knowledge of the organizational structure, the officials and the methods employed, but in this case in rather more detail. In the absence of more formal training methods, he will need to make a tour of the offices, spending a short time in each to familiarize himself with the work generally. Care must be taken that the trainee does not try to acquire too detailed a knowledge of all the office systems at this stage. It may be helpful if he studies one or two representative systems in detail and in this his study should be guided by a senior member of the office organization, so that he does not spend time unnecessarily. In the main, however, he should confine himself to understanding *what* each section of the office produces rather than the precise *way* in which it is produced.

Office Equipment

The trainee has to acquire a knowledge of office machines, devices and furniture. In addition to studying textbooks and attending courses at a technical college (where one is available) he will do well to visit exhibitions and the showrooms of office-equipment manufacturers. His aim should be to get a general knowledge of the range of equipment and of the main classes which are available. He cannot expect to get an understanding of all the possible applications, but he will be able to extend his knowledge of applications by consulting with the representatives of equipment suppliers. He should try to avoid becoming obsessed with any one class of machine (for example, the electronic computer) and he should not expect to become expert in the mechanical workings of machines. He should try to view each class of machine dispassionately and be concerned to find out only whether it will or will not perform the functions required of it for the particular job under consideration. Expert knowledge can always be provided by the supplier, but to be sure of securing this the O & M specialist must know sufficient to be able to find all the suppliers who may be able to help on any particular problem.

Common Office Methods

The trainee needs to acquire a knowledge of office practices in relation to sales, purchases, stock control, costing, wages, cash control, general office services and any other functions with which he is likely to be concerned. He should acquire a knowledge of layout and working conditions. A good grounding in these matters can be obtained from textbooks and courses of lectures. Given this, he will be adding to his knowledge as long as he is engaged on O & M work. He should, therefore, try to acquire new knowledge constantly by taking part in the activities of the O & M Division of The Institute of Administrative Management, by visits to the offices of other concerns and by reading publications concerned with office administration.

O & M Techniques

The trainee has to acquire by theory and practice the basic techniques of the O & M specialist. Methods design and form design are dealt with in the four chapters which follow. These, and the attitude of mind which is essential to the O & M specialist, will only fully be learned with practice and experience. Basic knowledge can be acquired through textbooks, lectures and discussions with experienced methods specialists, but it is not until the trainee begins to try to put this knowledge into practice that he will learn to do his job.

Usually it takes some two years of practical work before a newcomer to the O & M field is able to produce practical results unaided. Even then he is still very much a beginner and several more years will be needed before he is able to produce effective results at speed. It is for this reason that the practice in some concerns of seconding men on loan to the O & M section for a limited period of, say, three to five years fails to produce the most satisfactory results. Those who are most successful in O & M work are those who undertake it as a career.

16 Designing Methods – (1) Gathering Information

Briefing

Before an investigation is undertaken, it is important that the management responsible for the work concerned and the investigator should be agreed upon its scope. An investigation may require weeks of study and planning by one or more specialists and the costs involved may be significant. Unless everyone concerned is agreed at the outset as to the extent and aims of the investigation very little in the way of useful results may be achieved. Vagueness during briefing will almost inevitably cause wasted time later, so that extra care at this stage is generally well repaid.

Clerical procedures need to be examined as a whole, and since it is in their nature to range throughout the departments of an organization, it is not unusual for the management of several departments to be concerned with the results of a single investigation. However many departments are involved, one member of the management must be expected to take the lead and sponsor the investigation. It is rarely satisfactory for the investigation to be sponsored by the investigator himself.

It is good practice for the investigator to make a preliminary survey of the job, taking perhaps no more than a few hours. The object of this survey is to determine such matters as the field of the investigation, whether it appears to be justified, the time and expense likely to be involved, who should undertake it and how it is to be undertaken. After such a survey the investigator should be in a position to discuss the matter with the manager primarily concerned and, if others also are involved, to draw up the agenda for an initial meeting.

Defining the field of the work to be investigated is of considerable importance. There are rarely any natural limits to a clerical procedure. Sales procedures start with the receipt of the customer's order and include the processes of editing the customer's order, arranging to prepare or obtain the goods, arranging to dispatch the goods, preparing the invoice, keeping sales ledger accounts, collecting payment and preparing sales statistics. Any investigation which attempted to cover so broad a field at one time would be unlikely to prove successful. Similar considerations might be expected to apply to almost any other clerical function. It is therefore necessary to set some limit right at the beginning. The scope as originally envisaged may be narrowed or broadened as the investigation proceeds. But if the scope is altered this should always be for reasons which are understood by, and have the consent of, those who are to meet the cost of the investigation and who are expected to put its results into effect.

Next it is necessary to decide to whom the investigator is to report, particularly if more than one department is involved. This will not necessarily be the manager who has sponsored the investigation. It is possible that different levels of management may be concerned with different aspects of the investigation; one may be appointed to discuss day-to-day problems while another may give final authority for the acceptance of the recommendations. There may yet be others who expect to be kept informed of developments. On the other hand, limitations as to contacts with persons may be imposed. It may be considered undesirable for the investigator to approach other departments until a measure of agreement has been reached with those primarily concerned with the work under review.

It is also desirable to find out in what form the investigator is expected to report. Some managers may expect detailed reports, others may prefer an outline of the suggested procedure. If the investigator finds out the wishes of the executive management who are to act on his recommendations, he will improve the chances of bringing his work to fruition, and save his own time.

Three questions of policy must be answered at the briefing stage, as they will influence what is likely to be acceptable in the end. Firstly, is there a limit to operating cost within which any proposal must lie? Secondly, is there a limit to capital expenditure, however advantageous it may appear? Thirdly, if staff are displaced, what will happen to them? Ideally, the quite common policy of "no redundancy" will apply, meaning that anyone displaced must be reabsorbed and any reduction in numbers achieved by "natural wastage". If employees of long service are to be retained in any case, methods may have to be designed so that they can be employed.

If the investigator has several jobs on hand, it may be necessary to settle the order of priority or to find out if it is necessary for the job to be completed by a particular date.

It is important to establish the reasons for the investigation. Although the investigator may have his own ideas as to the benefits which would accrue from a new procedure, it is important that he does not lose sight of the intentions of whoever has commissioned the investigation. The ultimate acceptance of any recommendations will depend upon proper consideration being given to the original aims. Among the reasons might be any one or a combination of the following—

(1) To enable management to exercise closer control.

(2) To meet new needs, as for example in dealing with an expansion of business or with a new development.

(3) To reduce costs or to simplify the procedure so as to give greater convenience in operation.

(4) To prevent or reduce errors.

(5) To improve security. This may include the security of cash, of goods, or of information.

(6) To overcome difficulties in timing, e.g. delays in producing management information or in the payment of wages.

(7) To improve appearance and legibility.

(8) To review or audit an existing system so as to satisfy some higher authority that efficiency is being maintained.

(9) To consider the advantages of new techniques or equipment.

Finally, the investigator should discuss, with those concerned, the general approach to the investigation. It may be desirable to divide it into stages, in which case agreement should be reached as to when he is expected to report back. Although from the investigator's point of view it may seem desirable to withhold the recommendations until he is able to present a complete plan, this is rarely satisfactory from the point of view of the executive management. He should be prepared, therefore, to report back stage by stage, if this is required. Following the wishes of the management in this respect will, in the long run, save time and ensure that the ultimate proposals are more readily acceptable.

Statement of Purpose

Before giving thought to the present procedure or to any future procedure, it is necessary to define its purpose. Distinction has to be made here between the purpose of the investigation (say, to reduce the cost of the procedure) and the purpose of the procedure under examination (say, to provide certain information to management).

The statement of the purpose is without doubt the most important and is sometimes the most difficult part of planning a new system. Without it an original and satisfactory solution is unlikely to be achieved. With it, the problem is well on its way towards solution.

The statement is concerned with ends rather than means. Most clerical procedures are not an end in themselves, but are only a means to an end, usually the provision of information to guide the management in taking action or for safeguarding the assets of a business. The statement should therefore show clearly the purpose to be achieved, the information required to achieve the purpose, and, unless this is obvious, the way in which the information will serve that purpose.

There may also be supplementary or exceptional purposes to which reference should be made, including statutory requirements or other requirements imposed by outside conditions.

The statement of the purpose is not concerned with the form in which the information is required to fulfil that purpose. This needs to be determined later, but at this stage it is desirable to leave the precise form unspecified so as to give the greatest possible flexibility in arriving at a solution.

At the same time that the purpose is examined, consideration should be given to the qualities required in the final product. Generally these are concerned with accuracy, appearance and timeliness. The degree of accuracy required will depend upon the use to be made of the information. In some classes of work accuracy is of vital importance, in others less so, and since absolute accuracy can only be obtained by increasing the cost, the need in this connexion should be borne in mind right from the beginning of the investigation. A similar consideration applies to appearance. Appearance is usually more important in records intended for external use than those for internal use. But even in an internal record good appearance may sometimes be of importance if proper attention is to be paid to the information provided.

Finally, the requirements as to timeliness must be considered carefully. Some information must be available at once, otherwise it might just as well not be made available at all. Other information could be delayed without loss of usefulness. Since it is often more expensive to produce information at speed, it is necessary to be clear as to what are the requirements in this respect.

Consideration should also be given to the overall importance of the procedure and this also should be noted in the statement. An attempt should be made to sum up all that has gone into the statement of purpose, so that some judgment may be made as to the amount which may be spent in operating the procedure, that is to say on the capital cost of the equipment, on the running cost of labour and materials and on the cost of the investigation itself.

Much of the information shown in the statement of purpose will in the first instance be obtained from the management. At this stage it is likely to be in broad outline, and it will be subject to amendment later as a result of discussion with the management and as a result of subsequent detailed investigation. The aim, however, must be kept clearly in mind: to write a complete and concise statement of what the procedure is intended to produce, and how this will be used to serve the interests of the enterprise. This is the end-product of the investigation, and all that follows must be directed towards this end-product.

Study of Existing Procedure

Unlike the two preceding stages, which are likely to be based on discussions with management, this stage is concerned with the study of the actual clerical work wherever it is carried out.

The first reason for this study is that the purpose of the procedure may be checked. However well informed the responsible management and supervision may be, some part of the results obtained from a particular procedure may be temporarily overlooked during discussions. Moreover, there are often many exceptions to normal procedure which, since they are not recorded, can only be ascertained by detailed study. It is often only by a detailed examination of the procedure and a careful marshalling of facts that it is possible to ensure that nothing has been forgotten.

The second reason for the study of the existing procedure is to trace the sources of all the information used. The primary records, upon which all subsequent clerical operations must depend, are no less important that the statement of the purpose itself, as will be seen in the section which follows.

The nature of the examination necessary to achieve this dual information (the primary records and the end-product of the procedure) will depend upon circumstances. A complex procedure may call for a careful study of every operation, whereas a simple procedure may require no more than a brief survey. There are, however, certain principles which can be stated.

The survey must be conducted in a manner that will win the confidence of the management and clerks and at the same time enable the investigator to uncover all relevant information. The pattern of questions at all levels should as far as possible be decided in advance. The object of the survey should be understood by all parties.

When the investigator has been introduced to the manager directly concerned and the appropriate personal relationships have been established (if this has not already been done in the early stages), the arrangements for the survey should be discussed with the manager, and agreement should be reached as to where a start is to be made.

The responsibilities of the supervisors involved in the procedure should be discussed both with the management and with the supervisors themselves. Use should be made of an up-to-date organization chart and of any statements of the existing procedure which may be available.

Most of the information obtained during the course of an office survey must be obtained verbally from the individual clerks, and it is important that the correct approach is made. For example, the investigator should be properly introduced to the clerk who is to be interviewed, discuss the job at the workplace and keep the individual at ease. He should always be frank about what is being done and try to make it clear that he appreciates the importance of the job and intends to get a thorough understanding of the work. Above all he should avoid upsetting a supervisor or a clerk by criticizing the existing method or hinting at extensive changes.

The individual responsible for the work should be encouraged to explain the job he is doing and the investigator should, as always, apply the mental drill of "Why," "What," "When," "How," "Where" and "Who" to each of the points as they are explained to him. Any written instructions should be obtained and on occasions it may be desirable to interview more than one clerk on the same job and to compare the results. The investigator should also try to see and make use of any informal records or notes which may be kept by the clerks.

As far as possible operations should be studied in the sequence in which they occur, since first impressions are often important. The investigator will need to take notes, but these should be made as quickly as possible, so as not to break into the sequence of what is being explained. If necessary, only the main points should be noted and the notes amplified subsequently.

The investigator should be ready to consult anyone who is concerned with the system (e.g. the factory or sales manager) to learn their special difficulties and any suggestions for improvement which they may have to offer.

In some cases time spent in interviewing and note-taking can be reduced by asking clerks to fill in a questionnaire or to write out details of their jobs. For most purposes, however, direct interviewing is preferable, since a clerk is rarely able to give in writing an adequate description of his job. It is preferable, therefore, for questionnaires to be limited to a specific purpose, such as a record of the dates on which the various clerical operations are carried out.

The kind of information obtained as a result of the study of the existing procedure will include the following:

(1) The object of each operation.
(2) The method of achieving the object.
(3) Who does each operation and the amount of skill required.
(4) The location and layout of the place where the operation is performed.
(5) The time by which the information for the performance of an operation becomes available, and the time by which the operation needs to be performed.
(6) The flow of information used, showing from whom each item is received and to whom each item is passed.
(7) Samples of each of the forms used, preferably complete with specimen entries.

(8) The number of documents or items handled, together with details of any peak loads or troughs which may occur.

(9) The frequency or distribution of different types of transaction. If proper statistics are not available for this and the previous item, it may be necessary for them to be taken out over a fairly long period.

(10) Any special requirements which govern the conduct of the work, including those which relate to legal matters, the needs of other departments or the safeguarding of assets or information.

(11) The overall cost of the existing system before any changes have been made.

Not all this information will be required in every case, and the investigator needs to guard against the automatic collection of data merely for the sake of completeness. Where it is clear that an entirely new procedure needs to be designed, the investigator is not concerned with studying, still less with recording, the precise method of carrying out each operation. He is only concerned with what is achieved. To set down the detail of a system about to be superseded can only be a waste of time and effort.

Where, however, it is considered that an entirely new method is not necessary or desirable, the existing method must be studied so as to determine which parts of the system are to be improved and which parts are to remain basically unaltered. In these circumstances consideration must be given to the method of recording the data.

It is advisable to establish an agreed pattern according to which the investigator will set out his information. Reports which follow a familiar plan are easier to prepare and more easily read and understood. The particular forms of report which are adopted must depend to some extent upon the reactions of the people who receive them. Some managers may prefer written statements, others charts and diagrams. Four methods of presentation which may be usefully employed are briefly described below.

Procedure Narrative

This consists of a written account of each step in the procedure. The precise nature of each step may be emphasized in one of three ways:

(*a*) Make the initial word of each step (which should be a verb) the operative word (Fig. 18); it should be precise—such expressions as "handles" or "deals with" should be avoided.

(*b*) Repeat the operative word as a sub-title to each step.

(*c*) Precede each step with the appropriate charting symbol or combination of symbols.

Invoicing

Junior Clerk	receives	blank invoices and pack of carbon paper
	inserts	carbon paper in invoices
	passes	prepared invoices to Invoice Typist
Invoice Typist	receives	delivery note from factory
	types	invoice
	passes	delivery note and invoice to Checker.
Checker	checks	invoice
	passes	1st copy of invoice to Sales Dept
	passes	2nd, 3rd & 4th copies to machinist
	files	delivery note
Machinist	lists	totals of Invoices on tally roll
	passes	2nd copy of Invoices and tally roll to Control clerk.
	passes	3rd copy to Cost Office
	files	4th copy.
Control clerk	posts	total of tally roll to Control Ledger
	posts	values of Invoices to Personal Ledger & balances
	files	2nd copy of Invoice

Fig. 18

Method Analysis Sheet

On this is written a step-by-step account of the operations performed on a single form in the procedure (Fig. 19). The descriptions of the steps are kept as short as possible and are listed on the sheet together with the appropriate charting symbols.

Procedure or Flow Chart

This is a pictorial means of analysis (Fig. 20) used either on its own or in conjunction with the procedure narrative or method analysis sheets. It is of particular use in a complicated procedure to ensure that all facts have been obtained and to assist in analysing the method in use. The degree of detail may be varied to suit the circumstances.

METHOD ANALYSIS—UNIT DOCUMENT

SYSTEM	PROCEDURE FOR
Day Books	Invoicing

FORM	FORM REF.
Invoice	2/T/29

OPERATION SYMBOLS

Ⓒ	CLERICAL OPERATION	◇	INSPECTING (FOR QUALITY) OPERATION
Ⓣ	TYPEWRITER OPERATION	▽	PERMANENT STORAGE OPERATION
Ⓜ	MACHINE OPERATION	⛛	TEMPORARY STORAGE OPERATION
⇨	TRANSPORT OPERATION		

OPERATION SYMBOL	DESCRIPTION OF OPERATION
⇨	Receive blank invoices and pack of carbon paper
Ⓒ	Insert carbon paper in invoices
⇨	Prepared invoices to Invoice Typist
⇨	Receive delivery notes from factory.
Ⓣ	Name + address and body of invoice
⇨	Delivery note and invoice to checker
Ⓒ	Check invoice
⇨	1st copy of invoice to Postal Dept for mailing to customer
⇨	2nd 3rd + 4th copues to machinist
⛛	Delivery note
Ⓜ	List invoices to total on tally roll
⇨	2nd copy of invoice and tally roll list to Control clerk
⇨	3rd copy to Cost Department
⛛	4th copy.
Ⓜ	Post value of tally roll to Ledger control.
Ⓜ	Post values of invoices to Personal Ledgers + balance
	with Ledger control.
⛛	File 2nd copy of invoices and tally roll.

DATE 20/10/76 PREPARED BY J.E. Browne.

Fig. 19

Specimen Chart

Reduced to its simplest form this consists of completed specimens of the forms in a procedure pasted on to a large backing sheet in the order in which they are prepared. These charts may be further elaborated by the addition of marginal notes, coloured tapes to show movement, or the colouring of form panels to show duplicated entries.

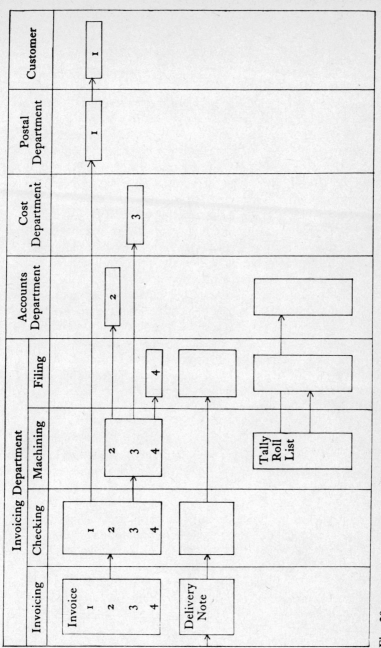

Fig. 20

Study of the Sources of Information

Assuming that at this stage the investigator has decided to try to design an entirely new procedure rather than to make piece-meal improvements to the old one, it is necessary to turn to a detailed examination of the sources of information.

Much of the information used in offices comes originally from outside sources; from the general public, from the sales force, from the factory and from other operative departments. In short, the office depends for its records upon people who are primarily concerned with physical transactions rather than records of transactions. It is not enough for the office to assume responsibility only at the point of receiving a record; it must go back to the source.

The primary reason for this study is to ensure that the investigator has an adequate knowledge of the conditions at source, so that these may be taken into consideration when designing the new procedure. Only when the investigator has made a proper study of the source can he be sure that he is in a position to design records for the entry of the basic information. He needs to know where it comes from, how it is prepared, by whom and under what conditions, and what scope there is for recording his information in a more convenient way should this be desirable.

In tracing the information back to its source the investigator will also make himself familiar with any other existing records relating to the subject of the procedure. Sometimes it may transpire that a part of the information required is already being compiled elsewhere, or that there are other jobs being carried out which can very well be combined with the procedure being designed.

Finally the source of information is often the best point at which to analyse, classify and measure the different types of transaction. Existing records do not always clearly display transactions in their essential units and studying the source may lead to a reclassification of some of the information obtained during the study of the existing system.

The preparation of a statement of the purpose, amplified by a study of the present procedure and the close examination of conditions at the source of the information used, completes the task of gathering information. Only when this has been done should the investigator turn his thoughts to the solution of the problem—the design of a new procedure. This next phase of the work is described in the chapter which follows.

17 Designing Methods – (2) Design and Installation

Design of a New Procedure

As the result of the investigations described in the previous chapter, the investigator is at this stage in possession of two sets of facts—

(*a*) The source of the basic information, the conditions under which it is recorded and the scope for altering the form in which it is recorded.

(*b*) The purpose for which the information is required and the general form in which it is required to fulfil that purpose.

He will check this information in every way open to him. He should as far as possible have armed himself with indisputable facts. Whatever system is adopted these at least should be unchanged. He is not concerned with the details of the existing system, only with the physical conditions which give rise to the information and the form in which that information is required to fulfil the purpose of the procedure.

The object at this next stage of the investigation is to discover the shortest and simplest way to bridge the gap between the information at source and the product required.

The investigator is now ready to design a procedure for the particular circumstances which have been brought to light by the previous stages. There may be something unique about these circumstances which makes it possible and desirable to design an original system. There may be some particular aspect of which it is possible to take advantage, such as the repetitive nature of some predominant type of transaction. Alternatively, it may be appropriate to adopt and adapt a system which is already in existence elsewhere.

The first step will be for the investigator to review the information he has already gathered. He will review the purpose of the procedure and, if there is more than one purpose, consider the relative importance of each. He will review the ways in which the initial information can be recorded at source. He will review the volume of work and establish the characteristics of the job. He will note any limitations ascertained in the earlier stages and assess what freedom he has in making changes as to calibre and number of clerks, situation, layout and equipment.

Although he is about to try to design an original procedure he will call to mind any knowledge he has of similar problems and the methods employed in dealing with them.

The aim is to devise the simplest possible procedure. This means if possible no paper work at all. If not, the fewest and simplest operations necessary to turn the initial information into the form required by the purpose.

All clerical work, including that done by the most elaborate equipment, carries out only the following basic processes:

(1) Writing (making original records).
(2) Reading.
(3) Copying (including posting, duplicating and punching cards etc.).
(4) Computing (adding, subtracting, multiplying and dividing).
(5) Comparing (checking).
(6) Sorting (classifying and collating).
(7) Filing and indexing.
(8) Communicating (conveying verbal and written information).

If the new system is to be kept as simple as possible, with no unnecessary operations introduced, it is best in the early stages of planning to think of the work in terms of these basic operations.

Having clearly in mind what has to be done to the information to put it into the form desired, the next step will generally be to design the form on which the information is to be recorded in the first instance. Often enough the initial form will provide the key to the whole system which follows. By giving careful thought to the way in which the information is set out on the source record it may be possible to keep to a minimum all the clerical operations which follow.

The object then is to determine how the initial information can be transformed into the final state required in the smallest number of simple operations. These should be written down in a brief procedure statement, which should be complete but concerned only with what is normal. The treatment of exceptions should be deferred until the main procedure has been established.

When, after careful consideration and further attempts to simplify the basic operations, the investigator is satisfied that this basic procedure is logical and straightforward, the remaining forms can be designed. The result at this stage may well be a simple manual system or one using only elementary machines and devices. The substitution of more elaborate machinery may be seen to be desirable when the volume of work to be handled is calculated. It is not desirable to make any assumption as to which type of equipment should be recommended until the job has been analysed and stated in its simplest terms.

When this concise statement of procedure, supported by specimen forms, is completed it should be offered for criticism to colleagues and to those members of the management concerned. It is important that the investigator should invite criticism and suggestions; it is essential that he should never resent the contributions of others or seek to defend his proposals at all costs merely because they are of his own creation. His object should be to profit from the experience of other people, whilst not following blindly their interpretation of it. Discussion and criticism will almost inevitably lead to some modification of the original proposals. Because the statement is brief and in outline only, such modifications can easily be made. It is axiomatic in this work that frequent consultation and the obtaining of agreement to proposals stage by stage saves hours of labour in preparing detailed procedures which may need far-reaching amendment.

If and when the new procedure, or some modification of it, survives this critical stage it should be expanded into a complete procedure. This should show the details of each operation, how the work is to be divided, when and by whom it will be undertaken. Wherever there are known exceptions to the normal, a note of these should be included with instructions as to the action to be taken in each case.

The entire procedure should then be examined yet again in an attempt to discover and eliminate any unnecessary work. Finally, after checking for difficulties and for any co-ordination necessary with related procedures, it should be confirmed that the result fulfils the purposes as originally designed.

Because the investigator has been thinking in terms of basic operations, it is probable, as already stated, that the system will be largely a manual one, dependent upon good form-design rather than upon elaborate and advanced equipment. Having produced this simple system he is ready to consider the use of alternative mechanical means.

Machines and appliances will perform all the basic operations referred to above, i.e. Writing, Copying, Computing, Comparing, Sorting, Filing and indexing, and Communicating. Largely because of their ability to combine operations they may give one or more of the advantages of greater speed, a saving of labour, greater control of accuracy or improved legibility.

The investigator should decide with which classes of equipment his problem is mainly concerned and study the possibilities of the various makes available. It is essential, therefore, for the investigator to be aware of the full range of appliances, but whilst he should be watching for opportunities to employ advanced equipment such as a computer, he must avoid the pitfall of trying to make the problem fit a preconceived solution.

However desirable a full knowledge of every type of equipment might be, it is doubtful if this is possible to attain. No one man is likely to understand fully the possibilities of all the machines and appliances which are available. He will do well, therefore, to offer his problem openly and freely to the manufacturers of likely machines. He will not only benefit from their ideas on the problem in hand but he will widen his own knowledge of the large number of alternative ways of achieving his objective.

Many possible alternatives can be considered and unlikely ones eliminated without going to the length of drawing up a complete procedure. Where a reasonable number of possible alternatives emerge some formal statement of costs may be necessary in order to make a comparison between them.

In most cases it will not be necessary to do more than make an estimate of costs and for this to cover only the principal items of labour, equipment and stationery. The labour cost can usually be estimated on the basis of experience, but if any completely new operations are involved it may be desirable to carry out a few experiments, to determine how long they are likely to take. The capital cost of any new equipment should be ascertained and it is usual to reduce this to an annual cost by spreading it over a period of, say, three to five years, depending upon the policy of the organization. Finally any significant stationery costs should be estimated. These three costs, labour, equipment and stationery, should be sufficient basis for the comparison of the various alternative systems. If one system does not emerge as being clearly superior to the others, more detailed tests and estimates may become necessary. It may even be necessary to stage experiments or trial runs and to record the results.

To summarize, this important stage comprises two tasks. First there is the design of a basic and comparatively elementary system to provide, at least, a yard-stick against which to measure other alternatives. Secondly, there is the offering of the problem to equipment manufacturers to see if the use of more elaborate equipment will produce additional savings which will in turn justify the capital cost involved.

Obtaining Agreement

Whilst the investigator has the task of proposing a procedure he cannot enforce its acceptance. He is an adviser; the responsibility for operating the procedure will lie with the executive. It therefore follows that the executive must have the right to accept or reject what is proposed. The investigator may be firmly convinced that he has devised an efficient system, but he has to convince others of this. And he may have to do so against the quite illogical prejudice of those to whom change is an irritation; or against the feelings of those who, perhaps years before, designed the system which is to be superseded. He has to obtain the agreement of management and the co-operation of those supervisors and clerks who will implement his plans. Nothing will bring success to the new procedure like the willing co-operation of those who are to operate it; nothing can condemn a procedure more easily than opposition from those same people.

The investigator has not only to create but to "sell" his product. This requires that he shall understand the people that he has to convince and he must make conscious efforts to this end. He must try to discover their prejudices and preferences, and develop good relationships with management and staff from the beginning. His function is to help them and his approach should at all times suggest this rather than that he has come to show how much more clever he is than they. Although this matter is here considered separately, there is no particular point in the sequence of events, from briefing to installation of the system, at which agreement is obtained. It is rather a continuing process in which first the management and later the staff are made parties to the proposals by frequent consultation and discussion.

In general it is advisable to discuss the procedure in broad outline first. By discussing the essentials of the procedure before attempting to obtain agreement in detail, the reaction of management to the proposals can be tested. Any criticisms or objections voiced at this discussion can be borne in mind when elaborating the plan into greater detail. Every opportunity should be taken to emphasize achievement of purpose. Whatever method of obtaining agreement is used it should prove quickly and concisely that the suggested procedure has achieved the purpose of the assignment with the least possible cost.

The use of lengthy reports should be avoided whenever possible; such reports waste management time. Very often they are not properly digested, the recipient fails to get a clear idea of what the suggested procedure achieves, and further time is wasted in explanation or no action is taken at all.

If reports have to be used they should start with a summary outlining the recommendations made, so that the recipient does not necessarily have to study the whole report (see Procedure Statements below). In some instances it may be necessary to give an outline of the existing routine, but this should be avoided if possible. Often the use of simple charts showing the old system against the new system and emphasizing the improvements that have been made will take up less time and will be more effective in obtaining agreement than a long report.

It is usually wise to avoid criticizing the existing procedure. Undue criticism of the existing system often leads those concerned to turn to its defence, with the consequence that the new proposals are rejected. The investigator should concentrate on the new proposals and the benefits which they can afford.

Obtaining agreement to the proposals will be made easier by getting to know the idiosyncrasies of the persons concerned. This prior knowledge will help in the diplomatic handling of the situation as it develops. If the investigator takes trouble to anticipate the possible objections it will probably enable him to deal with them sympathetically.

It is never wise to conceal weaknesses. If there are any weaknesses in the proposed procedure these should be pointed out and an attempt should be made to get all concerned interested in solving the problems. This will create a personal interest in the procedure and help to overcome any prejudice against it.

If the management are doubtful about the practicability of the method a demonstration can be arranged. This should be made as real as possible, so as to obtain and hold interest. Those concerned should be encouraged to point out any snags and produce ideas for further improvement. Experiments under actual operating conditions, however, if made in the face of opposition or doubt, are not likely to be effective. Where it is known that a comparable system is being operated successfully in another organization, it is often useful to arrange a visit.

With their first-hand knowledge of past difficulties, exceptions and abnormalities, the supervisors and clerks themselves can usually make a very useful contribution to the investigation. They may, however, feel diffident about putting their ideas forward unless actively invited to do so. They should be made aware of the proposals and given every encourage-ment to make suggestions; and having made them they should be given full credit for them. A procedure to which the staff have contributed, in however small a way, will be more readily received and operated than one which they may feel has been imposed on them. Resistance and even hostility to change is at a minimum where everyone concerned can feel a personal interest in a new scheme.

The investigator should not fail to emphasize the advantages of the new system to the staff. Most people are somewhat fearful of change. These fears, however groundless, must be met. Often this can be done by pointing out the benefits which will accrue from, e.g., improving working conditions, reducing peak loads of work and removing the drudgery from work.

It is not easy to obtain agreement to a new procedure. Some of the criticisms received will be valid and will be of considerable help, whilst others may be based on prejudice or fear. The investigator must try to keep an open mind and judge each point on its merits. If a point is of fundamental importance he must stand firm. If not, it may be helpful to the overall purpose if he is prepared to give way. He must always remember that the final system is unlikely to be the product of one mind. It is well that this should be so.

Preparation of a Procedure Statement

It is usually necessary to prepare a full description of a new procedure, setting out in logical sequence all the operations involved. The statement may be variously described as a "procedure statement," "method summary," "procedure record," or even "operating instruction," although the latter term is usually reserved for a very detailed exposition.

It is important to establish the purpose of the procedure statement before embarking on its preparation. It is usually to provide one or more of the following:

A means of presenting proposals in order to obtain approval.
A record for management of the system that has been agreed.
A means of instructing local supervisors.
A part of an office procedure manual.

Generally a procedure statement is not an effective means of training the clerks who are to operate the system. Most clerks are unable to learn their duties by merely reading a report and direct instruction by the supervisors is necessary. The procedure statement is, of course, of value in that it provides supervisors with the basis for their instruction. Many concerns use the T.W.I. Job Instruction method (see Chapter 12), drawing the necessary data from the procedure statement.

Once a procedure has been installed and is being operated satisfactorily the procedure statement will have fulfilled its primary purpose. In theory it may appear desirable to maintain a procedure manual always up to date. In practice this has often been found difficult, probably because it is not so essential as to make revision imperative for those operating the system. Once management, supervision and clerks have become familiar with its provisions they will no longer refer to the written statement.

In any live organization it is necessary to make minor changes in procedure from time to time to meet changing circumstances. These are usually made by the local management and supervision, and again the need for revising the record of the procedure will not be felt so long as the amending instruction is issued and obeyed. If the procedure is amended by the O & M section some purpose would be served by amending the manual—it would enable them to define their intentions in relation to the change. In general, however, it is not considered necessary or desirable to involve the specialist investigator unless a major review is to be undertaken.

Where a procedure must be followed at several dispersed points, the expense of maintaining a manual may well be justified. If, for example, a number of branches are to follow the same routine in order to fit in with the procedure at Head Office, an up-to-date instruction in some standard form can be of great assistance. It is certainly preferable to a file of

INVOICE-PASSING PROCEDURE

Purpose

To pass suppliers' invoices for payment by ensuring that—

the goods listed on the invoice are as ordered in regard to description, quantity, price and terms;

the goods listed have been received in acceptable condition;

the invoices are arithmetically correct;

and to dissect them to the appropriate nominal and departmental accounts.

Principles

There must be an Official Order, signed by an authorized buyer.
There must be a Goods-in Docket, originated by the department receiving the goods.
The invoice must agree with the Official Order as to description and must not exceed the order as to price of goods ordered; the invoice must agree with the Goods-in Docket as to quantity and description of the goods received.
All extensions and casts on the invoice must be checked.

Forms and Equipment

Official Order (spec. 1) used by an authorized buyer of the company for transmitting orders and conditions of purchase to a supplier.
Goods-in Docket (spec. 2) used by goods-in clerks for entering details of goods received from outside suppliers.
Grid Stamp used for printing on the invoice, the grid for the necessary passing signatures and registration details and the date of receipt.
Numbering Stamp with which the invoices are marked with a registration number.

Routine

Buyer

The buyer completes the Official Order and sends the original copy to the supplier. At the end of the day he sends the second copy of the order to the cost office.

Goods-in Clerk

The goods-in clerk checks goods received to ensure that they are in satisfactory condition and enters description, quantity, supplier's name and other details on the Goods-in Docket. The acceptance copy of the docket is sent with a daily summary to the cost office at the end of the day.

Fig. 21 (continued on page 199)

INVOICE-PASSING PROCEDURE (*contd.*)

Office

Order Control. Copy Official Orders sent in by buyers are controlled by checking that the numbers of all orders purporting to come from a given buyer are from the book issued to him, and that all orders from that book are received. The signatures on the orders are checked against the specimens held in the signature book.

Goods-in Docket Control. Goods-in Dockets are checked to ensure that they are from the book issued to the goods dock shown, and that all dockets are received.

Invoice Registration. Suppliers' invoices are back-stamped and marked with a registration number.

Invoice Verification. Official Orders are paired with the corresponding invoice and Goods-in Docket. The details on the invoice are checked against those on the docket and, when correct, the docket number is entered against each item on the invoice. The details on the invoice are checked against the order and, when correct, the order number is entered against each item on the invoice. The invoice is checked for arithmetical accuracy.

---

memoranda giving piecemeal alterations and additions which in time are almost impossible for new staff to assimilate.

There can be no definite rules applicable to the content and arrangement of procedure statements. The amount of detail to be shown, for example, will depend on the purpose of the statement, and for whose guidance it is intended. Generally there should be no more detail than the supervisor needs to control the system properly. The statement must be prepared in a readily intelligible fashion. A number of logical approaches are usually possible of which the following are the most common—

Chronological Order

This is usually the best for ease of understanding and is well suited to short procedures or those in which only a few sections of the organization are involved. The operations are described in the sequence in which they occur.

Departmental or Sectional Grouping

Here the operations of the procedure within each department or section are recorded in a sequence as nearly chronological as possible.

It is usually helpful if the statement (Fig. 21) includes introductory matter, such as some, or all, of the following:

(1) Purpose and scope of the procedure.

(2) Principles on which the procedure is based.

(3) A list of key forms and explanatory notes on any equipment which may be fundamental to the routine.

(4) Definition of important terms if these are liable to misinterpretation.

(5) Effective date of commencement.

By starting off with the purpose and principles, the reader is able to gather a general appreciation which will enable the details of the procedure to be followed more readily. By giving explanatory notes on equipment, forms and important terms, it becomes unnecessary to interrupt the description of the procedure by explanatory notes on unfamiliar matters when they are first mentioned.

In writing the main narrative it is advisable to keep a standard pattern of headings, sub-headings and of numbering of paragraphs. Every effort should be made to use clear and simple English and to avoid technical terms. The same terms should always be used to describe similar operations. Elegant variations have no place in a procedure statement, since if the same operation is described in two places in different terms the reader may well be led to believe that the operations are themselves intended to be different.

Where a printed form is mentioned the exact title should be given, using, for example, initial capital letters followed by a specimen number. If a title is unduly long and is frequently used it can be abbreviated, provided there is no risk of confusion. Consecutive numbers should be allotted to the specimens and if the statement is bound in any way these should be included so that they can be studied in conjunction with the text.

It is as well not to attempt to interrupt the flow of the narrative by dealing with exceptions to the routine as they arise. These are better shown separately at the end of the procedure with appropriate cross-references. Lists or schedules referred to in the narrative should also be kept separate as appendixes.

It is usually helpful to express the procedure in the present tense, even when it is being presented as a statement of future intention. This has the advantage that when the procedure is in actual operation it is not necessary to rewrite it with a change of tense.

The need for care in writing procedure statements cannot be over-stated. Brevity, so far as this is consistent with clarity, is always an advantage. It reduces the cost of producing the statement and adds to the likelihood of its being read thoroughly and understood. The investigator should read and reread all that he has written and, before circulating the statement generally, should submit it to others for criticism. The criterion is whether the statement makes clear to others the intention of the writer.

Installation

The installation of a new procedure must be the responsibility of the executive management and supervision in charge of the clerks who are to carry it out. The investigator should not be required to take executive responsibility, even though it may be accepted that at this stage he is better informed than anyone else on the requirements of the new procedure. He should, however—

Draw up the installation plans.
Assist and advise in the actual installation as may be necessary.
Inspect the working of the procedure when it is first in operation.

Where special difficulties obtain it may be helpful to second the investigator for a time to the department responsible for carrying out the procedure, but this should be avoided as far as possible.

An installation schedule should be prepared showing the tasks to be accomplished and the projected completion dates. The schedule should show who is to be responsible for dealing with each task; although the installation is the responsibility of the executive management, the investigator may, with their agreement, undertake to deal with certain aspects.

The installation schedule may include such items as the following.

Equipment
Details of new machines and equipment, including—
Specification of equipment.
Responsibility for ordering.
Date of delivery.
Responsibility for installation.
Responsibility for testing.
Responsibility for training operators.

Changeover Programme
The dates of the changeover and any special arrangements, e.g.—

New system to run in parallel with the old system for a period.
Staggered dates for commencing the new system in different sections or departments.
Staggered dates for introducing different processes.

The clerks cannot be expected to learn their new duties merely by reading the procedure statement or having it explained to them. If they are to become proficient quickly, they must be taught each step of each operation and, where appropriate, be given the opportunity to practise on samples of work. Any change of routine is likely to cause disruption, error and inconvenience; a major change undertaken without preparatory training can result in chaos. Time spent in detailed preparation is seldom if ever wasted. In the first place the supervisors must be instructed so as to be familiar with the procedure, its purpose and its implications. They in turn must prepare the clerks by systematic training according to a programme which is co-ordinated with the general installation plan.

During the initial stages additional staff or overtime may be required until normal working speeds have been attained and unforeseen difficulties overcome. These should be provided for in the installation programme, but specific arrangements should be made for follow-up and withdrawing surplus staff.

The clerks affected by the change should be kept informed of those matters which will concern them, including the procedure generally and the dates when changes will be made. It is preferable that they know the true intention, even if it be subject to amendment, than that they should learn by the spreading of rumours which may or may not be founded on fact.

Just as careful arrangements must be made to ensure that the clerks understand what is required of them, so must equally careful arrangements be made for informing other departments upon whom the new procedure will impinge. Usually this is best done by arranging a series of meetings with these departments, giving them a detailed statement of what is required of them, an opportunity to express their point of view and adequate time in which to make their arrangements.

It will probably be desirable for the investigator to be present on the first days when the new system is put into operation. He should, however, withdraw as soon as possible. A date should be agreed for subsequent review, when the procedure has been in operation for a few months.

Summary

The steps which have been described in the foregoing should not be considered as essentially separate entities; it is only necessary for the purpose of description that they should be shown as such. In practice they tend to merge one into the other, and the stages may not always be taken in the order given. Concentration of effort at one stage may reduce the work to be done at another. The techniques have been set out in full, but experienced investigators will have developed their own ways of shortening the process.

The stages as they have been given in this and the preceding chapters are:

Briefing.
Statement of Purpose.

Study of Existing Procedure.
Study of the Sources of Informaton.
Design of a New Procedure.
Obtaining Agreement.
Preparation of a Procedure Statement.
Installation.

These steps are no more than a logical approach to be followed until a satisfactory idea has been evolved and applied. And in this connexion it should be remembered that there is very little which is really new; much of the O & M specialist's work consists of adopting and adapting. Much, indeed, of his skill lies in an ability to appreciate the true needs arising from a situation and in selecting from his knowledge and experience the means to fill it.

18 Designing Forms –
   (1) Layout

To carry on any modern business, in the complex state of our society, it is necessary to have ready access to a mass of vital informaton. The best all-round method of recording and communicating this information is to put it on paper. The majority of the documents created for this purpose are forms. A form can be defined as one of a series of standard documents bearing descriptive matter intended to define subsequent entries. The documents serve as a means of recording and communicating the information entered on them, and the use of forms establishes a routine method of dealing with that information. This makes it easier both to add to the existing store of information and to use it.

The form designer should aim at ensuring, firstly, that a form will suit the work in which it is used and, secondly, that the clerical cost of using it will be as low as is consistent with efficiency. The form is a clerical tool and, as in the case of every tool, proper design will produce better results. Skill in form design can be achieved only by experience together with close and intelligent observation.

A form designer's task includes solving a number of problems, each of which concerns a basic element of the form. There are certain general principles which apply throughout every aspect of form design; if they are applied to each problem they will help to solve it. These principles include the following.

Reduce the number of different types of form in current use, in order to attain a simple system of recording information
This will be achieved by using standard forms and by insisting that no new forms be created unless either they form part of a new clerical procedure or they are sanctioned by a responsible authority as an improvement on an existing clerical procedure. In this case, care should be taken that the new, improved form is adopted throughout the organization and that all the old forms are withdrawn from the departments which were using them.

Reduce the number of forms in use and the number of copies made of each particular form, by designing each one to serve more than one purpose
Where the form is intended to let one person know two sets of facts, only

204

one copy of the form should be used. Where the information is for two users, who are at separate points, care must be taken that the increase in clerical cost, due to the fact that only one person can use one copy of the form at one time, does not make the application of this principle wasteful.

Reduce the number of operations necessary in the use of the form

This will reduce the clerical cost. Care must be taken that the correct balance is maintained between this principle and the one enunciated immediately above, so that the clerical cost is kept low and the efficiency high.

Make the form easy to read and to use

Let the form appear simple and let it please the eye as well as the mind. Let the purpose of the form and the significance of each part of it leap to the mind's eye, so that the originator of it will know what he is to enter on it, and so that every user of it will know what he must gather from it.

Where a form is to be used with other documents, relate the form to those documents, for example by designing the layout in a similar way

This will reduce the time and effort necessary either to transcribe information from one document to the other or to extract and assimilate information for subsequent use. Relate the form to the characteristics of the machines and equipment available, so that both production of the blank forms and reproduction of the completed forms will be achieved economically.

These principles indicate what must be achieved if the form is to fulfil its purpose with the maximum saving of effort and time. In the remainder of this chapter, these principles will be applied to the problems which arise in the selection of information to be entered on a form and the method of presenting it. In Chapter 19 these principles will be applied to the problems which arise in selecting the paper or other material on which the form is to be printed and in selecting the method of producing the actual blank form.

The main problems which confront a designer concern the selection of information to be recorded on a form in accordance with a procedure record or list of items, the appearance, size, contents and identification of a form, the instructions as to its use, the entry spaces and methods of making entries on it.

Information to be Recorded

A form should be designed only within the framework of a clerical procedure, i.e. a connected series of operations involving clerical work, necessary for an administrative action. The designer should prepare a list of items by reference to the procedure statement to show:

(1) The purpose, source and destination of each proposed entry on the form.

(2) The relationship of the form to other documents with which it will be used.

(3) The occasion, frequency and period of the form's use.

(4) The working environment of the user in each operation.

The contents of a form should be restricted to that information for which there is a definite continuing use, otherwise there will be a waste of effort among those who enter the information and those who use it. Within the limits set by the procedure statement, they must, however, be sufficient to achieve the objectives outlined in that statement.

Appearance

A well-contrived and attractive form stimulates the user to make an entry of the same high standard, whilst an indifferent form is likely to lead to an indifferent entry. These reactions are probably subconscious, but because of them, a well-designed form will produce better work from those who use it. Forms should be well balanced and the type used should be clear and uniform, unless there is a particular reason why one section of the form should stand out more than another.

Masses of close printing should be avoided so as to achieve apparent simplicity of design. Colour should be used with care and only for a definite purpose. There should be a minimum of printing on internal copies and any lines necessary should be feint to prevent the obliteration of badly registered entries, especially if the copies are made by using carbon paper.

Size

What size should a particular form be? This problem confronts the form designer when he has fixed the limits of the information that will appear on a form. The most important factors which govern the size of a form are its contents and the use which will be made of it. The form must be large enough to contain all the necessary information that will appear on it, and the size must be such as to assist the originator and any subsequent users of the form in their work. The designer must also consider any limits on size imposed by the machine on which the form will be produced, any machines which will be used in dealing with it, the filing facilities available and the postal regulations, if the form is to be mailed. If the form is being sent through the post and is not enclosed in an envelope, the size, shape and method of folding the form must accord with the postal regulations.

The designer must consider the effect which size will have on the clerical cost of the form. The clerical cost of a form is the cost both of its production and of its use. Production cost, although important, is not always the major part of the total clerical cost.

Use should be made of the standard sizes of paper shown below or cuts taken from these without waste. Office machines, carbon paper, folders, files, envelopes, etc. are generally designed in relation to standard sizes or reasonable deviations from them. The metric International sizes have been converted to the approximate equivalent sizes in inches to aid comparison.

British	International	inches	millimetres
Brief		13×16	
	A3	$11\frac{3}{4} \times 16\frac{1}{2}$	297×420
Foolscap Folio		8×13	
	A4	$8\frac{1}{4} \times 11\frac{3}{4}$	210×297
Quarto		8×10	
	A5	$5\frac{7}{8} \times 8\frac{1}{4}$	148×210
Octavo		5×8	
	A6	$4\frac{1}{8} \times 5\frac{7}{8}$	105×148
	A7	$2\frac{7}{8} \times 4\frac{1}{8}$	74×105

Identification and Instructions

The time spent in sorting, selecting, arranging and filing forms accounts for a great part of their clerical cost. Each form should, therefore, be easily identifiable so as to reduce the time spent on these incidental operations. Each form should bear a title prominently placed at its head, and printed horizontally. This title should be concise and should express the purpose of the form. Beneath it should be an indication of the origin and destination of the form. There should be a printing reference number in an inconspicuous position either at the head or at the foot of the form.

Other devices exist as aids to identification; coloured paper, coloured ink, corner symbols or numbers, and serial numbering. Serial numbering is a process whereby numbers are allotted in sequence to each form (copies being given the same number). When serial numbers are used, it is advisable to consult with the printer, since the precise position of the number may have a considerable effect on the cost. The aim should be to make the numbering part of the printing process and not a separate operation. Ideally, such numbers should be placed in the top right-hand corner of the form.

Instructions should be included only if the title and layout cannot fully indicate the purpose and methods of completing the form. Instructions as to how an entry space is to be completed should be placed as near the space as possible. Where instructions as to folding are included, the folding marks should be at the places to which the edges of the forms are to be folded and not where the creases are to be made. Any other printed instructions necessary should be placed either at the head or foot of the form.

Entry Spaces

Where possible, the information to be entered on a form should be divided into its principal sections. A portion of the form should be allotted to each section so that the entries relating to one subject or one distinct application of the form will be grouped together (Fig. 22). Wherever the information is accumulated or used in more than one place, the portion of the form allotted to it should be in a dominant position.

Customers' Orders					Dispatches			
Date	Name	Ref.	Qty.	Bal.	Date	Ref.	Qty.	Bal.

Fig. 22

Where entries are transcribed from another form, a similar order and arrangement of entry spaces on both forms is advisable; captions referring to the same information should be identical. Entry spaces should be arranged so that they are in the most natural order for the person making the entries or for a subsequent user if it is more important to assist him. Where possible the layout should be so planned that addition and subtraction are made vertically. Where cross-computation is unavoidable, addition should be from left to right and subtraction from right to left. In this case every fifth line should be printed heavily to serve as a guide line for the originator and subsequent user. Where a calculation such as multiplication of quantity by price per unit, is to be made, then the items should be side by side.

The usual types of entry space consist of columns, panels and spaces for ticking or completing pre-printed entries (Figs. 23 and 24). Columns are used where many entries have a common description. These should bear a short title printed horizontally wherever possible. Panels should be used for individual entries. They should bear a caption that describes their contents concisely (Fig. 25). The clarity of captions will greatly assist trainees to master a job. Entries should be pre-printed where the range of entry is small and predetermined (Fig. 24). The question-and-answer method is not recommended, since this leads to untidy entries, and consequently the possibility of error.

COLUMNS

Date	Item	Price

Preferred Method

Nat. Insurance	Nat. Savings	Pension

Preferred Method (Narrow Columns)

Gross Wages	Income Tax	Standard Deductions

Not Recommended

PANELS

Service to Machine	Date of Purchase
	Date of Rebuild
Details of Repairs	Date of Sale/Disposal

Preferred Method

When was the machine purchased? ....

Has it been rebuilt? If so, when? ....

When was the machine sold? ....

Details of repairs—

(i) ....

(ii) ....

(iii) ....

(iv) ....

Not Recommended

Fig. 23

Ballot Box

Road ☐

Rail
 Passenger ☐

Goods ☑

Deletion of Alternative

This order is complete/part sent

Completion of Part-printed Entry

Quantity		Price	Value
②ⁱ	lb. Oranges	10p	(20p)
	lb. Apples	15p	
⑦	lb. Plums	15p	(105p)
	lb. Pears	17p	

Ticking the Appropriate Entry

The Weight of the order is

under 1 ton

between 1–4 tons ✔

between 4–8 tons

over 8 tons

Fig. 24

Making Entries on Forms

Where a form is to be completed by typewriter, vertical lines should be so arranged that the tabulation stops can be used to the best advantage. Vertical ruled lines at tabulation stops should be continuous to avoid staggered entries and to provide a neat appearance (Fig. 26). An entry may be emphasized by stippling, shading or enclosing it with heavy lines (Fig. 27), or by arrows, variations in type, etc., but where stippling or shading is used care must be taken that entries on carbon copies, for instance, will not be obscured.

Where a form is one of a set, a degree of tolerance in the size of the spaces should be allowed, to offset any imperfect registration between the forms whilst the entry spaces are being completed. Such misalignment is sometimes caused by bulk after interleaving with carbon paper or by a typewriter platen slipping. The amount of space which must be allowed will vary according to the type of person who is making the entry and the method by which it is made.

Entries by hand: A horizontal space of one inch for eight characters and a vertical space of at least one-quarter of an inch for each line should be allowed. If the originator of an entry is not accustomed to clerical work, the vertical space should be one-third of an inch.

Entries by typewriter: It is necessary to allow a horizontal space in accordance with the size of the type; this will vary. A vertical space of at

PURCHASE REQUISITION	
Supplier	Buying Dept. Reference
	Date of Order/Inquiry
	Order No./Inquiry No.
Terms	
Deliver to	By (Date or Time)

Fig. 25

least one-sixth of an inch should be allowed. Where entries are partly typed and partly handwritten, it is necessary to allow a horizontal space that can contain at least eight characters, and a vertical space of at least one-third of an inch or any larger multiple of one-third of an inch. No typed entry should be within half an inch of the top of the paper or within one inch of the bottom of the paper unless continuous stationery is used.

Entries by accounting machine or visible record computer: Forms should be designed to suit the particular machine and guidance should be obtained from the supplier.

Computer printers: Because of the high speed of printing, paper is usually continuous stationery with sprocket holes on both sides to ensure a positive movement to each line or sheet position. For any particular printer, the width of paper is fixed and related to the maximum number of character positions available. Plain paper is often used, any headings being printed in the same type as the entries under control of the computer program. This method permits a change from one form to another without stopping the computer to change paper. Specially printed forms must be designed to match the capabilities of the machine. Where the full paper width is not required, it may be possible to print two or more forms across the sheet, thus saving paper and computer time.

Date	Description	Works Order No.
Drawing No.	Qty. Rejected	Operation
Qty. for Scrap	Reason for Rejection	Insp. Stamp

Fig. 26A Preferred Method

Date	Works Order No.	Drawing No.
Description	Operation	
Qty. Rejected	Reason for Rejection	Insp. Stamp

Fig. 26B Not Recommended

Addressing machines: Forms which are related one to the other should be designed so that entries to be made on them by an addressing machine can be derived from the same plate or stencil. The size of the entry space must be large enough to hold the maximum number of letters or figures to be entered. By masking a portion of the plate, only a portion of the embossed information will be printed; the designer may by this means select a particular portion of the information and print that only.

One of the most common methods of copying entries on a form involves the use of carbon paper. Where a handwritten entry is to be copied, the maximum number of copies that may be obtained is seven. Where a typewritten entry is to be copied as many as twenty copies may be obtained if an electric typewriter is used. The actual number of copies that can be produced depends on the machine and paper which are used.

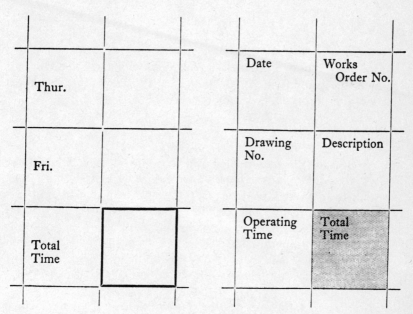

Fig. 27

Various forms of carbon paper may be used for the complete or partial reproduction of entries. One-time carbons, with or without cut-out areas, or carbon backing behind only those parts to be reproduced, may be included in the make-up of a form. They may decrease slightly the time needed to prepare the material before the copying process commences or increase slightly the number of copies, but raise their own problems of expense and deterioration in storage. As an alternative to carbon copying, use may be made of chemically impregnated papers which will produce a limited number of copies as pressure is applied by ball-pen or machine type.

Hectographic duplication provides an economical and flexible method of copying. Some models are line and item selective. All models can reproduce several colours at once. Closely competitive with this, from the point of view of operating costs, are the various photo-copying processes.

19 Designing Forms – (2) Production

The remaining problems which confront a designer concern the choice of material, the method of production, the question of cost and the task of informing the printer of the requirements. The last problem resolves itself into the preparation of a draft and specification.

Material

Before selecting the material on which a form will be printed, the designer must determine the requirements which the material must fulfil. He should bear in mind the occasion, frequency and period of the form's use, the method of printing, originating and copying it, the working environment of its users and the number of copies that are necessary. In the light of this information, he must select the type and grade of material which will be most suitable. To do this he should be aware of the advantages and disadvantages of different types of material and different grades of paper.

The occasion, frequency and period of the form's use are matters determined by the very nature of the form itself; they may vary with each different form. Certain methods of printing the forms can only be adopted if the material is of a certain type: thus, smooth non-absorbent paper should be used with hectographic duplicators, semi-absorbent paper should be used with stencil duplicators and special sensitized paper should be used with the dye-line process.

There are four common methods of making original entries on a form: pencil, ink, typewriter, accounting and other machines. Where entries are made in ink, the material should have a shiny, smooth surface; if coloured inks are used, they should be tested on the proposed paper, because often they penetrate the paper quickly and blur the entry. If a computer print-out is required, the material will have to be the type specified for the machine.

The method of copying entries and the number of copies which must be made will also affect the designer's choice. If carbon-copying is envisaged, the type and grade of paper must be selected to give the required number of copies. If the form is to be used in the open air, the paper should be such that it will stand up to use in inclement weather as far as this is possible.

In the case of forms designed to be filed vertically, the designer should consider the grain of the paper. Paper which stands on an edge cut across the grain is less likely to slip than paper standing on an edge cut along the grain. The designer should take into consideration the number of erasures which may be necessary, the ease with which they may be made and the writing quality of the spaces from which entries have been erased.

The most commonly used types of material are card and paper. Card is not easily folded and, unless of good quality, presents difficulties if erasure and rewriting are necessary. It may impose limitations on machine writing and reproduction. Papers are of different types and weights. The heavier the paper is, the more handling it will stand.

Method of Production

The form designer should advise which method of production is most suitable to a particular form and should be aware of the main technical considerations which underlie different methods. Firstly he must consider whether the job is one for office printing and duplicating equipment or for a professional printer. The decision will depend on the purpose and usage of the form and on the facilities available within the organization. The designer must consider the number of copies necessary, the possibility that the job will be repeated, the accuracy of registration necessary, and whether the form will be used only within the organization or sent, for example, to customers.

Normal office duplicating equipment consists either of offset litho machines, stencil duplicators, hectographic duplicators or machines which produce copies by photographic process. Offset litho machines are the most suitable from the point of view of accuracy and registration. They may be used to produce forms either from a coated paper master or from a thin metal plate. In either case, the master copy can be made by ruling, typing or writing directly on to its surface or by photographic processes. If a master copy is prepared photographically, the original draft can be made by a combination of typing, hand ruling, press-on characters and printed matter cut from existing forms. This method enables forms of "professional appearance" to be turned out quickly and cheaply. Paper masters are of varying quality and give up to about 500 copies. Metal plates, which can be stored and re-used, will give as many as 50,000 copies.

Stencil duplicators yield about five thousand copies from one master which may be stored and used again. Hectographic duplicators produce one hundred good-quality copies or more if care is exercised. These figures refer to sheets of paper. A small form may be repeated on the same sheet.

Where a large number of forms is required, and ancillary work such as numbering in sequence and perforating must be performed, it is usually better to have the form printed. Where the number of copies is within the range of an offset litho machine and the job is repetitive, the use of a master plate and the litho process is recommended. Where a limited number of copies is needed and the job is not repetitive, then the use of paper masters and the litho process is recommended.

Cost

The cost of forms is a subject which the designer must consider carefully. At the outset, the purchase costs of particular machinery, stationery and ancillary equipment may appear excessive. This may deter him from what is, in fact, the most promising line of approach. By looking beyond production costs, and estimating the clerical cost of using the form, the real valuation of it may be made. Where a particular clerical procedure has been evolved and forms are being designed to implement this procedure, care should be taken that apparent economy resulting from a reduction in production costs does not involve a real increase in clerical cost. Apart from this general consideration, the designer should attempt to reduce all costs as much as possible, provided that this reduction does not render the form a less-efficient clerical tool.

The various methods of producing forms differ in cost as they differ in results. The course of action eventually adopted will usually be a matter of compromise. As long as the general principles of form design are applied with understanding the result will be satisfactory.

Instructions to the Printer

Printers, compositors and plate makers should be assisted as much as possible by the form designer. The designer should always make certain that his requirements are clearly expressed and that there will be no doubt in the compositor's mind as to what is required. The only sure way to guarantee that the compositor will interpret the instructions correctly is to give him a visual impression of the complete form corroborated where necessary by written details. This is the "draft."

The "draft" should be an accurate, full-sized drawing of the proposed form. All columns and panels should be drawn showing precisely the areas and widths. This is particularly important when machine entries are to be made. The relative importance of captions, instructions and lines should be indicated by the use of appropriate sizes and densities of print on the draft. The extent to which details of the type of print are left to the discretion of the printer will vary, depending upon the relationship between the form designer and the printer. It is safer to be absolutely

6 point Gill Sans

A GOOD TYPOGRAPHER IS ONE WHO CAN
arrange type so as to produce a graceful and orderly page that puts no strain on the eye. This is the

8 point Gill Sans

A GOOD TYPOGRAPHER IS ONE W
arrange type so as to produce a graceful

12 point Gill Sans

A GOOD TYPOGRAPHER IS ONE WHO CAN ARRAN
produce a graceful and orderly page that puts no strain on

18 point Gill Sans

A GOOD TYPOGRAPHER is one who

6 point Gill Sans Italic

A GOOD TYPOGRAPHER IS ONE WHO CAN ARR
so as to produce a graceful and orderly page that put
no strain on the eye. This is the first and last fundam

10 point Gill Sans Italic

A GOOD TYPOGRAPHER IS ONE
and orderly page that puts no strai

12 point Gill Sans Bold

A GOOD TYPOGRAPHER IS ONE WHO CAN
type so as to produce a graceful and orderly page th

18 point Gill Sans Bold

A GOOD TYPOGRAPHER is one w

6 point Old Style

A GOOD TYPOGRAPHER IS ONE WHO CA
type so as to produce a graceful and orderly page
that puts no strain on the eye. This is the first and
last fundamental requisite of book design, and lik

8 point Old Style

A GOOD TYPOGRAPHER IS ONE
CAN ARRANGE TYPE SO AS TO PRODUC
and orderly page that puts no strain on

10 point Old Style

A GOOD TYPOGRAPHER IS
A GRACEFUL AND ORDERLY PAGE
and last fundamental requisite of

12 point Old Style

A GOOD TYPOGRAPHE
TYPE SO AS TO PRODUCE A
on the eye. This is the first a

6 point Old Style Italic

A GOOD TYPOGRAPHER IS ONE WHO CA
type so as to produce a graceful and orderly page that
puts no strain on the eye. This is the first and last fu

8 point Old Style Italic

A GOOD TYPOGRAPHER IS ONE
arrange type so as to produce a graceful

10 point Old Style Italic

A GOOD TYPOGRAPHER IS
a graceful and orderly page that p

12 point Old Style Italic

A GOOD TYPOGRAPHE
so as to produce a graceful a

8 point Old Style Bold

A GOOD TYPOGRAPHER IS O
can arrange type so as to produce

10 point Old Style Bold

A GOOD TYPOGRAPHER I
produce a graceful and orderl

Fig. 28 Specimen Type Faces

FORM PRINTING SPECIFICATION

To: Date

Form or Set No.	Title

PAPER/BOARD STOCK	No. and title—if different from above	Quantity and unit	Kind	Weight	Colour
Original—1					
Part —2					
Part —3					
Part —4					
Part —5					
Part —6					

Size   Deep X   Wide

Tolerance   On depth   On width

GRAIN	Grain of stock must run with .... dimension of form

PRINTING — Colour(s), face and reverse

☐ One side   ☐ Two sides head to head   ☐ Two sides tumbler

REGISTER
Forms must register exactly in sets of............
Forms must register exactly with measurements of form(s) No.(s)
☐ Specimens of these forms are attached

LINE SPACING   Vertical (down depth)   Horizontal (across width)

ORIGINAL ENTRY METHOD   ☐ Manuscript   ☐ Typewritten   ☐ Machine-pasted

PUNCHING	No. of holes	Diameter and shape	Distance	Centre to centre

PERFORATING	Centre of	Hole(s)	Holes centred on	Inch edge	Distance
	All sheets ☐	Other (specify)		Across the inch way of form	Position of perforation From the top/left
	Slotted ☐	Round ☐	Do not specify unless essential ☐	Across the inch way of form	Position of perforation From the top/left

GUM-TIP	Collate and gum-tip	Sheets to a set in the following order:

PAD	Sheets/sets to a pad	Padded on inch edge, top/left	Backing board ☐	Sheets of carbon per pad

BIND	Sheets/sets to a pad	Bound on inch edge, top/left		Sheets of carbon per book

NUMBER	Number consecutively:	All parts of sets ☐	Only sheets ☐	From	Start renumbering

FOLD	No. of times across the	Inch way of form	Inches from the top/left

CORNERS	After folding these words should appear on the outside front of the form:	Round ☐	Square ☐	Other

SPECIAL INSTRUCTIONS	e.g., carbon backing, continuous stationery, etc.

QUANTITY	Required for use by (Date)	Proof — Yes ☐ No ☐	Estimated annual usage	Signature

Fig. 29

specific wherever a particular type of print is required. The layout of the form should be drawn to the exact measurements required. Where registration with other forms is important, the printing expression "dead register" should be used. This will indicate to the printer that the highest degree of accuracy must be achieved.

Although most printers can be relied upon to avoid undue elaboration in type style, the form designer should be aware of the æsthetic values involved. The overall effect should be one of simplicity together with neatness. One style of lettering should be used throughout the form, unless particular emphasis must be given to any portion of it. Serif and sans-serif type should not normally be used in the same form. Capital letters may be used for short captions, but initial capitals and lower case letters should be used for long captions or text, since they are more easily read. The precise size of letters and the thickness of lines should be indicated in the draft by representing them visibly rather than by quoting printer's "points," since the latter are not always interpreted in the same way by different printers. Examples of type faces and sizes suitable for use on forms are given in Fig. 28.

In those few instances where a form will be printed in several colours, this must be indicated on the draft. The exact measurement for all punched holes should also be specified on the margin of the draft and their precise position indicated on the drawing. The printer should be informed of the position of any perforations, and unless the precise nature of the perforation is specified, marginal notes should be included as to their purpose. The draft should resemble the required form as closely as possible. This will help the printer to avoid mistakes.

Before the draft is sent to the printer the designer will be well advised to send it to those who will use the form so that they can make a final check to ensure that the dimensions are satisfactory. If it is thought necessary, a form data-sheet may be prepared to contain an analysis of the various points which form part of the design, and to serve as a check list.

The designer should always prepare a summary of the physical features of the form. This is the "specification." It consists of written instructions concerning the production of the form. The instructions should be clear and concise, and may either consist of narrative or of a series of entries on a pre-printed form (Fig. 29). Where instructions are lengthy they should form part of the specification and not be included on the draft. Instructions must be given as to the size of the form, the grade, weight and colour of the paper or card, the thickness and colour of lines, the size and style of type face and the position of the printing, whether it is on one or both sides of the form.

"Make-up" is a term used to describe the physical arrangement of the forms at the moment when they are ready for use. The term may be applied to the method of presenting the information contained in one form. A form may consist of one sheet of paper or of several sheets of paper, in which case it will be a multi-part form. In deciding whether he will use a single sheet of paper or a multi-part form, the designer must consider the purpose of the form, the locations in which it is to be used and the ease with which the necessary copies of it may be made.

"Make-up" is a term also applied to the physical presentation of many forms. As well as being supplied loose, forms may be made into pads, in which case the forms are covered and gummed along one edge with or without a backing board. They may be bound into books by means of stapling or sewing. In this case some form of perforation must be provided so that the forms may be detached. The forms may be printed on continuous stationery, in which case there are usually perforations between the forms. Since such forms must usually be printed on rotary presses this make-up is only economical for long runs. Moreover, the fact that the forms are printed from reels of paper may restrict the designer's freedom in choosing the size.

Normally printers are asked to provide proofs, but these can be dispensed with if the draft is well drawn and easy to understand. The proof should be regarded only as a means of checking that the printer has interpreted the draft and specification accurately. Changes at the proof stage should be avoided, since they can be expensive and inevitably waste time.

20 Designing Computer Methods

The basic O & M techniques described in the foregoing chapters are applicable whether or not a computer is to be employed. There are, however, some variations in detail and procedure which are important and the purpose of this chapter is to discuss these.

Where a computer is used, the O & M department's function must be co-ordinated with those of the Data Processing department. There must be a complete understanding between the two departments as to when they should operate independently and when they should collaborate. If the lines of demarcation of responsibilities are not clear, misunderstanding and friction may result.

Some organizations have established a separate O & M service for computer projects only, but this can lead to difficulties. If an assignment is given to a "computer" O & M specialist, this infers that a computer will be used, whether or not it is the best tool for the job. The result may be that work is done by computer at a cost far in excess of that incurred by more traditional methods. Even though computer time is available, the cost of systems analysis and programming may not be recoverable over a reasonable period. It must be borne in mind that data must usually be collected by people, and that, with suitable machines, these people might complete the job in little extra time.

The procedure to be followed in establishing a computer system follows lines similar to those for establishing any other system and it is perhaps helpful to compare the two. The initial stages are identical: briefing, statement of purpose, study of the existing procedure (if any), study of sources of information, designing the simple logic of a new procedure leading from the sources of information (data) to the required end products (results). At this point, the investigator comes to consider alternative methods, manual and mechanized, and may conclude that the computer is a valid possibility. His enquiries then include a computer feasibility study (or justification survey) to see whether or not this possibility is worth pursuing. Costs, including those of systems analysis and programming, must be estimated and compared with those of other methods. Only when the computer is shown to have clear cost or other advantages should it be selected as the means to be used.

Once the decision to use a computer has been reached, the methods design procedure follows a different path. The procedure statement must now include a computer job specification, set out in such a way as to be the basis for computer systems analysis and programming. The procedure statement as a whole must, of course, still cover the operations of data collection, control and recording, which will be done by clerical and possibly non-clerical staff outside the sphere of data processing. It may also be concerned with operations to be carried out after the computer has done its share of the work.

Although divisions of responsibility differ from one organization to another, there appears to be good reason for limiting the tasks of the data processing department to those matters which closely concern the operation of the computer and which require an expert knowledge of its characteristics. If this principle is applied, the division of duties might be as follows:

Organization and Methods Department
Investigation leading through a feasibility study to the preparation of a procedure statement and computer job specification.

Data Processing Department
From the computer job specification, the design of the detailed sequence of computer operations and the writing, testing and proving of programs.

There must, of course, be close collaboration between the two departments once the decision to use a computer has been reached. The computer systems analyst must understand fully the intentions of the O & M specialist's job specification. The O & M specialist must specify within the computer's technical limitations.

In the smaller organization, it may be necessary to require one person to carry out all functions, even including the writing of the computer programs. This is not, however, the ideal arrangement. To ask for too much specialist knowledge from one person is to create a jack-of-all-trades who is master of none.

Feasibility Studies

In order to carry out a feasibility study the investigator needs some basic knowledge of computers, sufficient to know the areas in which limitations of capacity are significant. The task certainly does not demand a knowledge in depth of any particular computer. Indeed, the study may be made in order to discover what sort of computer would be necessary to do the work economically. To an increasing extent use is made of computer bureaux and the enquiry must then be entirely without prejudice, the object being to obtain a basis on which competitive quotations for service can be obtained.

The feasibility study must establish facts which are significant in computer operation: information to be stored, data to be fed in, the output – whether printed, punched, or otherwise recorded. It must also state significant times, such as when data can be made available and when results are required. The sort of questions which must be answered are as follows:

Storage

What items of information must be stored?
How many letters and digits are needed to express each item?
How many of such items must be stored at any one time?

Input

What blocks of data must be collected and recorded?
From what sources will data be obtained?
How many letters and digits will each block of data contain?
How many blocks of data must be fed into the computer at each operational run (e.g. daily, weekly, etc.)?

Output

What prints are required on plain paper or on pre-printed forms?
What punched or other output records are required?
How many such records are to be made and how many letters or digits are to appear on each?

Timetable

When will data be ready for input?
When will printed and other output records be required?

From the answers to these and other questions appropriate in the particular case, it should be possible to make preliminary estimates of the necessary computer capacity and running time to do the job. Computer service bureaux (and some private users) can quote running costs per unit of data, per line of print, per card punched, etc., and from these it is possible to make rough but reliable estimates of cost with little effort. To the running costs must be added a sum to cover initial systems analysis and programming written off over an appropriate period of operation, perhaps three to five years, and a sum to cover program amendment from time to time over the same period.

In general terms, the O & M investigator, is trying to discover whether the work is likely to be done economically by computer, having regard to the volume of data to be processed in any one run and in any year. There is an initial cost in the work leading up to and including programming, which represents a burden to be spread over the total units of output to be produced before the system becomes obsolete. There is a basic minimum cost for setting up and running a computer on any one job irrespective of the number of units of data processed at that time. With high volumes of work, the overall cost per unit will be small; as the volumes reduce, they will reach a point at which other machines and manual methods can compete.

Computer Job Specification

In any revision of methods, it is necessary to prepare some written statement of the procedure to be followed. If this statement is to be used for the guidance of supervisors in training their clerks, it need not be completely detailed; it can assume certain existing knowledge. A clerk entering a customer's name and address manually on a form does not have to be told how many alphabetical letters he may write on a line. He will exercise discretion, varying the size of his handwriting and making use of intelligible abbreviations when necessary. The computer, on the other hand, is a moronic device, devoid of discretion in the human sense. The computer job specification must therefore be more precise than the usual procedure statement. It is the means whereby the O & M specialist conveys to the computer systems analyst—and through him to the programmer—what management has agreed as the output requirements, and what data are to be provided. It will be amplified verbally in discussion to ensure complete understanding, but must contain all the "hard facts" of the case. Its contents may be summarized as follows.

General Introduction and Statement of Purpose, providing the background knowledge against which the detail may be better understood.
Summary of Output, listing what is to be produced and giving brief descriptions as necessary.
Summary of Data, stating how it is proposed that each type of data shall be recorded ready for input to the computer.
Coding Systems, giving complete lists of codes and their meanings.
Volumes, relating to both data and output.
Output Specimens, being precise and realistic representations of printing, punching, etc.
Data Specimens, being precise and realistic representations of the forms, punched cards, tapes, etc., to be used in the collection and recording of data.
Output Descriptions, defining each item of output and how it is to be obtained from the data, and commenting on any aspects which may not be self-evident from the specimens.
Data Descriptions, defining each item of data, its source and significance.

The O & M specialist's work has not been completed on handing over the job specification to the computer systems analyst. The latter may have technical problems which can be solved by some adjustment of the system. Although each of the two parties has a definite job to do, the final outcome will depend to a great extent on their joint efforts as a team.

Installation

Once programs have been written and thoroughly tested, the computer systems analyst's contribution is complete, subject to any amendments that may prove necessary. The main tasks of installing the system lie either side of the computer: in the collection and recording of data and in making use of the output. The O & M specialist is here involved in the writing of procedure statements and in monitoring the changeover in the same way as he would be in introducing any other new manual or mechanized method.

Computers and Organization

The use of a computer frequently, if not always, calls for changes in organizational structure, and it is part of the O & M function to identify the need for such changes and advise management accordingly.

In the office, the reduction in repetitive routine work will obviously result in the contraction of some sections. It may be desirable to set up a separate data recording section. It is almost certain that a computer control section must be established where knowledgeable senior clerks can assemble data, subject it to appropriate scrutiny and pass it to the computer at the due time. This section may also be required to settle queries when data are rejected or questioned by the computer as directed by its programs. According to the nature of the system, senior clerks may have to examine the printed output and possibly interpret its meaning before passing information to management.

In departments outside the office, methods of collecting data in suitable forms may call for a redistribution of duties. Foremen, supervisors, storemen, drivers, cashiers, etc., may be required to take complete responsibility for the recording of data, possibly in a form which will pass straight to the computer input. This may entail some decentralization of clerical work and the establishing of small local offices which, in the interests of economy, may be required to take over other duties not directly connected with the computer data.

The ability of the computer to provide rapid and comprehensive information for the guidance of management can create a new climate in which the old divisions of responsibility are seen to be no longer appropriate. The need for reorganization may well extend beyond the changes directly associated with clerical operations and involve the business structure as a whole.

Appendix: Legal Aspects of Office Management

In the last edition of this book, the law relating to employment in offices was summarized. It was considered reasonable that an administrative manager should be fully aware of legal requirements and even be his employer's lay expert in this field. In the last decade, however, Parliament has seen fit to enact many laws which define in detail the relationships between employer and employee, and the duties of employers in relation to working conditions, trade unionization, etc. At the time of producing this edition, still more legislation is expected. In some cases, the Acts of Parliament provide broad guidelines within which a Secretary of State may make regulations from time to time.

The scope of the law now makes it a separate study. The administrative manager should not seek to be his own expert, but rather rely on professional legal guidance when deciding matters of policy and practice. In order to be able to seek such help, he must, of course, be aware of the areas in which there may be restrictions on his freedom of action. To offend against the law may lead to the employer being prosecuted in the Courts, or having to defend cases taken before tribunals. It must be noted that under some Acts the legal responsibility falls not only on the employer (which may be a Company) but on the Director or Manager concerned personally.

The following defines the general scope of the principal Acts involved.

Offices, Shops and Railway Premises Act, 1963

Requires employers to maintain working conditions in offices to minimum standards set by the Act or by Regulations issued by the Secretary of State. Scope includes:

Cleanliness—of premises, furniture, equipment, etc.

Overcrowding—rooms must allow 40 sq. ft of floor space per person (including space occupied by gangways, equipment, etc.), or 400 cu. ft where the ceiling is lower than 10 ft from the floor.

Temperature—minimum of 16° C (60.8° F) after the first hour (with some exceptions); thermometers to be provided.

Ventilation—adequate fresh or purified air.

Suitable lighting–with windows kept clean and lighting equipment maintained.

Sanitary conveniences—according to numbers employed.

Washing facilities—with hot and cold running water, soap, towels or equivalent.

Drinking water—with jet or drinking vessels provided.

Accommodation for clothing not worn at work.

Facilities for drying wet clothes.

Suitable seating—with footrest if necessary.

Floors, passages and stairs—safe, sound and unobstructed.

Safe machinery—fenced as necessary and cleaned only by staff aged 18 and over if risk is involved.

Heavy work—staff not required to lift or carry heavy loads likely to cause injury.

First Aid—materials and trained personnel to be available.

Fire precautions—adequate means of escape and fire-fighting equipment; premises to be inspected and certified as having adequate safeguards.

Notification of accidents—if causing death or disabling a person from working for more than three days.

Inspectors—to be admitted to premises at any reasonable time.

Health and Safety at Work etc. Act, 1974

Concerned with the promotion of health and safety of employees generally; requires a written statement of related policy, organization and arrangements to be provided to employees and also information given as to risks and training in safe practices.

Contracts of Employment Act, 1963 as amended

Requires a minimum period of notice to terminate employment after a qualifying period of employment; requires employers to give written particulars of terms and conditions of employment including rate of pay, intervals between payments, hours of work, sick pay, pension, holidays, trade union membership, grievance procedure, length of notice to be given and date of expiry of the contract (if for a fixed period).

Race Relations Act, 1968

Makes it unlawful to discriminate against a person on grounds of colour, race, ethnic or national origins in advertisements, employment, training, promotion or dismissal; employers may discriminate to secure a balance of different racial groups. This Act was about to be amended when this edition was produced.

Sex Discrimination Act, 1975

Makes it unlawful to discriminate directly or indirectly on grounds of sex or marital status in matters of employment, e.g. staff advertising, recruitment, promotion, transfer, training, benefits or facilities, except where the sex of a person is a genuine qualification for a job.

Equal Pay Act, 1970

Requires that employers shall accord equal treatment to men and women as regards terms and conditions of employment (including pay), except in matters which are (a) subject to laws regulating the employment of women; (b) concerned with childbirth; and (c) concerned with pensions, retirement, marriage or death.

Redundancy Payments Acts, 1965, 1969 as amended

Require employers to compensate employees made redundant by a scale of redundancy pay related to rate of pay and length of service.

Trade Union and Labour Relations Act, 1974

Concerned principally with trade union practices and the rights of trade union members, including the right to strike; lays down procedures for the settlement of disputes as to fair and unfair dismissal.

Employment Protection Act, 1975

Concerned with: (a) industrial relations and the settlement of disputes by conciliation or force of law; (b) the provision by employers of information to trade unions; (c) the rights of employees in relation to payment, medical suspension, maternity pay and reinstatement, trade union membership, time off for union or public duties and dismissal.

Industrial Training Act, 1964

Provides for the training of people over compulsory school age for employment in industry and commerce; establishes Training Boards with power to raise funds by levy on employers, to make grants to employers to cover training costs, and to provide training facilities and services.

Employers' Liability (Defective Equipment) Act, 1969

Makes an employer responsible for compensating an employee suffering personal injury resulting from defective equipment, even though the defect arose from a cause not under the employer's control.

Employers' Liability (Compulsory Insurance) Act, 1969

Requires employers to maintain approved insurance against liability for bodily injury or disease sustained by employees in the course of their employment.

Reading List

The following is a short list of books recommended for further reading—

General Reference

Better Offices, (Institute of Directors, London).
Developments in Office Management, J. Batty (Heinemann, London).
Filing, Oliver Standingford (The Institute of Administrative Management, Beckenham).
Introduction to the Theory and Practice of Management, Noel Branton (Chatto & Windus, London).
Management and Computer Control, T. R. Thompson (Gee and Co., London).
Management of Change – The Role of Information, John R. M. Simmons (Gee and Co., London).
Office, Oliver Standingford (BBC Publications, London).
Office Organization and Method, G. Mills and O. Standingford (Pitman, London).
The Open Plan Office, E. John Brown (The Institute of Administrative Management, Beckenham).

Control

Clerical Quality Control, D. C. Arnall and T. S. Hall (The Institute of Administrative Management, Beckenham).
Office Work Measurement, H. W. Nance and R. E. Nolan (McGraw Hill, New York).
Work Measurement in Typewriting, W. W. Burke and J. Maxim Watts (Pitman, London).
Work Study in the Office, H. P. Cemach (Applied Science Publications, Barking).

Staffing

Office Job Evaluation, Keith Scott (The Institute of Administrative Management, Beckenham).

Office Job Evaluation Grade Framework, (The Institute of Administrative Management, Beckenham).
Office Salaries Analysis, (The Institute of Administrative Management, Beckenham).
Office Staff – Holidays, Turnover and Other Procedures, (The Institute of Administrative Management, Beckenham).
Interviewing for Managers, J. D. Brake (Allen & Unwin, London).
Office Hours and Payment Practices, (The Institute of Administrative Management, Beckenham).

Supervision

A Guide to Effective Office Supervision, (The Institute of Administrative Management, Beckenham).
The Office Supervisor, Niles, Niles and Stevens (Chapman & Hall, London).

Planning

Design of Forms in Government Departments, Management Services Division of the Civil Services Department (H. M. Stationery Office, London).
Effective Use of Secretarial Services, D. L. Wallace (The Institute of Administrative Management, Beckenham).
Form Design, (The Institute of Administrative Management, Beckenham).
How to Design a Procedure (The Institute of Administrative Management, Beckenham).
Procedure Charts for Administrative Work, (The Institute of Administrative Management, Beckenham).
Setting up an Organisation and Methods Section, L. G. S. Mason (The Institute of Administrative Management, Beckenham).
Simplifying Office Work, Oliver Standingford (Pitman, London).

Index